# A2

# ENGLISH LITERATURE

## for AQA B

Tony Childs
Jackie Moore

Consultant: Peter Buckroyd

Heinemann Educational Publishers,
Halley Court, Jordan Hill, Oxford OX2 8EJ
A division of Reed Educational & Professional Publishing Ltd

OXFORD  MELBOURNE  AUCKLAND
JOHANNESBURG  BLANTYRE  GABORONE
IBADAN  PORTSMOUTH NH (USA)  CHICAGO

© Tony Childs and Jackie Moore

First published 2001

05  04  03  02  01
10  9  8  7  6  5  4  3  2  1

ISBN 0 435 10981 2

## Acknowledgements

The publishers gratefully acknowledge the following for permission to reproduce copyright material. Every effort has been made to trace copyright holders, but in some cases has proved impossible. The publishers would be happy to hear from any copyright holder that has not been acknowledged.

Extract from 'Twelve Songs IX' from *Collected Poems* by W. H. Auden, published by Faber and Faber Limited. Reprinted by permission of Faber and Faber; 'Valentine' from *Mean Time* by Carol Ann Duffy, published by Anvil Press Poetry in 1993. Reprinted by permission of Anvil Press Poetry; Extracts from *Birdsong* by Sebastian Faulks, published by Hutchinson. Reprinted by permission of The Random House Group Limited; Extract from *To The Lighthouse* by Virginia Woolf. Reprinted by permission of The Society of Authors as the Literary Representative of the Estate of Virginia Woolf; Extracts from *The Color Purple* by Alice Walker, published by The Women's Press. Reprinted by permission of David Higham Associates Limited; Extract from *Sacred Hunger* by Barry Unsworth, published by Penguin Books. Reprinted by permission of Penguin Books Limited; Extract from *The Invisible Man* by Ralph Ellison, published by Random House Inc. Reprinted by permission of Laurence Pollinger Limited on behalf of the author; Extracts from *Beloved* and *Jazz* by Toni Morrison. Copyright (c) Toni Morrison. Reprinted by permission of International Creative Management, Inc.; Extract from *The Great Gatsby* by F Scott Fitzgerald, published by Heinemann. Reprinted by permission of David Higham Associates Limited; Extract from *The Death of a Salesman* by Arthur Miller. Copyright (c) 1949 by Arthur Miller. Reproduced by permission of Rogers, Coleridge & White Ltd., 20 Powis Mews, London W11 1JN in association with International Creative Management, Inc, New York; Extract from *Nineteen Eighty-Four* by George Orwell. Copyright (c) George Orwell, 1949. Reprinted by permission of Bill Hamilton as the Literary Executor of the Estate of the Late Sonia Brownell Orwell and Martin Secker & Warburg Limited, c/o A. M. Heath & Co. Ltd; Extract from *Translations* by Brian Friel, published by Faber and Faber Limited. Reprinted by permission of Faber and Faber; Extract from *Wilt on High* by Tom Sharpe, published by Martin Secker & Warburg. Reprinted by permission of The Random House Group Limited; Extract from *Catch 22* by Joseph Heller. Copyright (c) Joseph Heller 1955. Reproduced by permission of A. M. Heath & Co. Ltd; Extract from *Captain Corelli's Mandolin* by Louis de Bernières, published by Vintage (May 1995). Reprinted by permission of The Random House Group Limited; Extracts from *The Female Gaze* by Lorraine Gamman & Margaret Marshment, published in Great Britain by The Women's Press Ltd, 1988, 34 Great Sutton Street, London, EC1V 0LQ. Reprinted by permission of The Women's Press Ltd; Extracts from *In Search Of Our Mother's Gardens* by Alice Walker, published by The Women's Press Ltd. Reprinted by permission of David Higham Associates Limited; Extracts from *Sons and Lovers* and *The Letters of D. H. Lawrence Vol 1* published by Cambridge University Press. Reprinted by permission of Lawrence Pollinger Limited and the Estate of Frieda Lawrence Ravagli; Extract from *The Forked Flame: A Study of D. H. Lawrence* by H. M. Daleski, published by Faber and Faber in 1965. Reprinted by permission of the author; A. B. Kuttner *A Freudian Appreciation* from *Psychoanalytic Review* July 1916.

Typeset by TechType, Abingdon, Oxon

Printed and bound by Bath Press in the UK

ii

# Contents

# Introduction

## How this book will help you

This book is designed to help students following AQA Specification B in Advanced English Literature through their course. Most students approaching this Specification will already have studied AQA Specification B in Advanced Subsidiary (AS) English Literature, and this book has been written with that in mind. It is important to recognise from the start, however, that A Level is different from AS Level in that two of the Assessment Objectives (AOs) change. This is dealt with fully below. The book is not specifically a guide to individual set texts – after all, each of you will choose different texts to work on. Rather, it is a guide to what you have to do with your texts in order to succeed.

This Introduction deals with the Assessment Objectives for Specification B. Please don't overlook this part and go straight to the modules, however tempting that may be – the Assessment Objectives underpin all the work in the course, and an understanding of them is the key to gaining good marks. Remember, the marking is based entirely on these Objectives. The final module, Exploring Texts, tests all the Objectives.

The rest of this book deals with each of the three assessment modules for the course. For each module, we take you through its design and content with practical advice and exercises. The work you will be asked to do has been tailored to the type of assessment involved in each module; this might be external assessment, open or closed book, or coursework. We also provide examples of the sorts of questions and tasks that will be used to test each module as part of the examination.

You will find a glossary for this book on page 223; you will also find the glossary in the previous book, for AS English Literature, helpful.

# The key to success: understanding the Assessment

## Objectives

The Assessment Objectives for the module require that you:

| Assessment Objectives | |
|---|---|
| AO1 | communicate clearly the knowledge, understanding and insight appropriate to literary study, using appropriate terminology and accurate and coherent written expression |
| AO2ii | respond with knowledge and understanding to literary texts of different types and periods, exploring and commenting on relationships and comparisons between literary texts |
| AO3 | show detailed understanding of the ways in which writers' choices of form, structure and language shape meanings |
| AO4 | articulate independent opinions and judgements, informed by different interpretations of literary texts by other readers |
| AO5ii | evaluate the significance of cultural, historical and other contextual influences on literary texts and study |

## What the Assessment Objectives mean

The Assessment Objectives were dealt with in the book accompanying the Advanced Subsidiary (AS) Specification, and you will have worked with them during your AS course. It's important to recognise, though, that at A Level, AO2 and AO5 change, and so make new demands on students. At AS, AO2i asks candidates to 'respond with knowledge and understanding to literary texts of different types and periods'. At A Level, this becomes: 'exploring and commenting on relationships and comparisons between literary texts.' As you can see, this is quite different, reintroducing a requirement to compare texts that you were probably used to in your GCSE English Literature course.

AO5i at AS asks candidates to show 'understanding of the contexts in which literary texts are written and understood'. At A Level this becomes: 'evaluate the significance of cultural, historical and other contextual influences on literary texts and study.' What you have to think about, therefore, is how various factors have shaped the writing of the texts you're studying – and how they affect your reading of them. This is the first step. The second is to think about which **contexts** are important in reading the text, and of these, which are the *most* important. For a full response, therefore, you may need to explore not only the contexts informing the text, but also your characteristics as a reader.

Here are some of the relevant types of context which you might look at (questions of context will be fully developed later).

- The context of period or era including significant social, historical, political and cultural processes, which could include period-specific styles. This could concern the period when the work was written, or the period that is being written about. These may not be the same, of course. A knowledge of the nineteenth-century Irish evictions, for instance, would affect your reading of Brian Friel's *Translations* – moreover, this play was first performed in the early 1980s in Derry in Northern Ireland, and so audiences would have seen it in the context of the continuing Troubles. If you evaluate how important this context is to their response, or to yours now, then you will be 'evaluating the significance' of the context.

- The context of the work in terms of the writer's biography or **milieu**. This could involve considering, for example, how a personal experience of war or racial prejudice had influenced a writer's works.

- The literary context, which includes looking at works in terms of the genre to which they belong; a play, for instance, could be seen in terms of the genre of **Revenge Tragedy**. This can also be a period-specific context, an example being the genre of **Restoration Comedy,** which you would consider when reading Congreve's *The Way of the World* – the extent to which his play fits into this genre, and ways in which it might go beyond it, would be an evaluation of significance.

- The language context, including relevant episodes in the use and development of literary language, the question of colloquial and dialect styles, and so on.

- The different contexts for a work established by its reception over time – works may well have different meanings and effects in different periods.

## Breaking down the Assessment Objectives

As you can see, the Assessment Objectives define the literary skills that you have to show in the course. It is vital to understand that they are awarded a different number of marks in different modules, and even for different texts. For example, in Module 5, which is the Set Texts module, the 30 marks available are divided like this:

| | |
|---|---|
| **AO1** | 5 marks |
| **AO3** | 5 marks |
| **AO4** | 10 marks |
| **AO5ii** | 10 marks |

In this module, you have to choose a pre-1770 drama text and a pre-1900 poetry text. The marks are divided between the texts like this:

| | | | |
|---|---|---|---|
| **Poetry: AO3** | 5 marks | **AO4** | 10 marks |
| **Drama: AO1** | 5 marks | **AO5ii** | 10 marks |

So it is important to remember that the marks depend on the Assessment Objectives, and that the marks are different in the different modules, and sometimes in the different sections, too. That's why there are boxes at the beginning of each of the three modules to show you exactly which Assessment Objectives count in that module, and the percentage of the marks each one carries.

## An exercise in the new A Level Assessment Objectives

### STOP ALL THE CLOCKS

Stop all the clocks, cut off the telephone,
Prevent the dog from barking with a juicy bone,
Silence the pianos and with muffled drum
Bring out the coffin, let the mourners come.

Let aeroplanes circle moaning overhead
Scribbling on the sky the message He Is Dead,
Put crêpe bows round the white necks of the public doves,
Let the traffic policemen wear black cotton gloves.

He was my North, my South, my East and West,
Mt working week and my Sunday rest,
My noon, my midnight, my talk, my song;
I thought that love would last forever: I was wrong.

The stars are not wanted now: put out every one;
Pack up the moon and dismantle the sun;
Pour away the ocean and sweep up the wood,
For nothing now can ever come to any good.

W. H. AUDEN

### SONNET 18

Shall I compare thee to a summer's day?
Thou art more lovely and more temperate.
Rough winds do shake the darling buds of May,
And summer's lease hath all too short a date:
Sometime too hot the eye of heaven shines,
And often is his gold complexion dimm'd;
And every fair from fair some time declines,
By chance, or nature's changing course, untrimm'd;
But thy eternal summer shall not fade
Nor lose possession of that fair thou ow'st;
Nor shall Death brag thou wand'rest in his shade,
When in eternal lines to time thou grow'st;
    So long as men can breathe or eyes can see,
    So long lives this, and this gives life to thee.

WILLIAM SHAKESPEARE

## VALENTINE

Not a red rose or a satin heart.

I give you an onion.
It is a moon wrapped in brown paper.
It promises light
like the careful undressing of love.

Here.
It will blind you with tears
like a lover.
It will make your reflection
a wobbling photo of grief.

I am trying to be truthful.

Not a cute card or a kissogram.

I give you an onion.
Its fierce kiss will stay on your lips,
possessive and faithful
as we are,
for as long as we are.

Take it.
Its platinum loops shrink to a wedding-ring,
if you like.
Lethal.
Its scent will cling to your fingers,
cling to your knife.

CAROL ANN DUFFY

Although you might have come across these poems before, the aim here is to look at them in the context of the A Level Assessment Objectives. In other words you now need to look at them in a different way.

## Assessment Objective AO2ii

> AO2ii respond with knowledge and understanding to literary texts of different types and periods, exploring and commenting on relationships and comparisons between literary texts

Beginning to compare these poems is easy – all three are concerned with love and time. All three are personal poems written in the first person: 'Stop all the clocks' mourns the death of a loved one, while the other two make declarations of love, though not in a straightforward way. 'Valentine' in particular concerns itself with the realities of love ('I am trying to be truthful'), in other words with love's difficulties and dangers.

To compare the poems in a more detailed way, it is a good idea to use AO3 as a framework, comparing how the three poets use *form*, *structure* and *language* to shape meanings. Work your way through the poems using the following suggestions.

## Form

There are three different forms illustrated by these poems – but simply identifying the forms is not enough; you need to compare how form expresses meaning in each case.

(1) The four separate verses of 'Stop all the clocks' suggest that each verse deals with a separate aspect of the subject. Is this in fact the case? How do punctuation and rhyme give a sense of finality?

(2) *Sonnet 18* is unpunctuated by verse divisions. Is it one continuous argument? If there are changes, how are they indicated by the form? Think about rhyme as well as page layout.

(3) 'Valentine' does not follow a set pattern of verse, or of rhyme, though there are repetitions and echoes. Can you find any of these? How does the author use the form to suggest unconnected but related thoughts about love, and about this particular relationship?

Now review your conclusions, and think about the relationships and comparisons between these texts.

## Structure

In all three poems form is closely related to structure.

(1) You have already worked out the subjects of each of the verses in 'Stop all the clocks'. Is there a logical structure? How does the poem build to the last verse, and to the last line in particular?

(2) How does the first line of *Sonnet 18* set the agenda for the whole poem? Where does the view of time alter, and which word at the beginning of a line marks the shift? The final change is to introduce the idea of the life of the poem, not just the person. Where does this begin?

(3) 'Valentine' looks different from the others on the page, not only because of the lack of verse pattern, but also because of the varying line lengths. Look at the effects of some of the very short lines, and the three single lines. Why do you think the poem begins the way it does, and then ends the way it does?

Now review your conclusions, and think about the relationships and comparisons between these texts.

## Language

There's a lot to say about the ways in which language is used to express meanings in these three poems. Here are a few questions to get you started.

(1)   Look at all three poems for sentence forms. Where can you find commands, or questions? Why has the poet used a particular form?

(2)   Two of these poems make use of repetitions, and one doesn't. What are the effects of the repetitions where they are used, and what does the lack of repetition in the other one tell you about that poem?

(3)   Each of the three poems is characterised by a particular uses of language: look at the verbs in 'Stop all the clocks'; the word-play in *Sonnet 18*; and the unorthodox sentences in 'Valentine'.

(4)   Imagery is a central feature of all three poems.

- Look at the imagery in the last two verses of 'Stop all the clocks'. What is the effect of all of them taken together? How does each image contribute to the whole? Notice particularly the line about the moon and the sun, bearing in mind the other two poems.

- Both the other poems dwell on a single image. In 'Valentine', what gifts does the speaker *reject*, and why? Why does she find an onion appropriate, and what view of love does this reveal? Look at the further comparisons that stem from this central idea.

- *Sonnet 18* works on one image, introduced in the first line. As in 'Valentine', the conventional love comparison is here rejected. Look at the ways in which Shakespeare uses the idea to praise the object of the poem, developing more imagery along the way.

Now review your conclusions, and think about the relationships and comparisons between these texts.

## Assessment Objective 5ii

> AO5ii   evaluate the significance of cultural, historical and other contextual
> influences on literary texts and study

At A Level it is not enough simply to recognise the contexts of each text studied. You also have to *evaluate their significance* for your reading of the text, particularly when you start to think about forming an interpretation. The thoughts and questions that follow should help you to see what this might mean, and to see how the Assessment Objectives are inter-related.

'Stop all the clocks' is an interesting poem to start with when thinking about contexts. You might already have two contexts for your reading of the text – as part of GCSE English Literature study you may have studied it in the context of other poems, or in the context of the film *Four Weddings and a Funeral*. If you have heard it read in this film, this context may well be significant in your response. In the film, the reading of this poem at a funeral is a very emotional moment, designed to move the audience, who may well also associate it with homosexual love. The first two verses of the poem were first published, however, in the prose/verse drama *The Ascent of F6*, by W. H. Auden and Christopher Isherwood. When you study the rest of the poem in this original version, you might well come to a very different interpretation of the verses.

## ACTIVITY

Re-read the first two verse of 'Stop all the clocks' (page vii), then read the following three verses, which completed the piece in *The Ascent of F6*.

Hold up your umbrellas to keep off the rain
From Doctor Williams while he opens a vein;
Life, he pronounces, it is finally extinct.
Sergeant, arrest that man who said he winked!

Shawcross will say a few words sad and kind
To the weeping crowds about the Master-Mind,
While Lamp with a powerful microscope
Searches their faces for a sign of hope.

And Gunn, of course, will drive the motor-hearse:
None could drive it better, most would drive it worse.
He'll open up the throttle to its fullest power
And drive him to the grave at ninety miles an hour.

The poem may well look more like a satirical parody of love poetry now. How has the writer worked to create this tone? Think about:

- the effects of particular words
- the effects of particular rhymes
- the actions of the characters, and how they are described.

Clearly these two contexts – the film and the play – give rise to interpretations that are quite opposed to each other. Does this mean that the satirical reading of the poem is the 'right' one? No. If it did, it would mean that anybody's response to the poem based on the film alone would somehow be invalid. AO5i, the building block for AO5ii, concerns both the contexts in which literary texts are *written* and the contexts in which they are *understood* – but these need not be the same. Here, the poem is written in one context, and understood in another by the film's audience. Two meanings, or interpretations, are generated, and neither is invalid. Nor does it make any difference that the writer did not intend, or indeed know about, the film context. Once the text is written, the writer is merely one interpreter of its meaning.

In the other two poems – 'Valentine' and *Sonnet 18* – *gender* is an important context. Unlike 'Stop all the clocks', neither identifies the gender of the person addressed. Some research might reveal significant contexts here. If you assume that the speaker in the poem – the persona – is meant to be the poet (although that might not be the case), what might the sexual preferences of the writer tell you? When you have researched this, you might think about these issues:

- Does this information make any difference to your reading of the poems? In other words, are the contexts significant? Is there any indication in the poems that these contexts were significant to the writing – and if so, how significant were they?

- If you respond to the poems differently when you know about these contexts, why is that? Is it to do with the poems, or with you? This may lead you to evaluate yourself as a reader – to decide what it is that is most important to you.

- What evidence are you using in coming to a view about the poems? Context is a form of evidence in itself, as are the details of form, language and structure. The tone of 'Stop all the clocks' can perhaps be read either way, depending on how you view the evidence – but what evidence of context can you find in the other two poems?

You could, of course, investigate other contexts, and if you were studying these texts as part of your A Level course you would have to choose which to pursue – to decide which contexts might prove to be significant in the writing and the understanding of the texts. You might want to look at the features of the poems that place them in their historic and social contexts. With *Sonnet 18*, for example, you could look at the literary context of the sonnet form in this period, and at how Shakespeare uses it, or at how ambiguity appears in other Shakespeare sonnets. If you were tackling this as an A Level task, you would also need to evaluate the significance of these contexts to ask: which of these contexts are central to my understanding of the texts, and why?

You will have noticed that as you investigated and thought about contexts, more relationships and comparisons between the three texts occurred to you, taking you back to AO2ii. This is the real point. The A Level course, like the AS course, divides the subject into Assessment Objectives to test your knowledge of the ways that English Literature works, but these areas are very closely inter-related, and sometimes overlap. In the final module in the course, Exploring Texts, all the Assessment Objectives are tested, to see what you have learned about the study of English Literature during the whole A Level course. In working through these three poems, you have already done exactly that – explored texts using each of the Assessment Objectives.

# MODULE 4  Comparing Texts

The Assessment Objectives for this module require that you:

## ASSESSMENT OBJECTIVES

**AO1**   communicate clearly the knowledge, understanding and insight
appropriate to literary study, using appropriate terminology and accurate
and coherent written expression
(5% of the final A2 mark; 2½% of the final A Level mark)

**AO2ii**   respond with knowledge and understanding to literary texts of different
types and periods, exploring and commenting on relationships and
comparisons between literary texts
(10% of the final A2 mark; 5% of the final A Level mark)

**AO3**   show detailed understanding of the ways in which writers' choices of
form, structure and language shape meanings
(5% of the final A2 mark; 2½% of the final A Level mark)

**AO4**   articulate independent opinions and judgements, informed by different
interpretations of literary texts by other readers
(5% of the final A2 mark; 2½% of the final A Level mark)

**AO5ii**   evaluate the significance of cultural, historical and other contextual
influences on literary texts and study
(5% of the final A2 mark; 2½% of the final A Level mark)

## Content

This module meets the requirements for a *prose* text. Though this text may be
taken from any period, there are some restrictions:

- The second text must be *substantial*, but it can be from any genre.

- The two texts must be of different *types*. This does not mean that they
must be of different genres (though you may use different genres if you
like). It means that they must employ different approaches. For example,
you would be allowed to compare a novel concerned with racial issues
such as Toni Morrison's *Beloved*, which is written with flashbacks, with
Alice Walker's *The Color Purple*, which is written in letter-form.

- The two texts must be of different *periods* (a 'period' consists of about 30
years). For example, you would be able to compare an early detective
novel, such as Raymond Chandler's *The Big Sleep* (1939), with a novel in
the same genre but from a different period, such as Michael Dibdin's *The
Long Finish* (1998).

This is also the module dealing with coursework, and it will be assessed in the same way as the examination modules, by moving up the ladder of the marking scheme.

## Aim

The aim of this module is to provide you with the opportunity to compare two texts in order to focus on the ways in which they relate to each other. It involves all the Assessment Objectives listed, but gives a special emphasis to AO2ii, as you might expect. This means that whichever texts you use for this module, and however you tackle it, you must keep the requirement to explore *comparisons* at the centre of your work.

The next section, therefore, will deal with the ways in which you can start exploring comparisons, and then look at coursework issues (page 30).

## Ways of looking at texts for comparison

It's important to identify at least two or three ways in which comparisons can be made, so that the individual texts are effectively illuminated by the comparison. That's one of the central points of AO2ii: by looking at a text in the light of another, you come to understand more about it. A good way to think about similarities and differences between texts is to focus on the other Assessment Objectives: after all, they are the basis of your course in English Literature.

The rest of this Section looks at these different ways of comparing texts:

**AO3** Form
Structure
Language
Meanings

**AO4** Critical perspectives

**AO5ii** Historical contexts
Social contexts
Socio-cultural contexts
Socio-economic contexts
Language contexts
**Generic** and literary contexts

Obviously, you will not be writing about all these different ways in your essay; you will need to choose the ones that are most appropriate to the texts you are comparing. There may in fact be other contexts, not treated here, that are particularly relevant to your chosen texts. What is important is that you write something about each of the targeted Assessment Objectives, and this means that you will have to plan your essay so as to ensure that you are covering AO3, AO4 and AO5ii. Coverage of AO1 will be dealt with by the end of this module, and because you are comparing texts all the time in your essay, you will always be addressing AO2ii.

The ideas and related activities that follow are intended to offer you a wide range of possibilities for comparison.

## Assessment Objective 3

> AO3 show detailed understanding of the ways in which writers' choices of form, structure and language shape meanings

### Form

Form is an interesting starting point for a comparison, as you can think about the ways that different forms can be used to explore the same subjects or ideas. You could, for instance, look at comparisons between the poetry of Wilfred Owen and the novel *Birdsong* by Sebastian Faulks. These texts, or any two concerned with the First World War, would also form a preparation for Module 6, Exploring Texts. The following activities begin with comparing form, but move on to other issues – you should seek to do the same with your texts. The first text is Owen's 'Cramped in that funnelled hole'.

Cramped in that funnelled hole, they watched the dawn
Open a jagged rim around; a yawn
Of death's jaws, which had all but swallowed them
Stuck in the bottom of his throat of phlegm.

They were in one of many mouths of Hell
Not seen of seers in visions; only felt
As teeth of traps; when bones and the dead are smelt
Under the mud where long ago they fell
Mixed with the sour sharp odour of the shell.

In the following extract from *Birdsong*, Stephen, the main character of the novel, has taken refuge in a shell-hole during an attack.

Stephen dropped his face into the earth and let it fill his mouth. He closed his eyes because he had seen enough. You are going to hell. Azaire's parting words filled his head. They were drilled in by the shattering noise around them.

Byrne somehow got the boy back into the shellhole. Stephen wished he hadn't. He was clearly going to die.

Harrington's sergeant was shouting for another charge and a dozen men responded. Stephen watched them reach the first line of fire before he realized that Byrne was with them. He was trying to force a way through the wire when he was caught off the ground, suspended, his boots shaking as his body was filled with bullets.

Stephen lay in the shell hole with the boy and the man who had died in the morning. For three hours until the sun began to weaken he watched the boy begging for water. He tried to close his ears to the plea. On one corpse there was still a bottle, but a bullet hole had let most of it leak away. What was left was a reddish brown, contaminated by earth and blood. Stephen poured it into the boy's beseeching mouth.

## ACTIVITY 1

Compare the two extracts above, using these questions to help you.

- The *forms* are clearly different. The extract from the novel is exactly that, an extract. How do you know it is not complete in itself? What information might you expect to have been given before this point in the novel?

- The poem is a fragment – it was found after Owen's death, and thought to be incomplete. Can it stand by itself, though? How is it different from the prose in this respect, and why? Do you need to know anything else? These questions might lead you to think about the writer's intentions.

- Owen creates some effects with form not open to Faulks. Look at the effects of the end of the second line in each stanza, where the end of a line naturally creates a gap. You might look at the effects of rhyme, too – again not found in the prose.

- The ideas and situations – part of the *context* of the writing here – are clearly comparable. Sort them out. Think about the physical positions of the characters, their feelings and attitudes, the times of day, the sounds (or lack of them).

- The *language* used by each writer is revealing. In the poem, Owen uses from the beginning the idea that the shell-hole is like a mouth. Find where the idea begins and trace it through, noticing how he uses it to comment on the men's situation.

- Although the prose is not as packed with imagery – a difference resulting from form, perhaps – Faulks does use language to create emotive effects. Look at the first and last lines of the extract with this in mind.

- Both writers use the senses extensively to involve the reader. Look for the way they use sight, hearing, touch, smell or taste.

- What do you think is the attitude of each of the writers to the war? Notice that they both use the same key word to describe the nature of the experience.

If you had actually chosen this Owen/*Birdsong* pairing, the prose extract here might have led you to other poems by Owen, such as 'Anthem for Doomed Youth', 'Inspection', 'At a Calvary near the Ancre', or (as in Pair 2 below) 'Strange Meeting'.

Here are two more pairs of extracts from the same authors.

## Pair 1

The opening four lines of 'Dulce et Decorum Est' by Wilfred Owen:

Bent double, like old beggars under sacks,
Knock-kneed, coughing like hags, we cursed through sludge,
Till on the haunting flares we turned our backs
And towards our distant rest began to trudge.

And from *Birdsong* by Sebastian Faulks:

It was dark at last. The night poured down in waves from the ridge about them and the guns at last fell silent.

The earth began to move. To their right a man who had lain still since the first attack, eased himself upright, then fell again when his damaged leg would not take his weight. Other single men moved, and began to come up like worms from their shellholes, limping, crawling, dragging themselves out. Within minutes the hillside was seething with the movement of the wounded as they attempted to get themselves back to their line.

'Christ,' said Weir, 'I had no idea there were so many men out there.'

It was like a resurrection in the cemetery twelve miles long. Bent, agonized shapes loomed in multitudes on the churned earth, limping and dragging back to reclaim their life. It was as though the land were disgorging a generation of crippled sleepers, each one distinct but related to its twisted brothers as they teemed up from the reluctant earth.

## Pair 2

The first fourteen and last five lines of Owen's 'Strange Meeting':

It seemed that out of battle I escaped
Down some profound dull tunnel, long since scooped
Through granites which titanic wars had groined.

Yet also there encumbered sleepers groaned,
Too fast in thought or death to be bestirred.
Then, as I probed them, one sprang up, and stared
With piteous recognition in fixed eyes,
Lifting distressful hands, as if to bless.
And by his smile, I knew that sullen hall, —

By his dead smile I knew we stood in Hell.

With a thousand pains that vision's face was grained;
Yet no blood reached there from the upper ground,
And no guns thumped, or down the flues made moan.
'Strange friend,' I said, 'here is no cause to mourn.'

…

'I am the enemy you killed, my friend.
I knew you in this dark: for so you frowned
Yesterday through me as you jabbed and killed.
I parried; but my hands were loath and cold.
Let us sleep now…'

The next extract from *Birdsong* comes from the end of a chapter, and almost at the end of the account of the First World War in the novel. Stephen is pulled from a blown-up tunnel by a German soldier, who has also been trapped underground.

He looked up and saw the legs of his rescuer. They were clothed in the German *feldgrau*, the colour of his darkest dream.

He staggered to his feet and his hand went to pull out his revolver, but there was nothing there, only the torn, drenched rags of his trousers.

He looked into the face of the man who stood in front of him and his fists went up from his sides like those of a farm boy about to fight.

At some deep level, far below anything his exhausted mind could reach, the conflicts of his soul dragged through him like waves grating on the packed shingle of a beach. The sound of his life calling to him on a distant road; the faces of the men who had been slaughtered, the closed eyes of Michael Weir in his coffin; his scalding hatred of the enemy, of Max and all the men who had brought him to this moment; the flesh and love of Isabelle, and the eyes of her sister.

Far beyond thought, the resolution came to him and he found his arms, still raised, beginning to spread and open.

Levi looked at this wild-eyed figure, half-demented, his brother's killer. For no reason he could tell, he found that he had opened his own arms in turn, and the two men fell upon each other's shoulders, weeping at the bitter strangeness of their human lives.

## ACTIVITY 2

### Pair 1

- Consider what the use of dialogue in the prose adds to the effect.

- Compare the imagery used in the two pieces, this time noticing the intensity of the imagery in the prose.

- Look for words in the two pieces which are the same, or very similar. Why do both writers make these choices, do you think?

- Compare the situations depicted and the writers' attitudes to them.

### Pair 2

- There's a lot to say about the effects of the different forms here. In the poem, look at the effects of the **half-rhymes**, and at the last line. The prose is also a closure – how does it read like an ending? Putting the two together, you can compare the different effects of form.

- Both language and situations are similar here. Look at them together. The similarities should reveal something about the attitudes and intentions of the writers.

- What futures are suggested in these endings?

You've done a lot of work on this pair of texts. If you look at the section on the strategic planning of your coursework (page 34 below), you'll see how this sort of analysis can be used in a complete piece of coursework.

## Structure

Structure can be a key factor in making comparisons between texts. For instance, three novels that all deal with war, but differ significantly in structure, are Joseph Heller's *Catch-22* (1961), Martin Amis's *Time's Arrow* (1991), and Sebastian Faulks's *Birdsong* (1993). Although the central subject of each novel is war, there are significant differences in the way the writers use structures to present it. In *Catch-22* the emphasis moves from character to character and the narrative is shot through with flashbacks. *Time's Arrow* is in a sense chronological, for it tells the story of the Holocaust, but backwards, each chapter starting at a point before the previous one. *Birdsong* is chronological through the war episodes, but there are also significant leaps in time, a much later narrative being interwoven with the war episodes.

If you were to compare *Catch-22* with either of the other texts, you would be comparing texts of a different period. A key element here would be the effects of the choice of structure: how, to echo the words of the Assessment Objective (AO3), the writers had shaped meanings from their choices. The contexts could also be compared, as well as the writers' attitudes, which might be conveyed by language as well as by structure. To enable you to address AO4, you might also like to think about which approach you found the most effective.

## Language

Language can form key points for comparison between texts. There are texts, for instance, where *dialect* is a significant factor. Irving Welsh's novel *Trainspotting* could be compared with Peter Roper's play *The Steamie* (also set in Glasgow), or with a D. H. Lawrence novel in which dialect is used.

Changes in language over time could be looked at, if two texts from very different time periods are studied. Nathaniel Hawthorne's novel *The Scarlet Letter* (1850), for instance, which deals with the consequences of adultery, could be compared with A. S. Byatt's *Possession* (1990), which within itself has contrasting forms, with language shaped to reflect language changes over time.

Below is an activity centred on similarities and differences in the use of language. The two writers are depicting significant moments in the lines of their central characters.

### ACTIVITY 3

In these two depictions of a meal, the writers use a range of techniques to convey pleasure. Compare the passages, using the questions below to help you.

In this extract from *A Christmas Carol* by Charles Dickens, the Cratchit family are enjoying their Christmas meal:

Such a bustle ensued that you might have thought a goose the rarest of all birds; a feathered phenomenon, to which a black swan was a matter of course; and in truth it was something very like it in that house. Mrs Cratchit made the gravy (ready beforehand in a little saucepan) hissing hot; Master Peter mashed the potatoes with incredible vigour; Miss Belinda sweetened up the apple-sauce; Martha dusted the hot plates; Bob took Tiny Tim beside him in a tiny corner at the table; the two young Cratchits set chairs for everybody, not forgetting themselves, and mounting guard upon their posts, crammed spoons into their mouths, lest they should shriek for goose before their turn came to be helped. At last the dishes were set on, and grace was said. It was succeeded by a breathless pause, as Mrs Cratchit, looking slowly all along the carving knife, prepared to plunge it in the breast; but when she did, and when the long expected gush of stuffing issued forth, one murmur of delight arose all round the board, and even Tiny Tim, excited by the two young Cratchits, beat on the table with the handle of his knife, and feebly cried Hurrah!

There never was such a goose. Bob said he didn't believe there ever was such a goose cooked. Its tenderness and flavour, size and cheapness, were the themes of universal admiration. Eked out by the apple-sauce and mashed potatoes, it was a sufficient dinner for the whole family; indeed, as Mrs Cratchit said with great delight (surveying one small atom of bone upon the dish), they hadn't ate it all at last! Yet everyone had had enough and the youngest Cratchits in particular, were steeped in sage and onion to the eyebrows!

In the following extract, from *To the Lighthouse* by Virginia Woolf, Mrs Ramsay is serving a meal to her guests, and feels that the 'coherence' she had wanted has happened at last.

Everything seemed possible. Everything seemed right. Just now (but this cannot last, she thought, dissociating herself from the moment while they were all talking about boots) just now she had reached security; she hovered like a hawk suspended; like a flag floated in a element of joy which filled every nerve of her body fully and sweetly, not noisily, solemnly rather, for it arose, she thought, looking at them eating there, from husband and children and friends; all of which rising in this profound stillness (she was helping William Bankes to one very small piece more and peered into the depths of the earthenware pot) seemed now for no special reason to stay there like a smoke, like a fume rising upwards, holding them safe together. Nothing need be said; nothing could be said. There it was, all around them. It partook, she felt, carefully helping Mr. Bankes to a specially tender piece, of eternity; as she had already felt about something different once before that afternoon; there is a coherence in things, a stability; something, she meant, is immune from change, and shines out (she glanced at the window with its ripple of reflected lights) in the fact of the flowing, the fleeting, the spectral, like a ruby; so that again to-night she had the feeling she had had once to-day already, of peace, of rest. Of such moments, she thought, the thing is made that remains for ever after. This would remain.

'Yes,' she assured William Bankes, 'there is plenty for everybody.'

- Both writers suggest that the characters experience something unusual. How does each writer use viewpoint and narrative technique to get this idea across?

- Compare the physical effects of pleasure on the characters in both extracts.

- Look for movement and stillness in each piece, and how they are conveyed. You should look particularly at the repetition of words, at syntax, and at sentence length.

- Look for suggestions of:

  - religion
  - closeness or intimacy
  - the importance of family
  - humour.

- To sum up the differences between the two extracts: How are the tones of the extracts different? What could you conclude about the writers' intentions?

Language is a key feature in both novels. If you were comparing them, you could look at the ways each conveys childhood through sentence *forms*, differences in *structure*, and invented *language*.

## Meanings

The central meanings of texts could obviously form the basis for a comparison, but if you are choosing texts for coursework you would do best to choose texts where the relationships and comparisons can develop into different areas. A 'rites of passage' novel like James Joyce's *A Portrait of the Artist as a Young Man* could be compared, for example, with J. D. Salinger's *The Catcher in the Rye*. Both depict a boy growing up, but the language and settings are very different. Alternatively, a play could be chosen for comparison with a rites of passage novel – Neil Simon's play *Brighton Beach Memoirs*, for instance, or his *Broadway Bound*. In this case, differences of form in dealing with a similar subject could be analysed as well, as with Activities 1 and 2 based on Wilfred Owen's poetry and Sebastian Faulks's novel *Birdsong*.

## Assessment Objective 4

> AO4   articulate independent opinions and judgements, informed by different interpretations of literary texts by other readers

So far, you have looked primarily at AO2ii, so it might now be helpful to take a closer look at the complex AO4 and AO5ii. This will help you to make a more informed choice about which precise area of these Objectives you would like to target in your coursework.  Below is a more detailed look at AO4, and on page 15 you will find AO5ii broken down in the same way.

This Objective is targeted in coursework, and in the poetry section of Module 5. In the **Specification**, five areas are outlined for this objective. It states that 'Candidates will be expected to show awareness of the following' (note, you will *not* be expected to write about *all* of them):

## Area 1

That we, as readers, are influenced by our own experiences, actual or imagined, and that our cultural background has an effect on our interpretation: thus the interpretation of literary texts, or the determination of their significance, can depend on the interpretative stance taken by the reader.

*Unpicking this area*   Because we are the products of different personal experiences and different social and cultural backgrounds, we all look at a text in an individual way: we each form an independent, and to some extent unique, view of a text.

*Coursework*   This is something that you will do automatically as you form judgements on each text you study. You must always make your own judgement on a text clear.

## Area 2

That there might be significant differences in the way literary texts are understood in different periods, and by different individuals or social groups.

*Unpicking this area*   This means that people from different historical periods, or from different social groups – for example, African Americans, or those with religious beliefs – may see texts very differently. You will see that part of Area 2 overlaps with Area 4 below.

*Coursework*   This area can be addressed by looking at responses to a text over two different historical periods.

## Area 3

That texts do not reflect an external and objective reality; instead, they embody attitudes and values.

*Unpicking this area*   The key words here are 'attitudes' and 'values'. Whenever you study a text, you inevitably concern yourself with determining the 'attitudes and values' embodied in that text. You should also discuss what it is about the text that gives it a *universal* value: in other words, why a text can appeal to readers in different periods.

*Coursework*   In this module you will always be expected to look at the 'attitudes' and 'values' behind texts in order to discuss the elements that make a text 'important'.

## Area 4

That there are different ways of looking at texts, based on particular approaches or theories (for example, those of **feminists**, critics influenced by **Marxism** or **structuralism**, and so on). Discussing these theories will require some understanding of critical concepts and terminology.

*Unpicking this area*   This area, which overlaps with Area 2 above, is a very easy area to target. You should not be too alarmed by the need to understand such theories. You are not expected to study critical texts in detail; you simply have to have a broad a grasp of the principles behind certain key theories.

*Coursework*   An example of a feminist reading of a text will be discussed below using the novels *Jane Eyre* and *The Color Purple* below (Critical perspectives, page 12).

## Area 5

That literary texts are frequently open-ended, dialectical or controversial in method; thus ambiguity and uncertainty are central to the reading of texts, and examination tasks will therefore expect candidates to take part in genuine critical enquiry rather than simply to respond to tasks assuming the teacher/examiner already knows the 'right' answer.

*Unpicking this area*   This simply means that you must engage with the texts thoroughly, both in your coursework and in your study of texts for Module 5. You must be confident enough to form an independent opinion about the texts you are studying, and be able to offer a considered opinion about that text.

*Coursework*   While working through this module you will already have formed your own opinions about the texts, and of course will continue to do so.

## Critical perspectives

Thinking about critical perspectives can form a fruitful starting point for comparisons. One of the ways of illuminating texts such as *The Color Purple* by Alice Walker and *Jane Eyre* by Charlotte Brontë is to see them from a feminist perspective.

### ACTIVITY 4

Read these two extracts, and then consider them in the light of the critical perspectives that follow.

In this extract from *Jane Eyre*, the housekeeper, Mrs Fairfax, is questioning Jane, a mere governess, about her relationship with their employer, Mr Rochester.

'I am sorry to grieve you,' pursued the widow; 'but you are so young, and so little acquainted with men, I wished to put you on your guard. It is an old saying that "all is not gold that glitters"; and in this case I do fear there will be something found to be different to what either you or I expect.'

'Why! – am I a monster?' I said: 'is it impossible that Mr. Rochester should have a sincere affection for me?'

'No: you are very well; and much improved of late; and Mr. Rochester, I daresay, is fond of you. I have always noticed that you were a sort of pet of his. There are times when, for your sake, I have been a little uneasy at his marked preference, and have wished to put you on your guard: but I did not like to suggest even the possibility of wrong. I knew such an idea would shock, perhaps offend you; and you were so discreet, and so thoroughly modest and sensible, I hoped you might be trusted to protect yourself. Last night I cannot tell you what I suffered when I sought all over the house, and could find you nowhere, nor the master either; and then, at twelve o'clock, saw you come in with him.'

'Well, never mind that now', I interrupted impatiently: 'it is enough that all was right.'

'I hope all will be right in the end,' she said: 'but, believe me, you cannot be too careful. Try and keep Mr. Rochester at a distance: distrust yourself as well as him. Gentlemen in his station are not accustomed to marry their governesses.'

In this letter from Alice Walker's *The Color Purple*, Celie is describing the preparations for the funeral of Sofia's mother.

Harpo say, Whoever heard of women pallbearers. That all I'm trying to say.

Well, say Sofia, you said it. Now you can hush.

I know she your mother, say Harpo. But still.

You gon help us or not? say Sofia.

What it gon look like? say Harpo. Three big stout women pallbearers look like they ought to be home frying chicken.

Three of our brothers be with us, on the other side, say Sofia. I guess they look like field hands.

But peoples use to men doing this sort of thing. Women weaker, he say. People think they weaker, say they weaker, anyhow. Women spose to take it easy. Cry if you want to. Not try to take over.

Try to take over, say Sofia. The woman dead. I can cry and take it easy and lift the coffin too. And whether you help us or not with the food and the chairs and the get-together afterward, that's exactly what I plan to do.

These two extracts are taken from novels of two different periods: *Jane Eyre* was published in England in the middle of the nineteenth century, *The Color Purple* was published in the United States in the 1980s.

You could look at these extracts from several different critical perspectives. Here are five to consider:

- a social perspective
- a feminist perspective
- a cultural perspective
- the perspective of period
- your own critical perspective.

### A social perspective:

- What is there in the extracts that suggests how society may be organised in terms of a social *hierarchy*?
- What is there in the extracts that suggests how society may be organised in terms of social *structure*?

### A feminist perspective:

- What do you make of the situation and role of women in society in each extract and text?
- Are there any similarities?
- Are there any differences?

### A cultural perspective:

- What do you learn from the culture and cultural attitudes embedded in these extracts and texts?
- Is there a difference in the cultures?
- What do you learn of customs at work and at leisure?

### The perspective of period:

- What sense do you have of the historical periods in which these extracts are set?
- How is this indicated?
- Do either or both texts have a value for readers outside the specific period in which they are set?

### Your own critical perspective:

When setting out your own critical perspective you must make clear:

- which of these readings interests you
- which you consider to be the most useful way into the book for you, and why.

Offering your own critical perspective, 'your own interpretation', is *essential* to achieving AO4, which states that students ought to be able to 'articulate independent opinions and judgements, informed by different interpretations of literary texts by other readers'.

For this reason, it's always necessary to make your own interpretation abundantly clear.

A feminist comparison of these two texts might include:

- the treatment of sexuality

- the ways in which feminist issues are reflected in the type of narrative used in each text – letters in *The Color Purple*, and the autobiographical mode in *Jane Eyre*

- the power struggles between male and female in the two narratives, which have very different outcomes.

The position of women in society could also be an important element in looking at less overtly feminist texts. For example, this point of view could be used to compare Nathaniel Hawthorne's *The Scarlet Letter* and Margaret Atwood's *The Handmaid's Tale*.

Comparing the presentation of power and social class in texts – the Marxist perspective, in other words – could also be a good starting point. The novel *Hard Times* by Charles Dickens and J. B. Priestley's play *An Inspector Calls* offer similar perspectives on society, though they differ in social and historical contexts, and have different forms. *King Lear* is also open to a Marxist interpretation, and comparing it with Thomas Hardy's novel *Far From the Madding Crowd* would raise issues of family and power, gender and power, and nature and humankind. A **psychoanalytical** reading of the nature of obsession in *Enduring Love* by Ian McEwan and in either *Hamlet* or *Othello* would provide some illuminating relationships and comparisons.

## Assessment Objective 5ii

> AO5ii   evaluate the significance of cultural, historical and other contextual influences on literary texts and study

This Assessment Objective is targeted in coursework, and in the drama section of Module 5. In the Specification there are seven areas outlined for this objective (set out below).

This is a crucial objective for you to grasp as it marks the difference between AS and A2 Level of study. At AS Level, you had simply to show an awareness that certain contexts existed for or within the texts; but at A2 Level you *must* discuss the relationship between the text and selected areas of context.

You have looked at relationships between context and text throughout this module, and you will also be able to evaluate the significance of the context when *Pride and Prejudice* and *Wilt on High* are discussed as satires (page 27). In other words, you will see how each text operates within the framework of satire as a genre.

The seven areas outlined for this Objective in the Specification are:

## *Area 1*

The context of period or era, including social, historical, political and cultural processes.

*Unpicking this area*   This is probably the most accessible and useful form of context to analyse, as it involves so many different areas.

*Coursework*   You will look at this area over and over again in this module, for example in discussing *Catch-22* and *Captain Corelli's Mandolin* (page 39), where you will look at the context of war – a social, historical, and political context.

## Area 2

The contexts of the writer's biography and/or milieu.

*Unpicking this area*  It would not be wise to concern yourself too much with an author's life, as this might take you away from the study of the text – and it is the *text* that matters.

*Coursework*  You might of course refer to an author's life as *one* element in your response to a text; for example, knowing that Heller was a bombardier in the Second World War might help to explain the vividness of his portrayal of some of the horrors of war. But to make such biographical considerations into something more than a brief issue would be to diminish the importance of the text. A good guide is to refer to biography where it might have effected the ways in which a writer thinks or feels, but remember that it is merely a *part* of what that writer has offered in the text.

## Area 3

The context of the work in terms of other works, including other works by the same author.

*Unpicking this area*  You inevitably look at works by other authors when you compare texts.

*Coursework*  Throughout this module you will compare works by two different authors. Because of the period requirement, you will not often look at works by the same author, unless he or she has written in different literary forms; for example, you might look at the plays and novels of D. H. Lawrence, or at the poetry and novels of Thomas Hardy.

## Area 4

The different contexts for a work established by its reception over time, including the recognition that works have different means and effects upon readers in different periods.

*Unpicking this area*  This looks very much like Area 2 of AO4 (see page 11).

*Coursework*  You have already considered this issue under Area 2 of AO5 above.

## Area 5

The context of a passage in terms of the work from which it is taken, a part-to-whole context.

*Unpicking this area*  This simply refers to how an extract relates to the work from which it is taken.

*Coursework*  You inevitably discuss this area when you look at how different parts of a text come together to create the meaning of the whole text.

## Area 6

The literary context, including issues of genre and period-specific styles.

*Unpicking this area*   This involves, for example, looking at a text in terms of genre to see how far it complies with traditional forms, and where – and why – changes are made.

*Coursework*   We will consider genre when we look at satire (page 27); the context of period-specific styles overlaps with language context (Area 7, below).

## Area 7

The language context, including relevant and significant episodes in the use and development of literary language. This would include matters of style, such as the use of colloquial, dialect, or demotic language.

*Unpicking this area*   You have already paid some attention to language use on page 8 of this module.

*Coursework*   This may well form one of the areas which you choose to use for comparison.

Having set out the seven areas in this Specification, we can now look at the various contexts relating to AO5ii.

## Historical contexts

Many texts have historical contexts that are significant for the reader. In pairing texts, you may want to compare historical contexts, or the ways in which the writers *use* such contexts. For instance, Mary Shelley in *Frankenstein* and Barry Unsworth in *Sacred Hunger* both write about eighteenth-century society, but use the contexts in different ways. (You could also use Daniel Defoe's *Moll Flanders* here.)

### ACTIVITY 5

Read the extracts below, and then attempt the questions.

In this extract from *Sacred Hunger*, Paris is recalling his confinement in Norwich Jail.

In prison I was subject also to defect of heat, he thought, remembering the stone floor, the bare walls. At this interval of time Norwich Jail had assumed the shape of a pit in his mind, with descending levels of damnation. At the lowest level were those who had no money at all and small means of obtaining any. He had been one week here, on the orders of the outraged cleric who owned the prison, as punishment for printing seditious views concerning God's creation. Here men and women fought with rats in damp cellars for scraps of food thrown down to them through a trap-door, and huddled together for warmth upon heaps of filthy rags and bundles of rotten straw. Lunatics stumbled about here, women gave birth, people died of fever or starvation.

These were people yielding no profit. Higher in the scale were those who could pay for food and a private room and it was here that Paris, until redeemed by his uncle, had found lodging. Two shillings a week had provided him also with writing materials and given him access to the prisoners' common-room, where there were newspapers, and a fire in the coldest weather; but it had not been enough to free him from the stench of the place, nor the brutalities of some of his fellow-inmates – thieves and pimps mingled with debtors here. Higher yet, serenely above all this and freed from unpleasant associations, were the rich prisoners, who lived as the bishop's guests and entertained on a lavish scale.

Norwich Jail had given Paris his notion of hell, and its workings afforded an example of docility to law every bit as absolute as the motions of the blood postulated by Harvey. Money regulated every smallest detail of the place, from the paupers in the cellars to the profligate feasters above. All rents went to the bishop, who had spent a thousand pounds to acquire the prison and was laudably set on making his investment as profitable as possible, this being a time when the individual pursuit of wealth was regarded as inherently virtuous, on the grounds that it increased the wealth and well-being of the community. Indeed, this process of enrichment was generally referred to as 'wealth-creation' by the theorists of the day. The spread of benefits was not apparent in the prison itself, owing to the special circumstances there and particularly to the very high death-rate.

The keepers at their lower level sought to emulate the governor, pursuing wealth diligently through the sale of spirits, the purveying of harlots and the extortionate charges to visitors.

In the next extract, Frankenstein describes his surroundings, and his feelings, as he lies in prison.

But I was doomed to live; and in two months, found myself as awaking from a dream, in a prison, stretched on a wretched bed, surrounded by gaolers, turnkeys, bolts, and all the miserable apparatus of a dungeon. It was morning, I remember, when I thus awoke to understanding: I had forgotten the particulars of what had happened, and only felt as if some great misfortune had suddenly overwhelmed me; but when I looked around, and saw the barred windows, the squalidness of the room in which I was, all flashed across my memory, and I groaned bitterly.

This sound disturbed an old woman who was sleeping in a chair beside me. She was a hired nurse, the wife of one of the turnkeys, and her countenance expressed all those bad qualities which often characterise that class. The lines of her face were hard and rude, like that of persons accustomed to see without sympathising in sights of misery.

Her tone expressed her entire indifference; she addressed me in English, and her voice struck me as one that I had heard during my sufferings: –

'Are you better now, sir?' said she.

I replied in the same language, with a feeble voice, 'I believe I am; but if it all be true, if indeed I did not dream, I am sorry that I am still alive to feel this misery and horror.'

'For that matter,' replied the old woman, 'if you mean about the gentleman you murdered, I believe that it were better for you if you were dead, for I fancy it will go hard for you! However, that's none of my business; I am sent to nurse you and get you well; I do my duty with a safe conscience; it were well if everybody did the same.'

I turned with loathing from the woman who could utter so unfeeling a speech to a person just saved, on the very edge of death; but I felt languid, and unable to reflect on all that had passed. The whole series of my life appeared to me as a dream; I sometimes doubted if indeed it were all true, for it never presented itself to my mind with the force of reality.

As the images that floated before me became more distinct, I grew feverish; a darkness pressed around me: no one was near me who soothed me with the gentle voice of love; no dear hand supported me. The physician came and prescribed medicines, and the old woman prepared them for me; but utter carelessness was visible.

- List the similarities in the physical conditions of the institutions described.

- What principles govern the two institutions?

- What are the attitudes to money and women in the two institutions? What seems important about them to each writer?

- Look for the references that relate to hell or hellishness in each extract.

- What are the attitudes of Paris and Frankenstein to the conditions they see? How are they similar, and how are they different? How are their attitudes conveyed?

If you were looking at these texts as a pair, you would naturally look at (a) the wider picture each text offers of the period in which the action takes place, and (b) at the way each text uses different methods of telling its story. Language would also be a point of comparison, as one text represents the eighteenth century through twentieth-century eyes, and the other from the viewpoint of the nineteenth century.

## Social contexts

Many writers comment through their writing on the social context within which a story is set. Dickens is an obvious example: his descriptions of Coketown in *Hard Times* or of London in *Bleak House* could be compared with William Blake's treatment of urban life in poetry such as *Songs of Innocence and of Experience*. Or you might use George Orwell's *Down and Out in Paris and London*. Such an approach could be developed into issues of form and language.

Many writers also comment on their own society by setting their texts in other societies. As we have seen, Brian Friel's play *Translations*, for instance, is set in Ireland 1833; but for the audience at its first performance in Derry in Northern Ireland in 1980, the issues of change in society brought about by the presence of British soldiers would have been very relevant to their own lives.

## Socio-cultural contexts

Social context is often intertwined with the cultural context. Consider the following extracts from two books that deal with racism.

### ACTIVITY 6

In the first extract, from Ralph Ellison's *Invisible Man*, the narrator describes the events after a boxing match put on for the entertainment of white men.

Then the M.C. called to us, 'Come on up here boys and get your money.'

We ran forward to where the men laughed and talked in their chairs, waiting. Everyone seemed friendly now.

'There it is on the rug,' the man said. I saw the rug covered with coins of all dimensions and a few crumpled bills. But what excited me, scattered here and there, were the gold pieces.

'Boys, it's all yours', the man said. 'You get all you grab.'

'That's right, Sambo,' a blond man said, winking at me confidentially.

I trembled with excitement, forgetting my pain. I would get the gold and the bills, I thought. I would use both hands. I would throw my body against the boys nearest me to block them from the gold.

'Get down around the rug now,' the man commanded, 'and don't anyone touch it until I give the signal.'

'This ought to be good,' I heard.

As told, we got around the square rug on our knees. Slowly the man raised his freckled hand as we followed it upward with our eyes.

I heard, 'These niggers look like they're about to pray!'

Then, 'Ready,' the man said. 'Go!'

I lunged for a yellow coin lying on the blue design of the carpet, touching it and sending a surprised shriek to join those fishing around me. I tried to remove my hand but could not let go. A hot, violent force tore through my body, shaking me like a wet rat. The rug was electrified. The hair bristled up on my head as I shook myself free. My muscles jumped, my nerves jangled, writhed. But I saw this was not stopping the other boys. Laughing in fear and embarrassment, some were holding back and scooping up the coins knocked off by the painful contortions of the others. The men roared above us as we struggled.

'Pick it up, goddammit, pick it up!' someone called like a bass-voiced parrot. 'Go on, get it!'

In this extract from Toni Morrison's *Beloved*, the white men are approaching the house and shed were Sethe is hidden with her baby:

When the four horsemen came – schoolteacher, one nephew, one slave catcher and a sheriff – the house on Bluestone Road was so quiet they thought they were too late. Three of them dismounted, one stayed in the saddle, his rifle ready, his eyes trained away from the house to the left and to the right, because likely as not the fugitive would make a dash for it. Although sometimes, you could never tell, you'd find them folded up tight somewhere: beneath floorboards, in a pantry – once a chimney. Even then care was taken, because the quietest ones, the ones you pulled from a press, a hayloft, or, that once, from a chimney, would go along nicely for two or three seconds. Caught red-handed, so to speak, they would seem to recognize the futility of outsmarting a whiteman and the hopelessness of outrunning a rifle. Smile even, like a child caught dead with his hand in the jelly jar, and when you reached for the rope to tie him, well, even then you couldn't tell. The very nigger with his head hanging and a little jelly-jar smile on his face could all of a sudden roar, like a bull or some such, and commence to do disbelievable things. Grab the rifle at its mouth; throw himself at the one holding it – anything. So you had to keep back a pace, leave the tying to another. Otherwise you ended up killing what you were paid to bring back alive. Unlike a snake or bear, a dead nigger could not be skinned for profit and was not worth his own dead weight in coin.

- Who are the victims in these extracts?

- What are the attitudes shown towards them?

- How are these attitudes conveyed? You might consider viewpoint, narrative structure, and the distinctive use of language.

- Can you see the differences in language use that arise from the period difference? (*Invisible Man* was published in 1951, *Beloved* in 1987.)

- What are the similarities and differences in the writers' attitudes?

There are many socio-cultural areas that might yield interesting and illuminating comparisons. The novel *Trainspotting* by Irving Welsh and the play *Shopping and F***ing* by Mark Ravenshill, for instance, both deal with drug culture, and there would be comparisons of language and structure to be made. The novel *The French Lieutenant's Woman* by John Fowles and the play *Mrs Warren's Profession* by George Bernard Shaw both centre on issues of love, marriage and prostitution, but embody very different cultural assumptions about them. As well as exhibiting differences in form, the play is a chronological narrative and the novel is a non-chronological narrative, a difference that offers further room for exploration.

## Socio-economic contexts

A particular socio-economic theme that forms a context for many American texts is the 'American Dream' – the idea that working to acquire money and material goods will bring success, and with it happiness of every kind. Two texts that both reflect on this are the novel *The Great Gatsby* by F. Scott Fitzgerald and the play *Death of a Salesman* by Arthur Miller.

### ACTIVITY 7

Read the extracts below, and then answer the questions that follow.

In this extract from *The Great Gatsby*, the narrator, Nick, is describing the parties at the house of his new neighbour, the millionaire Jay Gatsby.

At least once a fortnight a corps of caterers came down with several hundred feet of canvas and enough coloured lights to make a Christmas tree of Gatsby's enormous garden. On buffet tables, garnished with glistening hors-d'oeuvre, spiced baked hams crowded against salads of harlequin designs and pastry pigs and turkeys bewitched to a dark gold. In the main hall a bar with a real brass rail was set up, and stocked with gins and liquors and with cordials so long forgotten that most of his female guests were too young to know one from another.

By seven o'clock the orchestra has arrived, no thin five-piece affair, but a whole pitful of oboes and trombones and saxophones and viols and cornets and piccolos, and low and high drums. The last swimmers have come in from the beach now and are dressing upstairs; the cars from New York are parked five deep in the drive, and already the halls and salons and verandas are gaudy with primary colours, and hair bobbed in strange new ways, and shawls beyond the dreams of Castile. The bar is in full swing, and floating rounds of cocktails permeate the garden outside, until the air is alive with chatter and laughter, and casual innuendo and introductions forgotten on the spot, and enthusiastic meetings between women who never knew each other's names.

The lights grow brighter as the earth lurches away from the sun, and now the orchestra is playing yellow cocktail music, and the opera of voices pitches a key higher. Laughter is easier minute by minute, spilled with prodigality, tipped out at a cheerful word. The groups change more swiftly, swell with new arrivals, dissolve and form in the same breath; already there are wanderers, confident girls who weave here and there among the stouter and more stable, become for a sharp, joyous moment the centre of a group, and then, excited with triumph, glide on through the sea-change of faces and voices and colour under the constantly changing light.

Suddenly one of these gypsies, in trembling opal, seizes a cocktail out of the air, dumps it down for courage and, moving her hands like Frisco, dances out alone on the canvas platform. A momentary hush; the orchestra leader varies his rhythm obligingly for her, and there is a burst of chatter as the erroneous news goes around that she is Gilda Gray's understudy from the Follies. The party has begun.


In this extract from *Death of a Salesman*, Willy Loman is contemplating killing himself so that his family can collect the insurance money. Willy, a salesman, is ill, and has been fired from his job. He feels guilty about his lack of success, the trouble his wife has had to endure, and the contempt that his son Biff feels for him. In this scene he is 'talking' to his Uncle Ben, who was a successful entrepreneur; the conversation takes place in Willy's imagination.

WILLY:    What a proposition, ts, ts. Terrific, terrific. 'Cause she's suffered, Ben, the woman has suffered. You understand me? A man can't go out the way he came in, Ben, a man has got to add up to something. You can't, you can't – [BEN *moves towards him as though to interrupt.*] You gotta consider, now. Don't answer so quick. Remember, it's a guaranteed twenty-thousand-dollar proposition. Now look, Ben, I want you to go through the ins and outs of this thing with me. I've got nobody to talk to, Ben, and the woman has suffered, you hear me?

BEN:    [*standing still, considering*]: What's the proposition?

WILLY:    It's twenty thousand dollars on the barrelhead. Guaranteed, gilt-edged, you understand?

BEN:    You don't want to make a fool of yourself. They might not honour the policy.

WILLY:    How can they dare refuse? Didn't I work like a coolie to meet every premium on the nose? And now they don't pay off! Impossible!

BEN:    It's called a cowardly thing, William.

WILLY:    Why? Does it take more guts to stand here the rest of my life ringing up a zero?

BEN:    [*yielding*]: That's a point, William. [*He moves, thinking, turns.*] And twenty thousand – that *is* something one can feel with the hand, it is there.

WILLY: [*now assured, with rising power*]: Oh Ben, that's the whole beauty of it! I see it like a diamond, shining in the dark, hard and rough, that I can pick up and touch in my hand. Not like – like an appointment! This would not be another dammed-fool appointment, Ben, and it changes all the aspects. Because he thinks I'm nothing, see, and so he spites me. But the funeral – [*Straightening up*] Ben, that funeral will be massive! They'll come from Maine, Massachusetts, Vermont, New Hampshire! All the old-timers with the strange licence plates – that boy will be thunderstruck, Ben, because he never realized – I am known! Rhode Island, New York, New Jersey – I am known, Ben, and he'll see it with his eyes once and for all. He'll see what I am, Ben! He's in for a shock, that boy!

BEN: [*coming down to the edge of the garden*]: He'll call you a coward.

WILLY: [*suddenly fearful*]: No, that would be terrible.

BEN: Yes. And a damned fool.

WILLY: No, no, he mustn't, I won't have that! [*He is broken and desperate.*]

BEN: He'll hate you, William.

- Look for the words and phrases in the first extract that suggest:

    - abundance and excess

    - that things are dream-like or unreal

    - that things are transitory

    - that things are false

    - that though an effect has been aimed for, it hasn't quite succeeded.

- In the second extract, look for evidence in Willy's language of his desire to succeed. What else seems to drive him?

- Willy is planning to kill himself, but he describes it as though it were a business deal. Find evidence of this.

- Find evidence of Willy's sense of his own failure.

- Willy has always deluded himself about his own achievements. Can you find evidence of this here?

Both texts end in the death and failure of the central figures. Taking all the evidence you've found, show how both passages present the American Dream.

## Language contexts

Of course all literary texts have a language context, but in some language is a particularly important feature. Brian Friel's play *Translations* and George Orwell's novel *1984* both deal with the power of language to affect society and the individual.

## ACTIVITY 8

Read these two extracts, and then respond to the questions that follow.

In this extract, from Orwell's *1984*, the central character, Winston Smith, is listening to a colleague in the Ministry of Truth telling him about the advantages of Newspeak. Newspeak is the language of Big Brother, who is the figurehead of the future totalitarian state in which the novel is set.

'Do you know that Newspeak is the only language in the world whose vocabulary gets smaller every year?'

Winston did know that, of course. He smiled, sympathetically he hoped, not trusting himself to speak. Syme bit off another fragment of the dark-coloured bread, chewed it briefly, and went on:

'Don't you see that the whole aim of Newspeak is to narrow the range of thought? In the end we shall make thoughtcrime literally impossible, because there will be no words in which to express it. Every concept that can ever be needed will be expressed by exactly *one* word, with his meaning rigidly defined and all its subsidiary meanings rubbed out and forgotten. Already, in the Eleventh Edition, we're not far from that point. But the process will still be continuing long after you and I are dead. Every year fewer and fewer words, and the range of consciousness always a little smaller. Even now, of course, there's no reason or excuse for committing thoughtcrime. It's merely a question of self-discipline, reality-control. But in the end there won't be any need even for that. The Revolution will be complete when the language is perfect. Newspeak is Ingsoc and Ingsoc is Newspeak,' he added with a sort of mystical satisfaction. 'Has it ever occurred to you, Winston, that by the year 2050, at the very latest, not a single human being will be alive who could understand such a conversation as we have having now?'

'Except –' began Winston doubtfully, and then stopped.

It had been on the tip of his tongue to say 'Except the proles,' but he checked himself, not feeling fully certain that this remark was not in some way unorthodox.

In this extract from *Translations*, Lancey, an English soldier, is warning the villagers of Ballybeg what will happen if his fellow officer, who has gone missing, is not found. In the play, set in the west of Ireland in 1833, Owen has been translating the officers' words into Irish, and has been helping to give English names to Irish places. Sarah, who is mute when we first meet her, learns to speak during the course of the play.

LANCEY: If that doesn't bear results, commencing forty-eight hours from now we will embark on a series of evictions and levelling of every abode in the following selected areas –

OWEN: You're not – !

| | |
|---|---|
| LANCEY: | Do your job. Translate. |
| OWEN: | If they still haven't found him in two days' time they'll begin evicting and levelling every house starting with these townlands. |
| | [LANCEY *reads from his list.*] |
| LANCEY: | Swinefort. |
| OWEN: | Lis na Muc. |
| LANCEY: | Burnfoot. |
| OWEN: | Bun na hAbhann. |
| LANCEY: | Dromduff. |
| OWEN: | Druim Dubh. |
| LANCEY: | Whiteplains. |
| OWEN: | Machaire Ban. |
| LANCEY: | Kings Head. |
| OWEN: | Cnoc na Ri. |
| LANCEY: | If by then the lieutenant hasn't been found, we will proceed until a complete clearance is made of this entire section. |
| OWEN: | If Yolland hasn't been got by then, they will ravish the whole parish. |
| LANCEY: | I trust they know exactly what they've got to do. |
| | [*Pointing to* BRIDGET.] I know you. I know where you live. |
| | [*Pointing to* SARAH.] Who are you? Name! |
| | [SARAH's *mouth opens and shuts, opens and shuts. Her face becomes contorted.*] |
| | What's your name? |
| | [*Again* SARAH *tries frantically.*] |
| OWEN: | Go on, Sarah. You can tell him. |
| | [*But* SARAH *cannot. And she knows she cannot. She closes her mouth. Her head goes down.*] |
| OWEN: | Her name is Sarah Johnny Sally. |
| LANCEY: | Where does she live? |
| OWEN: | Bun na hAbhann. |
| LANCEY: | Where? |
| OWEN: | Burnfoot. |

- How are language, and change to language, used to oppress people in each extract? Be as detailed and exact as you can.

- *1984* is about a society in the future, and *Translations* about a society in the past. What does each extract seem to be suggesting about the society in which it is set?

- In each extract one character does not speak – Winston starts to do so but stops. What might their silences suggest to the reader of *1984* and the audience of *Translations*? Look at the stage directions, and think how the play works differently from the novel.

If you were comparing these two works, you could go on to look at the importance of language in the complete texts. These two extracts would be good starting points.

Invented language is a feature of some texts, and could be an important element in comparing, say, *1984* and *A Clockwork Orange* by Anthony Burgess.

## Generic and literary contexts

It might be a worthwhile exercise to compare two texts within the same genre, but from different periods.

Satire is a useful genre to look at: styles and attitudes may have changed, but it is interesting to see how much satirical focus is universal. You might find that although conventions have changed, intentions and reactions remain remarkably similar.

## ACTIVITY 5

Below are the openings from two satirical novels, Jane Austen's *Pride and Prejudice*, and Tom Sharpe's *Wilt on High*.

From *Pride and Prejudice*:

It is a truth universally acknowledged, that a single man in possession of a good fortune, must be in want of a wife.

However little known the feelings or views of such a man may be on his first entering a neighbourhood, this truth is so well fixed in the minds of the surrounding families, that he is considered as the rightful property of some one or other of their daughters.

'My dear Mr. Bennet,' said his lady to him one day, 'have you heard that Netherfield Park is let at last?'

Mr. Bennet replied that he had not.

'But it is,' returned she; 'for Mrs. Long has just been here, and she told me all about it.

Mr. Bennet made no answer.

'Do not you want to know who has taken it?' cried his wife impatiently.

'*You* want to tell me, and I have no objection to hearing it.'

This was invitation enough.

'Why, my dear, you must know, Mrs. Long says that Netherfield is taken by a young man of large fortune from the north of England; that he came down on Monday in a chaise and four to see the place, and was so much delighted with it, that he agreed with Mr. Morris immediately; that he is to take possession before Michaelmas, and some of his servants are to be in the house by the end of next week.'

'What is his name?'

'Bingley.'

'Is he married or single?'

'Oh! single to be sure! A single man of large fortune; four or five thousand a year. What a fine thing for our girls!'

'How so? How can it affect them?'

'My dear Mr. Bennet,' replied his wife, 'how can you be so tiresome! You must know that I am thinking of his marrying one of them.'

'Is that his design in settling here?'

'Design! nonsense, how can you talk so! But it is very likely that he *may* fall in love with one of them, and therefore you must visit him as soon as he comes.'

'I see no occasion for that. You and the girls may go, or you may send them by themselves, which perhaps will be still better, for as you are as handsome as any of them, Mr. Bingley might like you the best of the party.'

From Tom Sharpe's *Wilt on High*:

'Days of wine and roses,' said Wilt to himself. It was an inconsequential remark but sitting on the Finance and General Purposes Committee at the Tech needed some relief and for the fifth year running Dr Mayfield had risen to his feet and announced, 'We must put the Fenland College of Arts and Technology on the map.'

'I should have thought it was there already,' said Dr Board, resorting as usual to the literal to preserve his sanity. 'In fact to the best of my knowledge it's been there since 1895 when –'

'You know perfectly well what I mean,' interrupted Dr Mayfield. 'The fact of the matter is that the College has reached the point of no return.'

'From what?' asked Dr Board.

Dr Mayfield turned to the Principal. 'The point I am trying to make –' he began, but Dr Board hadn't finished. 'Is apparently that we are either an aircraft halfway to its destination or a cartographical feature. Or possibly both.'

The Principal signed and thought about early retirement. 'Dr Board,' he said, 'we are here to discuss ways and means of maintaining our present course structure and staffing levels in the face of the Local Education Authority and Central Government pressure to reduce the College to an adjunct of the Department of Unemployment.'

Dr Board raised an eyebrow. 'Really? I thought we were here to teach. Of course, I may be mistaken but when I first entered the profession, that's what I was led to believe. Now I learn that we're here to maintain course structures, whatever they may be, and staffing levels. In plain English, jobs for the boys.'

'And girls,' said the Head of Catering, who hadn't been listening too carefully. Dr Board eyed her critically.

'And doubtless one or two creatures of indeterminate gender,' he murmured, 'Now, if Dr Mayfield –'

- What social 'institution' does each author satirise?

- How does each writer achieve her/his satirical effects?

- What are the similarities and differences in their methods? You might consider viewpoint, narrative structure, and use of language.

- Can you see the differences in language because of the periods in which they were written? (*Pride and Prejudice* was published in 1813, *Wilt on High* in 1984.)

- Which text appeals to you more, and why?

One clear literary context occurs when one text refers to another. This is the case, for instance, with *Jane Eyre* by Charlotte Brontë and *Wide Sargasso Sea* by Jean Rhys, with Rhys developing a character from the earlier novel; and with *Precious Bane* by Mary Webb and *Cold Comfort Farm* by Stella Gibbons – Gibbons's novel is a parody of the rural genre to which the earlier book belonged.

Literary forms and conventions can also form a context. In first-person narratives, for instance, the narrator might be 'reliable' or 'unreliable'. The 'unreliable' narrator in *The Remains of the Day* by Kazuo Ishiguro, for instance, could be examined through a comparison with the 'reliable' narrator in *David Copperfield* by Charles Dickens. On the other hand, comparing *The Remains of the Day* with a similar narrative of self-delusion, such as Dickens's *Great Expectations*, could also be fruitful.

Texts within particular literary genres can be compared. In detective fiction, *The Lady in the Lake* by Raymond Chandler could be compared with any of the Aurelio Zen novels by Michael Dibdin; or either of these could be compared with Ian McEwan's *Enduring Love*, which has strong elements of thriller writing, but used for different purposes. Another possibility is to use Gothic or horror texts from different periods.

# Coursework

## Preparation

For the coursework module, you will have to study and compare at least two texts, one of which must be a prose text, and produce an essay of between 2,000 and 3,000 words. You can write the pieces at school, at college or at home, and they will be marked by your teacher. The moderator from the Examination Board will then look at all the work from your centre, and decide on a final mark for each candidate's essay. In order to do well in your coursework, you need to think about the following:

- choosing a task
- reading the text
- planning your essay
- researching your essay
- writing your essay
- drafting and re-drafting your essay
- sticking to word and time limits.

## *Choosing a task*

It's vital to choose a task that's appropriate – which means a task that addresses the Assessment Objectives. Coursework represents 15% of the whole A Level examination, and 30% of A2. It addresses AO1, AO3, AO4 and AO5ii equally, and places particular emphasis on AO2ii. This means that you must choose a task that is not simply about two texts – one of them a prose text – but a task that also makes you *compare* them. You then have to remember to focus on comparison throughout your essay.

These are some things to think about carefully when you are choosing a task:

- Does it allow me to compare the writers' choices of form, structure and language?

You don't have to treat all three aspects equally; depending on which texts you have chosen, you might have much more to say about one of them than you do about the others. But you do have to make sure that your comments are supported by detailed reference to the ways the texts are written.

- Does it allow me to discuss different interpretations of the texts?

One way of answering this question is to read some critical comments on the texts you have chosen. These might be from critical essays or books, or from articles on the Internet. But these different interpretations might also include those you can think about for yourself – for example, a feminist interpretation as opposed to a Marxist one. In any case, you will need to determine your position in relation to these interpretations in order to show that you have established your *own* interpretation of the text.

- Does it allow me to deal with different contexts in which the texts were written and can be understood?

If you were comparing a novel with a play or with poems, for example, you might want to think about the writers' choice of genre. Why is the form of a play or a novel particularly appropriate for what they have to say? But you might also want to consider several of the contexts outlined on pages 15–29 above. It's always useful to ask yourself the following questions: 'What have I gained by seeing the text in this way?' and 'How useful is it to think about the text in this way rather than in other ways?' By doing this you will be able to evaluate the significance of the particular context you are examining. In some texts it will be especially helpful to think in terms of historical or cultural context; in others, such as drama texts, it might be more useful to think in terms of performance issues and problems; in yet others, it might be useful to focus on what they are saying about language or social behaviour.

You will find in most cases that the context in which the text was written is very different from the context in which you are reading or hearing it. For instance, expectations about the behaviour of men and women might be quite different from those in the society in which you live. Remember that your own assumptions will affect the way in which you respond to a literary work. You might discover, having considered several contexts, that some are more useful than others. A knowledge of the Bible, for example, might be essential to a reading of Milton's *Paradise Lost*, but not very useful for *Hamlet*.

- Is it achievable in terms of length?

It's easy when you are preparing your coursework essay to get wrapped up in covering subject matter and to forget that you have more to do. Your task needs to be *achievable*, too. If you're setting out to write 2,500 words, then there's no point in embarking on a task that will take 10,000. As a general rule, the more precisely and sharply defined your task, the better, for it will help you to focus and thus keep to the word count – and you *must* keep within the word limit.

## Reading the text

You'll probably read at least part of the texts in class, where you'll have the opportunity to discuss them with your teacher and with other students. But just as with your examination texts for Module 4, you'll need to read them again yourself. You need to demonstrate in your writing a 'knowledge and understanding' of the texts (AO2ii), and the more you read them the better your chances of finding and exploring relationships and comparisons between them. This will enable you to draw on a wide range of evidence when you write your final essay.

## Planning your essay

Now you need to plan your essay. There are three general points to consider here:

- Your plan needs to be helpful to you in writing your essay – so that in working through it you produce a logical sequence of ideas which develop an argument and lead to a clear conclusion.

- You need to check your plan against the Assessment Objectives – is it clear how and where you are going to meet them?

- Because you don't want to have to change your plan much once you start writing, it's worth thinking about the length of your essay again at this stage. By the time your plan is fleshed out with argument and evidence, does it look as though the word count will be about right? Too many words? Too few to create a solid argument? If it doesn't look right, change your plan now.

## Researching your essay

Research may well involve reading articles or essays about your texts. These can be found in books or journals or on the Internet, but the most important source of information is still the primary source – the texts themselves. For instance, if you decided to write about the ways the American Dream is presented in *The Great Gatsby* and *Death of a Salesman*, you'd begin with a selective re-reading of the texts, looking for ideas and passages which might be useful to you. You might then want to research the writers, or the concept of the American Dream, to see if you can add to the ideas you already have, to find some new angles to develop, or to provide additional evidence.

When you have read secondary sources as part of your research, you must mention them in the bibliography at the end of your essay (see Writing your essay, below).

## Writing your essay

A significant proportion of the marks available for this module are simply for writing, and in your coursework you have the chance to score well for it – far more easily than in timed examinations. Five of the 30 marks are for the ability to 'communicate clearly the knowledge, understanding and insight appropriate to literary study, using appropriate terminology and accurate and coherent written expression' (AO1). As long as you give yourself plenty of time to write, you can take more care over the accuracy and clarity of your writing than you can in an examination – and you can take the time to check, revise and improve it when you've finished the first draft. These are specific marks for this, as you can see; it would be silly not to take the trouble to collect them.

AO2ii is the dominant Assessment Objective here – after all, the module is called Comparing Texts and the second part of this Objective asks you to explore and comment on 'relationships and comparisons between literary texts'. You also have to meet the first part of the Objective, though, and show your ability to 'respond with knowledge and understanding to literary texts'. Your *understanding* will be shown by the quality of your argument; but *knowledge* has to underpin everything you write, both in examinations and in your coursework. In coursework you have the leisure to practise what you had to do under time pressure in the examinations – provide support from the text for what you say. There are appropriate ways of showing knowledge, too. You can show it by referring to details or echoes of the text, or by quoting extracts. Short quotations (which are usually the most effective) can be included in the body of your writing, while longer quotations can be written on separate lines, so that they are easier to read. If you're quoting lines of verse, remember to show the line divisions.

If you're quoting from a secondary source, such as a critical essay, you should give details of your source in footnotes or endnotes, numbering each quotation and providing a guide to the numbers at the foot of the page or at the end of your essay. Here is an example:

*Bernard is, in fact, living proof that the system's effectiveness, an affirmation of the proposition that persistent application of one's talents, small though they may be, pays off. And this, after all, is the substance of the American Dream.[1]*

The note at the bottom of the page or at the end of the essay would be:

*[1] R. H. Gardner, 'Tragedy of the Lowest Man' from Splintered Stage (1965), p.65*

If you use the words of other writers such as critics in your own writing, you *must* acknowledge them. You have to sign a declaration that the coursework is your own work, and if you 'lift' from other writers without acknowledging them – which is plagiarism – you might lose all your marks for the module.

## Drafting and re-drafting your essay

When you have completed a first draft of your coursework essay, your teacher may allow you to re-draft it – as long as there is enough time left to do so. Your teacher is allowed to give only general advice as to how you might improve the essay, not to correct it or rewrite it – it must be your work, after all. Of course, you should heed any advice that you get – but you should aim for your first draft to be *as good as you can make it*. It's a lot easier to make minor changes than major ones.

## Sticking to word and time limits

The word limit for A2 coursework is between 2,000 and 3,000 words. If you exceed it, you run the risk of being penalised – it's as simple as that. If your first draft comes to 3,500 words, you can probably trim it fairly easily, and you may want your teacher's guidance on which parts to prune. If it is 5,000 words, though, you're in trouble – cutting sentences here and there, and tightening expression, won't cut it by 50%. Too long an essay suggests that you made a mistake much earlier – in selecting the task, at the planning stage, or perhaps when you were part way through.

Your teacher will give you coursework deadlines, and it is important to stick to them – not just to please your teacher, but to improve your chances of success. You will only be able to cut/re-draft/re-think if you've got the time to do so.

## Strategies for planning your coursework

The first part of this module offered you a range of methods for comparing texts, and therefore a range of possible combinations of texts. When you've chosen and read your texts, though, and chosen or negotiated a task with your teacher (who has to get the agreement of the coursework moderator), it's then up to *you* to start planning. Below are several strategies you could adopt. They are listed according to complexity. The teachers and moderators who assess your work do not favour one method over another, but they do mark to the Assessment Criteria. The criteria for the two top bands for AO2ii for this unit are:

- evaluative discussion of comparisons/contrasts

- secure, well-informed knowledge and understanding of text and task.

Methods 1 and 2 below are based on the study of *Birdsong* by Sebastian Faulks and the war poetry of Wilfred Owen, but the principles will apply to any choice of texts.

The basic questions you need to consider are:

- How do you respond to the ways in which war is presented in both *Birdsong* and Wilfred Owen's poetry?

- How might other readers respond differently to these texts?

## *Method 1*

The simplest plan is to deal with one text first, then the other, and finally draw together the comparisons and contrasts. If you choose this method, you will need to make sure that the two sections are clearly parallel to each other. For instance, a plan might look like this:

| Birdsong | Owen |
|---|---|
| Nature of war | Nature of war |
| Presentation through:<br>• characters<br>• novel<br>• description<br>• dialogue<br>• echoes of earlier incidents in the narrative<br>• developing narrative | Presentation through:<br>• vignettes<br>• poems<br>• description<br>• dialogue<br>• images<br><br>• concise impact |
| Aspects of war | Aspects of war |
| Responses at time written | Responses at time written |
| Interpretations | Interpretations |
| Evaluation of significance of contexts | Evaluation of significance of contexts |
| Your own response | Your own response |

## Method 2

A similar method is to begin writing about one text but then to compare and contrast elements in the second *as you write*. In other words, the difference from Method 1 is that instead of working down the first column and then down the second column, you work *across* the columns. You would have to make sure that you have a detailed plan, so that you don't use material on one text for which you can't find a parallel in the other text.

## Method 3

The final method involves looking at the two texts alongside each other, but then organising your response to them according to a specific theme, focus or critical perspective. This method may make it easier for you to ensure that your responses will remain relevant and that you provide the reader with the required 'evaluative discussion of comparisons/contrasts'.

You could decide, for example, that the focus of your essay was going to be on different contexts and interpretations. You would then be able to address AO3 – which is concerned with how writers' choices of form, structure and language shape meanings – in order to gather your evidence.

You will already be familiar with the following material because you read it when you were working through the extracts from *Jane Eyre* and *The Color Purple* (page 12). However, you were probably not thinking at that point that you could use this material as the basis for a plan.

Looking at texts from a different critical perspective will usually give rise to differing interpretations, because in order to make an interpretation we need to select material that suits a specific purpose. We then put the material together to see what we have found. This is therefore one way of linking contexts and interpretations, rather than by dealing with them separately, as was the case in Method 1 and Method 2.

Because you have to explain your own interpretation of the text in the light of different interpretations by other readers, this structure for your essay could be a helpful way of allowing you to link the material you have selected to use. The evidence for your writing about the different contexts and interpretations, as well as the evidence for your own interpretation, would then come from a close examination of the methods chosen by the writers to present their material: in other words, their choices of form, structure and language, and the ways in which these allow you to create meanings from the text. Because you are looking at different interpretations in terms of particular contexts, you can evaluate the significance of the different contexts when deciding what your own interpretation is and how it differs from other readers' interpretations.

As noted before, these two extracts are taken from novels from two different periods: *Jane Eyre* was published in England in 1847, while *The Color Purple* was published in the United States in 1982. You could look at these two extracts from several different critical perspectives. Here again are the five critical perspectives we looked at earlier (page 13):

- a social perspective
- a feminist perspective
- a cultural perspective
- the perspective of period
- your own critical perspective.

**A social perspective:**

- What is there in the extracts that suggests how society may be organised in terms of social *hierarchy*?
- What is there in the extracts that suggests how society may be organised in terms of social *structure*?

**A feminist perspective:**

- What do you make of the situation and role of women in society in each extract and text?
- Are there any similarities?
- Are there any differences?

**A cultural perspective:**

- What do you learn from the culture and cultural attitudes embedded in these extracts and texts?
- Is there a difference in the cultures?
- What do you learn of customs at work and at leisure?

**The perspective of period:**

- What sense do you have of the historical periods in which these extracts are set?
- How is it indicated?
- Do either or both extracts have a value for readers outside the specific period in which they are set?

**Your own critical perspective:**

When setting out your own critical perspective, you must make clear:

- Which of these critical perspectives interests you.
- Which you consider to be the most useful way into the book for you, and why.

One way of using these perspectives is to apply the same perspective to both texts. Alternatively, you could consider each text from a different perspective and then consider the appropriateness and significance of these perspectives for the study of the texts.

An example of this second approach is a comparison of *Hard Times* by Charles Dickens, written in the middle of the nineteenth century, and *Enduring Love* by Ian McEwan, written at the end of the twentieth century.

*Hard Times* could be read from:

- a Marxist perspective
- a historical perspective
- a cultural perspective
- a feminist perspective.

While *Enduring Love* could be considered as:

- a medical case study
- a novel in the thriller genre
- a biography of Joe
- an investigation into physics and the laws of time and matter.

## Preparing your final draft

In order to make sure that you are addressing AO1 as well as you can, you need to be able to read your essay critically when you think you have finished your draft. You need to ask yourself the following questions:

- Is my argument clear?
- Have I expressed myself clearly?
- Have I used literary terminology correctly and appropriately?
- Is my choice of words and syntax as interesting as it could be?
- Will my essay interest and persuade the reader?

## Achieving high marks

When you've followed all the advice above about selecting texts and task, and about planning and writing your essay, you need to have an idea of how high a mark you're likely to achieve with it. Obviously your teacher will help you here, but it's worth knowing exactly what criteria teachers and moderators use to judge your essay. So far we have looked at all the assessment criteria; you now need to know how these will be used to measure the quality of your work.

The dominant Assessment Objective in this module is AO2ii: *candidates should be able to respond with knowledge and understanding to literary texts of different types and periods, exploring and commenting on relationships between literary texts.*

There are six mark bands. Here are the assessment criteria for three of the bands. (The bottom band in effect tells you what to *avoid*.)

## Top band (26–30 marks):

| | |
|---|---|
| AO1 | technically sophisticated expression and some originality of insight/approach/argument |
| AO2ii | secure, well-informed knowledge and understanding of texts and task |
| AO3 | conceptually/analytically links purposes/means |
| AO4 | synthesises/evaluates critical viewpoints and positions, and forms own judgement in context of other interpretations |
| AO5ii | analysis of a range of contextual factors related to meaning |

## Middle band (16–20 marks):

| | |
|---|---|
| AO1 | ideas expressed in a clear, accurate way with some degree of sustained argument, amplified and supported |
| AO2ii | informed knowledge of texts/consideration of comparison and contrasts |
| AO3 | commentary on how specific aspects of form/structure/language shape meanings |
| AO4 | coherent individual response with evident critical position |
| AO5ii | examination of a range of contextual factors with specific, detailed links between context/text/task |

## Bottom band (0–5 marks):

| | |
|---|---|
| AO1 | unclear line of argument with frequent technical lapses |
| AO2ii | simple narration or assertion/no sense of comparison between texts |
| AO3 | very limited discussion of how language features shape meaning |
| AO4 | very little (if any) understanding of different interpretative approaches or of personal response |
| AO5ii | very little awareness of significance of contextual factors |

By becoming familiar with these criteria – in other words with what your teachers and moderators are looking for in your coursework – you will be able to monitor your own progress as you move through the various stages in the preparation of your coursework essay. Your teachers will be able to show you the whole of the mark scheme that is used for the assessment of your coursework.

## Concluding exercise

Now that you have worked your way through Module 4, and have an understanding of both the Assessment Objectives and of methods you might use in comparing texts, here is a final exercise.

The following two extracts are from novels about war. Read them carefully, and then carry out Activity 10.

The first extract is from Joseph Heller's novel *Catch-22*, published in 1961.

Now Lieutenant Scheisskopf had confidence enough in his powers to spring his big surprise. Lieutenant Scheisskopf had discovered in his extensive research that the hands of marchers, instead of swinging freely, as was then the popular fashion, ought never to be moved more than three inches from the center of the thigh, which meant, in effect, that they were scarcely to be swung at all.

Lieutenant Scheisskopf's preparations were elaborate and clandestine. All the cadets in his squadron were sworn to secrecy and rehearsed in the dead of night on the auxiliary paradeground. They marched in darkness that was pitch and bumped into each other blindly, but they did not panic, and they were learning to march without swinging their hands. Lieutenant Scheisskopf's first thought had been to have a friend of his in the sheet metal shop sink pegs of nickel alloy into each man's thighbones and link them to the wrists by strands of copper wire with exactly three inches of play, but there wasn't time – there was never enough time – and good copper wire was hard to come by in wartime. He remembered also that the men, so hampered, would be unable to fall properly during the impressive fainting ceremony preceding the marching and that an inability to faint properly might affect the unit's rating as a whole.

And all week long he chortled with repressed delight at the officers' club. Speculation grew rampant among his closest friends.

'I wonder what that Shithead is up to,' Lieutenant Engle said.

Lieutenant Scheisskopf responded with a knowing smile to the queries of his colleagues. 'You'll find out Sunday,' he promised. 'You'll find out.'

Lieutenant Scheisskopf unveiled his epochal surprise that Sunday with all the aplomb of an experienced impresario. He said nothing while the other squadrons ambled past the reviewing stand crookedly in their customary manner. He gave no sign even when the first ranks of his own squadron hove into sight with their swingless marching and the first stricken gasps of alarm were hissing from his startled fellow officers. He held back even then until the bloated colonel with the big fat mustache whirled upon him savagely with a purpling face, and then he offered the explanation that made him immortal.

'Look, Colonel,' he announced. 'No hands.'

And to an audience stilled with awe, he distributed certified photostatic copies of the obscure regulation on which he had built his unforgettable triumph. This was Lieutenant Scheisskopf's finest hour. He won the parade, of course, hands down, obtaining permanent possession of the red pennant and ending the Sunday parades altogether, since good red pennants were as hard to come by in wartime as good copper wire. Lieutenant Scheisskopf was made First Lieutenant Scheisskopf on the spot and began his rapid rise through the ranks. There were few who did not hail him as a true military genius for his important discovery.

The next extract is from Louis de Bernières's novel *Captain Corelli's Mandolin*, published in 1994.

I will illustrate the pride of the populace by retailing what happened when we asked them to surrender. I had this story from Captain Corelli. He was prone to dramatic exaggeration in the telling of a story because everything about him was original, he was always larger than his circumstances, and he would say things for the sake of their value as amusement, with an ironic disregard for the truth. Generally he observed life with raised eyebrows, and he had none of that fragile self-pride that prevents a man from telling a joke against himself. There were some people who thought him a little mad, but I see him as a man who loved life so much that he did not care what kind of impression he made. He adored children, and I saw him kiss a little girl on the head and whirl her in his arms whilst his whole battery was standing at attention, awaiting his inspection, and he loved to make pretty women giggle by snapping his heels together and saluting them with a military precision so consummate that it came over as a mockery of everything soldierly. When saluting General Gandin the action was sloppy to the point of insolence, so you can see what kind of man he was.

I first came across him in the latrines of the encampment. His battery had a latrine known as 'La Scala' because he had a little opera club that shat together there at the same time every morning, sitting in a row on the wooden plank with their trousers about their ankles. He had two baritones, three tenors, a bass, and a counter-tenor who was much mocked on account of having to sing all the women's parts, and the idea was that each man should expel either a turd or a fart during the crescendos, when they could not be heard above the singing. In this way the indignity of communal defecation was minimised, and the whole encampment would begin the day humming a rousing tune that they heard wafting out of the heads. My first experience of La Scala was hearing the Anvil Chorus at 7.30 a.m., accompanied by a very prodigious and resolute timpani. Naturally I could not resist going to investigate, and I approached a canvas enclosure that had 'La Scala' painted on it in splashes of blanco. I noticed an appalling and very rank stench, but I went in, only to see a row of soldiers shitting at their perches, red in the face, singing at full heart, hammering at their steel helmets with spoons. I was both confused and amazed, especially when I saw that there was an officer sitting there amongst the men, insouciantly conducting the concert with the aid of a feather in his right hand. Generally one salutes an officer in uniform, especially when he is wearing a cap. My salute was a hurried and incomplete gesture that accompanied my departure – I did not know the regulation that governs the saluting of an officer in uniform who has his breeches at half-mast during a drill that consists of choral elimination in occupied territory.

Subsequently I was to join the opera society, 'volunteered' by the captain after he had heard me singing as I polished my boots, and had realised that I was another baritone. He handed me a piece of paper filched from General Gandin's own order pad, and on it was written:

TOP SECRET

By Order of HQ, Supergreccia, Bombadier Carlo Piero Guercio is to report for operatic duty at every and any whim of Captain Antonio Corelli of the 33rd Regiment of Artillery, Acqui Division.

Rules of engagement:

1)   All those called to regular musical fatigues shall be obliged to play a musical instrument (spoons, tin helmet, comb-and-paper, etc.).

2)   Anyone failing persistently to reach high notes shall be emasculated, his testicles to be donated to charitable causes.

3)   Anyone maintaining that Donizetti is better than Verdi shall be dressed as a woman, mocked openly before the battery and its guns, shall wear a cooking pot upon his head, and, in extreme cases, shall be required to sing 'Funiculi Funicula' and any other songs about railways that Captain Antonio Corelli shall from time to time see fit to determine.

4)   All aficionados of Wagner shall be shot peremptorily, without trial, and without leave of appeal.

5)   Drunkenness shall be mandatory only at those times when Captain Antonio Corelli is not buying the drinks.

Signed; General Vecchiarelli, Supreme Commander, Supergreccia, on behalf of His Majesty, King Victor Emmanuel.

## ACTIVITY 10

Work through all the parts of this task.

- As you do so, remember to sequence your ideas carefully to produce a well-constructed argument; take care with the expression of your ideas and check your spelling; use technical terms where appropriate. (AO1)

- Compare and contrast the attitude of each author towards war. (AO2ii)

- Compare and contrast the ways in which each author presents certain aspects of war. (AO3)

- 'War is a noble subject.'
  Basing your answer on the two extracts, how far do you agree with this comment? (AO4)

- What do these extracts tell you about different aspects of war? What might you deduce from them about the nature and purposes of war in general? (AO5ii)

This concludes your study for Module 4.

You should now be able to choose which specific areas of AO4 and AO5ii you want to include in your coursework. This will enable you to look at the examination questions for Module 5, Set Texts, and recognise which area(s) is (are) being targeted. You should be able to offer a firm response.

Remember: in both your coursework and your examinations, you must be able to take on other readers' views of the texts, assess them, and respond to them, whether agreeing or disagreeing, but you *must always* go on to offer a judgement of your own.

# MODULE ⑤ Set texts: Drama before 1770; Poetry before 1900

The Assessment Objectives for this module require that you:

---
## ASSESSMENT OBJECTIVES
---

AO1 communicate clearly the knowledge, understanding and insight appropriate to literary study, using appropriate terminology and accurate and coherent written expression
(5% of the final A2 mark; $2\frac{1}{2}$% of the final A Level mark)

AO3 show detailed understanding of the ways in which writers' choices of form, structure and language shape meanings
(5% of the final A2 mark; $2\frac{1}{2}$% of the final A Level mark)

AO4 articulate independent opinions and judgements, informed by different interpretations of literary texts by other readers
(10% of the final A2 mark; 5% of the final A Level mark)

AO5ii evaluate the significance of cultural, historical and other contextual influences on literary texts and study
(10% of the final A2 mark; 5% of the final A Level mark)

In this module the Assessment Objectives are allocated as follows:

- Section A: Poetry Before 1900, targets AO3 and AO4, with the emphasis on AO4

- Section B: Drama before 1770, targets AO1 and AO5ii, with the emphasis on AO5ii

## Introduction

### Content

This module meets the syllabus requirements for Drama and Poetry and for a pre-1770, and a pre-1900 text respectively. There is a list of Internet resources and a select bibliography on page 165 below.

### The examination

The examination is split into Section A, Poetry, and Section B, Drama. You have to answer one question from each section. The marks are weighted equally, and are scaled to achieve the final mark. You are not allowed to take your texts into the examination.

## Assessment

Your work will be assessed as you move through the bands of the marking scheme.

## Links to work at Advanced Subsidiary Level

This module is designed to build upon the skills you acquired in your work on AS Level Module 2, Genre Study – Poetry and Drama. The Assessment Objectives for the Poetry section again draw on AO3, with the addition of the dominant AO4. The Assessment Objectives for the Drama section again test AO1 and also AO5ii, which is the more complex level for the fifth, and the dominant, Assessment Objective.

As you will be answering questions on two specific texts, you will be studying only two sections of this module closely. But you might find it helpful to look across at the actual questions set on the other texts too, to see a wide range of question types targeting the same Objectives.

## Section A: Poetry before 1900

### Assessment Objective 4

At A2 Level this is a more complex Assessment Objective than it is at Advanced Subsidiary Level. There are several ways of approaching AO4, as this Objective may be presented in different ways in the questions. You should remember that:

- texts are capable of multiple interpretations, depending upon the experiences and cultural or social background of the individual reader

- interpretations may change over time

- different social or cultural groups may interpret texts in different ways

- there are different ways of looking at texts, based on particular approaches or theories, for example feminist, Marxist, structuralist, etc.

- texts embody attitudes and values rather than present objective realities

- texts may be open-ended or controversial, and ambiguity and uncertainty are legitimate and reasonable responses.

In the examination you will be assessed both on your own interpretations of your chosen poetry text, and also on your responses to other readers' interpretations of the text.

This means that you should have a thorough knowledge and understanding of your poetry text, be flexible enough to take on board other readers' experiences of the text, and be confident enough to express and justify your own responses in both areas. In discussing how various interpretations are justified, by referring to the choices the writer has made, you will also fulfil AO3.

### Exploring interpretations for Section A

For each poetry text you are offered six or seven critical perspectives to explore, looking at the ways in which the poet's uses of form, structure and language support this perspective. You can then develop these more fully in your own time.

## *The General Prologue* – Geoffrey Chaucer

In *The General Prologue*, Chaucer introduces the characters who will tell the tales during the pilgrimage to Canterbury. He does so in ways that bring out their vices or their virtues, their dedication to matters material or spiritual. Using the dual narration of 'Chaucer the Pilgrim' and 'Chaucer the Poet' he also supplies a commentary to nudge the reader into certain responses to these characters.

Six critical perspectives are offered on *The General Prologue*:

- *The General Prologue* as a 'concise portrait of an entire nation'

- Two methods of presenting character: by outward appearance; by 'inner characterisation'

- Chaucer's use of language

- Four stages in the development of *The General Prologue*

- Further aspects of the structure of *The General Prologue*

- Chaucer the Pilgrim and Chaucer the Poet

Quotations are taken from *The Canterbury Tales*, Macmillan Education.

## The General Prologue *as a 'concise portrait of an entire nation'*
### AO4

The claim that *The General Prologue* presents a 'concise portrait of an entire nation' was made by Neville Coghill. In considering this observation, you might ask yourself:

- whether you view *The General Prologue* simply as a series of portraits of individual characters, or

- whether the selection of characters offered may represent a whole nation; and if so, how this is achieved

- whether this portrait is 'concise' but fairly complete.

### AO3

You might consider this assertion in various ways, beginning with a portrait of society divided into the 'three estates' of the **medieval** age. These three estates are:

- the military or knightly class

- the clergy and their associates

- the commons.

The Knight and the Squire are of the military or knightly class; the Nun (Prioress), the Monk, and the Parson are of the clergy; and the Doctor, the Franklin, and the Wife of Bath are members of the commons. Does it seem reasonable to suggest that Chaucer does construct profile of the nation in this way?

## ACTIVITY 1

- Do you think that Chaucer uses general terms such as 'the Pardoner' rather than personal names in order to suggest the whole social structure?

- What happens if you arrange the groupings differently, for example:

  - according to wealth, or

  - according to the degrees of their virtue or sinfulness?

## Two methods of presenting character: by outward appearance; by 'inner characterisation'

### AO4

'The most interesting thing about Chaucer's characters is their physical description.'

Here you are offered an opinion with which you may agree or disagree. You may either:

- agree, and discuss characters such as the Miller and the Cook, showing in what way their presentation is 'interesting', or

- disagree, and discuss the presentation of characters by other means, as in the case of the Parson.

### AO3

*Presentation by outward appearances*

You might consider the presentation of the Miller, as he is described through his physical appearance:

He was short-sholdred, brood, a thikke knarre,
Ther nas no dore that he nolde heve of harre,
Or breke it at a rennyng with his heed.
His berd, as any sowe or fox, was reed,

(lines 549–552)

## ACTIVITY 2

- What features does Chaucer stress in these lines?

- Why do you think that Chaucer stresses these physical features?

- Why does Chaucer select specific details, use certain similes, and add other details? (This is probably the key question to ask yourself.)

- Why might Chaucer compare the Miller to these animals?

- Why does he add the details of breaking the door?

- Does the characterisation therefore move 'inward'?

You could look at Chaucer's portrait of the Cook to see a similar development.

### Presentation by 'inner characterisation'

For this, you might consider the portrait of the Parson. Chaucer offers very little physical detail about the Parson, who is introduced immediately by the use of the word 'Poure'.

He was a shepherde, and noght a mercenarie:
And though he hooly were and vertuous,
He was to synful man nat despitous.

(lines 514 –516)

By good ensample, this was his bisynesse:

(line 520)

## ACTIVITY 3

- Why might Chaucer immediately stress that the Parson was poor?

- Why might there be no 'outer' description at all?

- Is there any doubt about the goodness of this man?

- Look carefully at the words 'mercenarie' and 'ensample': might Chaucer be making a dig at other characters such as the Knight and the Prioress?

- You should always bear in mind how much of these descriptions Chaucer the Pilgrim might offer, and which aspects might reveal Chaucer the Poet.

To take this a stage further, you could look at the description of the Prioress, and see how both types of description overlap and inter-relate.

## Chaucer's use of language

### AO4

'Chaucer's language is most interesting when he is being satirical.'

With this observation you are being offered an opinion with which you may agree or disagree. You may either:

- agree, and look at Chaucer's use of satire, or

- disagree, and suggest and illustrate other important aspects of Chaucer's style and method.

### AO3

You might consider some of the ways in which Chaucer uses language. These include:

- his use of similes

- his use of 'loaded' words

- his use of irony.

Examples of these are discussed below, and you may continue with the work in your own time. Remember, these are just three of the possible areas of aspects of Chaucer's use of language; you may want to consider others.

### Chaucer's use of similes

You have already considered Chaucer's use of similes (in Activity 2 above). Here are two further examples. The Summoner is described as being 'as hoot . . . as a sparwe' (line 626), and the Squire 'as fresshe as is the Monthe of May' (line 92).

### ACTIVITY 4

- What does Chaucer suggest through the use of these particular similes?

- Do they help to extend your response to these characters?

Similarly, the Wife of Bath's hat is described as being 'As brood as is a bokeler or a targe' (line 471); and the eyes of the Prioress are described as 'greye as being as glas' (line 152).

### ACTIVITY 5

- Why should the Wife of Bath's hat be linked to the idea of war?

- Why should the eyes of the Prioress be described as though they were a lover's eyes? What might this suggest about your response to her?

### Chaucer's use of 'loaded' words

As you read Chaucer, you will soon realise that he repeats certain 'loaded' words in his various portraits. For example, the word 'worthy' in the portrait of the knight, 'gay' in the case of the Yeoman, and 'semely' for the Prioress.

---

## ACTIVITY 6

- What might the word 'gay' tell you about the Yeoman's character?

- Might the words 'worthy' and 'semely' be ironical? Is the Knight *really* 'worthy'? Should the Prioress be concerned with looking 'semely'?

---

### Chaucer's use of irony

You have just seen how Chaucer sometimes introduces an ironical note into his descriptions. You might also look at some of the comments which Chaucer makes about the pilgrims, such as that directed at the Doctor:

> For gold in phisik is a cordial;
> Therefore he lovede gold in special.
>
> (lines 443–444)

In modern terms, you might call this a 'snide' comment. Look through the portraits to see where and why these apparently harmless comments are made, often to 'undercut' the portrait offered. You will also see later how the placing of portraits side by side might create irony (see 'Further aspects of structure in *The General Prologue*', below).

## Four stages in the development of The General Prologue

### AO4

'The structure of *The General Prologue* seems clear when it begins by presenting characters of high social class. Then it becomes a jumble.'

Here you are offered an opinion that seems to suggest that there is no sustained structure in *The General Prologue* after the first few portraits. You may either:

- agree, and see the poem as simply a series of portraits, or

- disagree, perhaps tracing another type of structure in the poem, where the portraits of characters are just a part in the overall design.

### AO3

There are four different stages discernible in the development of *The General Prologue*. The first is the introductory – idealised – account of the purposes of pilgrimage (lines 1–18); the second, the description of the pilgrims (lines 19–714);

the third, the account of the evening at the Tabard, and the plan to tell the individual tales (lines 715–821); and finally, the drawing of lots to decide the sequence of tales (lines 822–858).

## ACTIVITY 7

- Look carefully at the ways in which these parts inter-relate. For example, how does the opening account of the pilgrims' motives throw light on:

    The individual portraits of the pilgrims?

    What the pilgrims do at the Tabard?

    The apparent necessity of entertainment?

- Are all these different elements compatible, or do they create ironies?

## Further aspects of the structure of The General Prologue

Chaucer's method of constructing this poem was discussed in 'Aspects of the poetry of Chaucer' in *AS English Literature for AQA B,* by Childs and Moore, page 68. It would be helpful to look again at that section. As a brief reminder, Chaucer did not work in the same way as modern authors. There is no linear development; rather, different elements are placed together in a specific way for specific purposes. The whole effect, like that of a medieval cathedral, is a juxtaposition of all the parts to make a whole that is **interlaced**.

One of the most important aspects of this approach is the *placing* of parts or portraits alongside each other. You have already glanced at this in Activity 7 above, and here is another example. The portrait of the worldly and material Merchant is followed by that of the unworldly and spiritual Clerk of Oxenford. Is there a purpose for this placement? Is it ironic? Does it help to enlarge your understanding of both characters?

But Chaucer goes further than just placing them side by side; there are other echoes. The Merchant is described in his conversations as obsessed with 'sowynge always thencrees of his wynning' (line 275) and the Clerk immediately afterwards as 'Sowyinge in moral vetu was his speche'.

## ACTIVITY 8

- Why might Chaucer use the word 'sowinge' for both characters? Irony?

- Look carefully through the text to identify other examples.

## Chaucer the Pilgrim and Chaucer the Poet

### AO4

'There is no significant difference between Chaucer as Pilgrim and as Poet.'

### AO3

In considering the relationship between Chaucer the Pilgrim and Chaucer the Poet, you must remember that the Pilgrim has only just met these characters. How much might you expect him to know about them? There will be physical description, perhaps accounts of conversations or attitudes. But you must be aware of the point at which the portraiture goes beyond what the Pilgrim can reasonably know. When there are assessments of character, when there are comments or asides, or when you come to consider any of the aspects of style or structure discussed above, you are working firmly in the area of Chaucer the *Poet*. You might also consider differences in tone: the naive, often over-enthusiastic descriptions offered by Chaucer the Pilgrim, in contrast to the irony or disapproving tone of Chaucer the Poet.

### ACTIVITY 9

- Look carefully through one of the portraits to see how these two areas are interwoven, for example in the portrait of the Knight.

- You might consider the effects of the combination of poet and pilgrim as source of humour or irony, or a means of adding depth to the characterisation.

## Conclusion

This completes your study of six critical perspectives on *The General Prologue* (remember that this list is not exhaustive). Using this model framework, you can go on to explore other critical perspectives on your own, such as Neville Coghill's comment that in *The General Prologue* Chaucer presents a picture of medieval life 'as robust as it is representative'. You should always bear in mind, however, that straightforward character studies are not in themselves sufficient for this level of work. Your views on character must always be seen within the perspectives on Chaucer's methods and purposes outlined above.

## *Prescribed Sonnets* – **William Shakespeare**

Shakespeare's *Sonnets* range widely in concerns, including love or lack of love; death and mortality; self-exploration on the part of the speaker; and what it means to be a writer. This wide range is reflected in the twenty-two *Prescribed Sonnets*.

Six critical perspectives are offered on the *Prescribed Sonnets* by Shakespeare:

- The problem of time

- The *Sonnets* as self-exploration

- Some aspects of form

- The use of language: ambiguity and dramatic effects

- Patterns in the *Sonnets*

- The use of imagery

Quotations are taken from the Arden Edition of the *Sonnets*, ed. Kathryn Jones, Methuen.

## *The problem of time*

### *AO4*

'In Shakespeare's *Sonnets*, the "problem of time" is not a metaphysical one.'

Here you might consider two areas: what the 'problem of time' is in the *Sonnets*, and whether Shakespeare presents this in a metaphysical way. The word 'metaphysical' usually suggests philosophical analysis in terms of such abstract concepts as time, change, death and immortality.

### *AO3*

You might explore this comment by considering the following:

- The effects of time

- Ways of defeating time

- Time transcended.

### *The effects of time*

Over half the sonnets in this selection are concerned with aspects of time. (Remember that only one or two examples may be discussed here; you can develop more on your own.)

Shakespeare is concerned to show the effects of time on people, on their relationships, and on nature. You see this in many of the sonnets, such as *Sonnet 73*.

That time of year thou mayst in me behold,
When yellow leaves, or none, or few do hang
Upon those boughs which shake against the cold,
Bare ruined choirs where late the sweet birds sang;

## ACTIVITY 1

- What sort of imagery is Shakespeare using here?

- What actual effects does the speaker discuss?

- Are they just the physical effects of ageing?

- Is time also being seen to affect poetic skills?

## Ways of defeating time

Shakespeare may seem to suggest that there are several ways of defeating, or at least of lessening, the impact of time. In *Sonnet 73*, a solution is offered: 'To love that well, which thou must leave ere long.'

## ACTIVITY 2

- What advice does the speaker offer to the 'lover'?

- Might he be suggesting that it is wise to make the most of the time available?

- Is there any sense of a denial of the inevitability of decay?

- Might the speaker be using the pressures of time to his own advantage?

There are at least two other suggestions about overcoming the pressures of time and the inevitability of death. In *Sonnet 3*, the speaker says:

But if thou live remembered not to be,
Die single, and thine image dies with thee.

Elsewhere, the speaker offers another way of escaping the oblivion of death, as in *Sonnet 65*, where he suggests:

O none, unless this miracle have might:
That in black ink my love may still shine bright.

## ACTIVITY 3

- What are the two solutions suggested in these sonnets?

- Might the speaker of *Sonnet 65* (like the speaker of *Sonnet 73*) be including a little twist, so that *both* the poet and loved one may retain some immortality on earth?

### Time transcended

The critic quoted on page 53 of this module suggests that the problem of time was not a 'metaphysical' one for Shakespeare. Consideration of time in the *Sonnets* is certainly very complex. There is a constant interest in its passing, and of the related problems of death and the inevitability of uncertainty and change in our lives. Perhaps the critic believed that Shakespeare relies on experience and sensation for the driving force of the *Sonnets*, rather than philosophical enquiry.

An example might be *Sonnet 116*, in which Shakespeare addresses the problem of finding any sort of continuity or permanence in human experience in the face of the inevitability of the passage of time and of death:

Love's not Time's fool, though rosy lips and cheeks
Within his bending sickle's compass come;
Love alters not with his brief hours and weeks,
But bears it out even to the edge of doom.

## ACTIVITY 4

- Does the speaker admit that change and the passage of time are inevitable?

- Might the speaker be concerned with how it is possible to achieve self-identity through love, which defeats the problems of change and impermanence?

- Is this a form of consolation?

You might go on to consider where the experience of the poem is *grounded*. Is it in contemplation? Or does the poem rely on physical experiences, such as the 'rosy lips'? You might conclude that there is a mixture of both. To complete this discussion, you might consider the different *types* of time included in the poem.

## ACTIVITY 5

- Is there a concern for time as immovable, *eternal* time, 'an ever-fixed mark'?

- Is there a concern for *natural* time in the seasons of nature, 'that looks on tempests'?

- Is there a concern for *human* time, with the 'bending sickle'?

Perhaps Shakespeare has presented the solution that, in the face of the inevitability of both death and the passage of time, the best that we can do is to find our own constant identity – as lover, parent or poet. You might consider *Sonnet 19* and *Sonnet 71* here to see how the problems related to time are transcended.

## *The* Sonnets *as self-exploration*

### AO4

'In the *Sonnets*, Shakespeare is addressing his own conscience.'

### AO3

To explore this idea, you may consider that in writing about his loved ones, Shakespeare is analysing his own response to the implications of being in love, a theme we have touched upon already. You must ask how far you think this comment is true. Here are just three of the stages of the complex process of falling in love as explored in the *Sonnets*:

- 'perfect' love, where the loved one is outwardly and inwardly ideal

- imperfect love, where outer beauty is not matched by inner beauty

- the lover's (or Shakespeare's) admission that love may be damaging.

### *'Perfect' love, where the loved one is outwardly and inwardly ideal*

You may see this stage at the beginning of *Sonnet 15*:

When I consider everything that grows
Holds in perfection but a little moment;

## ACTIVITY 6

- Is there any doubt in the speaker's mind about the 'perfection'?

- Is the love described as right and natural?

*Imperfect love, where outer beauty is not matched by inner beauty*

The flaws within the loved one are acknowledged in *Sonnet 129*:

> Th'expense of spirit in a waste of shame
> Is lust in action;

### ACTIVITY 7

- Might these words be applied to the speaker as well as to the loved one?

- How might *Sonnet 129* sound a warning note to the speaker/lover?

*The lover's (or Shakespeare's?) admission that love may be damaging*

The consideration of how love might affect a person may be seen explicitly in *Sonnet 144*, which contains a firm moral frame:

> To win me soon to hell my female evil
> Tempteth my better angel from my side,

### ACTIVITY 8

- Might Shakespeare be suggesting that we may face damnation or salvation in pursuing love?

- Might he be suggesting that love may be either redemptive or base and evil?

- Is there any solution offered to this dilemma?

This is a very brief outline for you to develop in your own time. But it should be clear that the *Sonnets* are not merely a series of flattering or accusatory poems, but an analysis of what it means, in emotional and moral terms, to love.

## Some aspects of form

### AO4

'The most important feature of Shakespeare's *Sonnets* is his use of rhyme.'

In this statement you are offered an opinion with which you may agree or disagree. You may either:

- agree, and discuss the uses and effects of rhyme in the *Sonnets*, or

- disagree, and look at other aspects of Shakespeare's poetry that are more important.

*AO3*

Just one of the *Sonnets* will be explored here; in your own time you can repeat the exercise on several of the others. The structure of the English sonnet form that Shakespeare uses is that of three quatrains (sets of four lines), followed by a concluding couplet. As you will see, because of the way Shakespeare develops most of the sonnets, the couplet is a logical and natural conclusion to what has been said earlier. The rhyming scheme plays an important role in the structure of a sonnet, but the form is also developed by the careful planting of words. Here are some lines from the first quatrain of *Sonnet 30*:

> When to the sessions of sweet silent thought
> I summon up remembrance of things past,
> I sigh the lack of many a thing I sought,

## ACTIVITY 9

- What type of imagery does Shakespeare use here?

- How are the language effects created? (You might look at the sibilance.)

- Why might Shakespeare be using the words 'sigh' and 'lack'?

In the next two quatrains, Shakespeare introduces financial metaphors: 'expense' and 'account'. It would seem that Shakespeare planted the word 'lack' in the first quatrain as a link to the financial imagery. You probably do not notice this at first, for this might be seen as typical of the 'organic' or natural-seeming development of the poem.

## ACTIVITY 10

- Look at the final couplet and work out how Shakespeare has pre-prepared for the ideas here, remembering the word 'sigh' in the third line.

- Look at the ways Shakespeare uses linking words (such as 'when', 'then', 'but') to build up the different stages of the argument in the poem.

- What is the patterning of sound here? Does it enhance the sense?

- How does the 'd' sound pick up and resolve patterns of earlier words?

- Might the final couplet with its idea of 'compensation' draw together and conclude the financial imagery of the sonnet?

## The use of language: ambiguity and dramatic effects

*Ambiguity*

*AO4*

'Verbal ambiguity confuses more than it clarifies.'

Here you are offered an opinion with which you may agree or disagree. You may either:

- agree, showing how verbal ambiguity may weaken the effect of the *Sonnets* by making the verse unclear, or

- disagree, showing that the verbal ambiguity strengthens the sonnets by increasing their range of meanings.

*AO3*

You have already looked at some aspects of word play in Activities 9 and 10. Here are some examples of ambiguity from *Sonnet 30*. You may have seen that the word 'sweet' can be linked to such words as 'dear', 'precious', and 'expense'. What are the two sets of meanings attached to these words? Do you think that there is an emotional range and a non-emotional range attached through the legal and financial metaphors?

Look at these lines:

> Then can I drown an eye (unused to flow)
> For precious friends hid in death's dateless night,
> And weep afresh love's long since cancelled woe,

## ACTIVITY 11

- Do you think that the speaker remembers past emotions in these lines?

- Look at the stresses on 'long since cancelled' in the third line above; might they emphasise that this love and pain are long gone?

- When you consider this, and the concluding couplet, do you think that the speaker is able to remember pain and past sadnesses *calmly*?

- Do you think that the double play on the words allows this detachment to be created?

Using this example, you could carry out your own analysis of ambiguity in the *Sonnets*.

*Dramatic effects*

The *Sonnets* could be perceived as the dramatisation of emotions related to love that are within the range of readers' experience. Shakespeare can be seen to do two things:

- express very clearly what it feels like to be in these situations

- relate these experiences to 'normal' situations.

Here are two lines from *Sonnet 3*.

> Thou art thy mother's glass, and she in thee
> Calls back the lovely April of her prime:

## ACTIVITY 12

- How do you know that the speaker thinks that the beloved is beautiful?

- Look at the experiences 'dramatised' in this poem: are they beyond the experience of a reader? Or are they familiar? Is it like looking in a mirror?

- Does it express the idea that parents somehow live through their children?

- Is the poem 'special' because it might present these experiences in a fresh way, for fresh purposes? – a new light on old ideas?

- Might part of the appeal of the *Sonnets* be that we can relate to them in this way?

## Patterns in the Sonnets

### AO4

'The *Sonnets* have a thematic rather than a narrative structure.'

Here you have three elements to consider: 'thematic', 'narrative', and 'structure.' You are asked to consider how the series of sonnets is put together and decide whether:

- the *Sonnets* are linked together by their themes; or

- they are linked by a narrative, a story which runs through them.

### AO3

You have already begun to consider a thematic development in 'The *Sonnets* as self-exploration' (page 56). To develop this aspect fully, you could work through all the stages of Shakespeare's analysis of what it means to love somebody.

### ACTIVITY 13

You could begin with *Sonnet 94*, in which the emotional and moral effects of love are explored.

- Does this sonnet express the idea that those who are beautiful need to act virtuously?

- How might the image of 'Lilies that fester' present this idea?

## The use of imagery

### AO4

'The *Sonnets* show a repetitive use of poetic symbolism.'

Here the concern is the symbolism of the poems, and whether it is repetitive or not. You might ask yourself:

- Do certain images, or groups of images, recur in the *Sonnets*?

- If they do, is it due to lack of imagination, or do such repeated images suggest something important about the nature of love?

### AO3

To explore this aspect of the *Sonnets*, you might consider the groups of predominant images, such as those relating to nature, time, the sun, the cosmos, precious metals, gems, and kingship.

### ACTIVITY 14

- You could begin with *Sonnet 29* and the ideas of kingship and royal wealth. Remember to consider what it is that these images say about love.

## Conclusion

This completes your study of six critical perspectives on the *Prescribed Sonnets* by Shakespeare (remember that this list is not exhaustive). Using this model framework, you can go on to explore other Shakespeare sonnets on your own, perhaps beginning with a discussion of Coleridge's comment that 'the *Sonnets* are all the same with a variety of expression'.

## Prescribed Poems – George Herbert

George Herbert was a devoted clergyman who saw in his gift for writing poetry a means of praising and serving God. His poetry is generally seen as 'plain' or 'simple'. But beneath this plain-seeming surface Herbert uses complex emblems and arguments to fashion his poetry, and to make the actual writing of poetry an act of prayer.

Six critical perspectives are offered on the *Prescribed Poems* by George Herbert:

- The use of patterning and **emblem** in Herbert's poetry

- Dramatic encounters in Herbert's poetry

- The use of the **conceit** in Herbert's poetry

- Herbert's views on writing poetry

- Plainness in Herbert's poetry

- The poem as prayer

Quotations are taken from *The Metaphysical Poets*, ed. Helen Gardner, Penguin.

## The use of patterning and emblem in Herbert's poetry

### AO4

'The poem and its pattern constantly insist that for man, only through the Fall is the flight possible.' (A comment on 'Easter-wings'.)

In this comment you are asked about both the ideas in the poem, and its shape on the page. You are invited to agree about the shape of wings and about Easter, and to link these ideas to those of the **Fall of Mankind** and redemption. You could disagree, arguing that it doesn't quite work.

### AO3

In the poem 'Easter-wings' you may see the actual pattern of the wings on the page, as an emblem of what the poem is about. But when you look closer into the poem you will see *how* the wings have been made:

> Lord, who createdst man in wealth and store,
> Though foolishly he lost the same,
> Till he became
> Most poore:
> With thee
> O let me rise
> As larks, harmoniously,
> And sing this day thy victories:
> Then shall the fall further the flight in me.

## ACTIVITY 1

- What does Herbert suggest about the Fall of Mankind here? What state was mankind in at first, and what happened then?

- How might the central part of the poem show impoverishment or 'thinness'?

- What might Herbert be suggesting about the effects of trust in God?

- What might be the effects of representing wings and 'flight' on the page?

The first part of the poem presents the Fall of Mankind in biblical terms, and the second can be seen to consider the physical problems of life over which mankind needs to 'take flight' in order to triumph.

## ACTIVITY 2

- Read the second verse: how are the processes of thinning and growing repeated?

- Look at the oppositions that Herbert sets up: sickness and health, folly and wisdom, death and resurrection. Why might he do this?

- Why might Herbert refer to Easter? What is the religious significance?

- Are the wings an image of mankind achieving resurrection?

You could also consider the patterning in 'Deniall', 'The Collar', or 'The Pulley'.

## Dramatic encounters in Herbert's poetry

### AO4

'Herbert's poems are over dramatic.'

Here you are offered an opinion about the nature of Herbert's poetry. You could:

- agree, producing evidence to support your view

- disagree, showing the effectiveness of his 'dramatic' poems, or

- disagree, looking at poems which are **lyrical** rather than dramatic.

### AO3

In this category, you could consider Herbert's poem 'Death', which establishes a dramatic note in the first verse:

> Death, thou wast once an uncouth hideous thing,
> Nothing but bones,
> The sad effect of sadder grones;
> Thy mouth was open, but thou couldst not sing.

## ACTIVITY 3

- What attitudes to death is established here?

- What tense is Herbert using, and why?

- Why might Herbert use the word 'once'?

As you read through the poem you may notice that the first three stanzas repeat this idea of death, but then there is a change in the fourth stanza when Herbert talks of death as 'fair and full of grace'. In the fifth stanza death is seen as 'gay and glad'. What has changed? The final stanza might give the explanation:

> Therefore we can go die as sleep, and trust
> Half that we have
> Unto an honest faithfull grave;

## ACTIVITY 4

- Why does Herbert use the word 'therefore'? Might it suggest that he has quietly made an argument that defeats the terror of death?

- Might Herbert be suggesting that this is due to the Saviour, who brings hope of redemption and resurrection?

- Do you think that Herbert might have dramatised his own attitudes?

Among other Herbert poems you could consider in this way are, for example, 'Discipline', 'Dialogue', 'Mortification', and 'Man'.

## The use of the conceit in Herbert's poetry

### AO4

'The conceit is used to persuade, rather than define or prove a point.'

In this statement you are offered an opinion about the use of the conceit – the far-fetched image – in Herbert's poetry. It is claimed that the conceit has only one use, to persuade. But two other possible uses are identified: to define or prove a point. To respond to this you could:

- agree, demonstrating the use of conceit in persuasion

- disagree, demonstrating either or both of the other uses of the conceit, or

- suggest other uses.

## AO3

To explore the use of the conceit in Herbert's poetry you might consider 'The Collar'. Critics generally believe that this complex poem is about a clergyman's struggle for self-discipline. It takes the form of a debate, probably between the Heart and the Will, which is resolved by the end of the poem. This extract begins at line 6:

> Shall I be still in suit?
> Have I no harvest but a thorn
> To let me bloud, and not restore
> What I have lost with cordiall fruit?
>                 Sure there was wine
> Before my sighs did drie it: there was corn
>                 Before my tears did drown it.

## ACTIVITY 5

- What do you think is the central imagery here?

- Might the words 'cordiall fruit' remind the reader of Adam in Paradise? The fruit lost him Eden, but gave him another life? (The adjective 'cordiall' meant life-giving or restorative.)

- In religious terms, what might the 'bloud' and the 'corn' represent?

- Might they represent the wine and bread of communion?

- Might they be connected to the 'thorn' (crucifixion)?

- Might there thus be an image of the Eucharist here?

Perhaps Herbert is offering a solution to the series of 'complaints' that the Heart is making, which suggests that at the core of the poem lies a Christian understanding of the purposes of life. But there is another kind of imagery here: think of the words 'still' and 'in suit'.

## ACTIVITY 6

- Might the phrase 'in suit' be a legal metaphor for a client putting a case to a figure in authority? Might this be the general frame of the poem?

- Might it also refer to the title of the poem? Might this legal metaphor call to mind a prisoner 'slipping the collar', i.e. escaping?

- Do the words 'cage' and 'rope', later in the poem, support this idea?

- Could the collar of the title, the central conceit, have a double significance as the clergyman's collar, and also the collar of discipline?

- Might the word 'still', therefore, mean quiet? A quiet acceptance of Christ's law? Quiet because resurrection is guaranteed through the Eucharist?

- Might this be why Herbert can reply at the end of the poem 'My Lord'?

You may conclude that the central conceit of the collar is both the real collar of the priest, and a metaphor for mankind's relationship with God. You might also consider 'The Pulley', 'Man', 'Affliction' and 'Redemption' here.

## Herbert's views on writing poetry

### AO4

'Herbert is most interested in writing about God with simplicity and sincerity.'

There are three elements to consider here: 'writing about God', 'simplicity', and 'sincerity'. To answer this question you should consider each element in turn, seeing whether you agree or disagree.

### AO3

Here you might consider Herbert's poem 'The Forerunners', where he explains why he will not write a certain type of poetry.

Farewell sweet phrases, lovely metaphors.
But will ye leave me thus? when ye before
Of stews and brothels onely knew the doores,
Then did I wash you with my tears, and more,

## ACTIVITY 7

- What sort of poetry might Herbert be thinking of here?

- Why are there references to 'stews and brothels'?

- Do you think Herbert appreciates the beauty of the language used?

- Why might this sort of poetry sadden him?

Herbert goes on to explain the necessity of leaving such poetry behind, because 'True beautie dwells on high'. He adds: 'Beautie and beauteous words should go together.'

## ACTIVITY 8

- From what you have learned about Herbert in your studies so far, what do you think of his idea of 'true beautie' in life is?

- Might he be suggesting in 'The Forerunners' that some poetry uses beautiful words for ugly subjects? That beauty might not always be truthful?

Herbert then makes his position clear:

For, *Thou art still my God,* is all that ye
Perhaps with more embellishment can say.

## ACTIVITY 9

- Might the 'true beautie' of poetry lie in its very plainness?

- Might the writing of this poetry 'chalk the door' of his house, and so link Herbert's house of poetry with the House of God?

- Might Herbert be able to see truth and beauty come together by the end of the poem?

For further research you could consider Herbert's poems 'Jordan' (I) and 'Jordan' (II).

## Plainness in Herbert's poetry

### AO4

'Herbert's plainness is an art by which he may tell the truth to himself and God.'

AO3

Here you might consider 'The Temper'. Herbert clearly lays out the purpose of the poem in the opening verse:

How should I praise thee, Lord! how should my rymes
   Gladly engrave thy love in steel,
   If what my soul doth feel sometimes,
      My soul might ever feel!

## ACTIVITY 10

- Do you think that the first sentence might be a question as well as an exclamation?

- What is it that Herbert wants to discover from his Lord?

- Work out the meaning of the image 'engrave thy love in steel'. (Might it refer to the engraving process used to print his poems, but also to a steely firmness in observing the love of God?)

- Might writing poetry and serving God come together as a way of life?

Why is this poem 'plain'? Herbert lays out a clear proposition with the words 'how' and 'if', and uses the middle four stanzas to present the problems of finding a way of trusting in God, and of expressing this trust. So he uses language that is rather grand, rather pretentious and very dramatic in stanzas 2–5. There is a change in the sixth stanza:

Yet take thy way; for sure thy way is best:
   This is but tuning of my breast,
      To make the musick better.

## ACTIVITY 11

- How does Herbert now respond to God?

- Is there any 'high-flown' language here?

- Why might Herbert refer to music?

- Might this reference suggest that the fit of 'temper' is now over and that a state of harmony has been achieved?

The answer is found at the end of the poem: whether the speaker 'flie[s] with angels' or 'fall[s] with dust', he now knows that 'Thy hands made both, and I am there'. The mood and the language now seem to be very plain and clear.

You could apply this sort of analysis to most of Herbert's poems, beginning perhaps with 'Love'.

## The poem as prayer

### AO4

'Herbert intended the form of a poem to be obvious.'

With this comment you are offered an opinion about the form of Herbert's poetry. You could either:

- agree that in the poems there is an obvious form, or

- disagree, and demonstrate that at times the form of the poem is unclear.

### AO3

You could consider here the poem 'Deniall'. It has been suggested that the poem may be seen to take the form of a prayer. It begins:

> When my devotions could not pierce
> They silent eares;
> Then was my heart broken, as was my verse:
> My breast was full of fears
> And disorder:

## ACTIVITY 12

- What is the difficulty Herbert presents in his relationship with God?

- How might this difficulty be represented in the *form* of the verse?

- Is there any regular pattern of construction, rhyme or rhythm?

- Alternatively, are both Herbert's thoughts and his poetic form disordered?

As in 'The Temper', the middle stanzas (here 2–5), show the difficulties Herbert felt, reflected in the broken patterns of the verse. But here again, in the last stanza all comes together:

O cheer and tune my heartlesse breast,
                    Deferre no time;
That so thy favours granting my request,
                    They and my minde may chime,
                              And mend my ryme.

## ACTIVITY 13

- How has the speaker moved from fear and distrust to contentment?

- How have the rhyme and rhythm of the last stanza been 'mended'?

- What is the significance of the music imagery?

- Might you conclude that the answer to his fears is prayer, and that this is demonstrated in the prayer of the last stanza?

You might also consider the poems 'Prayer' and 'Discipline' here.

## Conclusion

This completes your study of six critical perspectives on the *Prescribed Poems* by George Herbert (remember that this list is not exhaustive). Using this model framework, you can go on to explore other critical perspectives on your own, perhaps beginning with the use of a female voice in Herbert's poetry.

## *The Rime of the Ancient Mariner* – Samuel Taylor Coleridge

Coleridge believed that imagination was the driving force behind poetry, and it is thought that he celebrates this in *The Rime of the Ancient Mariner*. A variety of influences lie behind the poem, notably Coleridge's familiarity with the seafaring men he met at Bristol and, through his knowledge of German literature, the story of the **Wandering Jew** and of ships guided by the dead. From his wide reading of travel books he would have learnt of strange sea-creatures, of the glow of phosphorescence and lights at sea, of changeable tropical seas, and of the frozen seas of the North. All were combined in *The Rime of the Ancient Mariner* to create a strange and open-ended poem. Coleridge himself said that readers would have to **suspend disbelief** and accept the poem on its own terms.

Seven critical perspectives are offered on *The Rime of the Ancient Mariner*:

- The variety of voices in *The Rime of the Ancient Mariner*

- The narrative structure of *The Rime of the Ancient Mariner*

- Mankind and nature in *The Rime of the Ancient Mariner*

- A religious reading of *The Rime of the Ancient Mariner*

- A historical reading of *The Rime of the Ancient Mariner* I: the French Revolution

- A historical reading of *The Rime of the Ancient Mariner* II: the slave trade

- A literary reading: Coleridge's use of the **ballad** form

Quotations are from the 1798 text.

## *The variety of voices in* The Rime of the Ancient Mariner

### AO4

'It has been suggested that in *The Rime of the Ancient Mariner* there is a mixture of voices in subtle disagreement.'

### AO3

There seem to be a range of voices in, and related to, this poem; it is up to you to decide whether you think they disagree or not, and also what their function is. To respond to this critical comment you might consider the reactions of: the Pilot and the Pilot's boy; the Hermit; the Wedding-Guest; the Mariner; the narrator; the poet; and you as reader.

### The Pilot and the Pilot's boy

Both of these personae are terrified at the appearance of the Mariner. The Pilot's boy goes crazy, saying 'The devil knows how to row', and the Pilot is 'a-fear'd' and 'fell down in a fit'.

### The Hermit

The Hermit's response is very different. Not afraid, he urged them to 'Push on, push on!' to rescue the Mariner. He also fulfils the Mariner's hopes:

> He'll **shrieve** my soul, he'll wash away
>    The Albatross's blood.

## ACTIVITY 1

- What is the difference in attitudes of these three men?

- Do you think that the first two acted in fear and superstition?

- What difference is there in the Hermit's response?

- What might be the importance of the Hermit to the Mariner?

- What different perspectives might these three voices bring to the poem?

### The Wedding-Guest

At first the Wedding-Guest is moody, having to listen to this 'loathsome tale'. He is missing the wedding celebrations and hears the 'loud bassoon' ruefully. However, his attitude changes, and he becomes afraid, saying 'I fear thy skinny hand'. He doesn't speak at the end of the poem, but we are told he has been 'stunned'.

## ACTIVITY 2

- How does Coleridge use the Wedding-Guest at the start of the poem?

- What do you make of the changing responses of the Wedding-Guest?

- How might he affect your response to the Mariner?

- Might he represent the church or society that the Mariner seems to reject?

### The Mariner

The Mariner is described as 'ancient' – perhaps because he tells an old tale full of myth and legend; perhaps because, as he relates his story, it becomes obvious that he himself lived through it all a long time ago. He has a 'glittering' eye which 'holds' his listener, just as he 'holds him with his skinny hand'. The Wedding-Guest seems to be hypnotised: 'He cannot choose but hear', for the

Mariner exerts a strange and compelling power: 'The Mariner hath his will.' At times he seems to be old-fashioned, using the pre-Reformation Catholic prayer 'To Mary Queen'.

### ACTIVITY 3

- How many times has the Mariner told his tale? Do you actually know?

- Why do you think the Wedding-Guest feels compelled to listen?

- In the poem, the Mariner tells of supernatural events, but how much of them does he interpret for you or understand himself?

- Do you think the Mariner is fully alive, or is he in a state of death-in-life?

### The narrator

The narrator introduces the Mariner very briefly: 'It is an ancient Mariner'. Why do you think that this introduction is so brief? And why do you think he uses the present tense? Might it suggest that the Mariner is *always* in this state of life? In the last verse of the poem, the narrator adds the conclusion:

A sadder and a wiser man,
He rose the morrow morn.

### ACTIVITY 4

- Why might the narrator describe the Mariner at the end of the poem in the same way as he had at the beginning?

- Why might the narrator be made to draw a final moral for the reader?

### The poet

You are made aware of the poet's presence through his skilful use of the ballad metre and its variations, the selection and arrangement of episodes, and his ability to resolve the complexities in the poem. An example is the use of the Two Voices (Part the Sixth), which the Mariner hears even though he is in a 'trance'. Logically, these voices have to be included in order to explain the ship's movement to the reader. If you look at the gloss Coleridge wrote for the 1817 edition, you can also hear *his* voice as he tells you what to think: 'The ancient Mariner earnestly entreateth the Hermit to shrieve him: and the penance of life falls on him.' Why do you think that Coleridge added this and other glosses?

*You as reader*

You create another 'voice' in the context of the poem as you think about and discuss its possible meanings and interpretations, and so extend its significance.

### ACTIVITY 5

- What might be the combined effect of all these different voices?

## *The narrative structure of* The Rime of the Ancient Mariner

### AO4

'There is great clarity of design in this poem.'

In response to this claim about the design of *The Rime of the Ancient Mariner*, you may either:

- agree, and demonstrate a clear structure in the poem, or

- disagree, and demonstrate that there is no clear design in the poem. You may think that the poem is open-ended, or even confused.

### AO3

One of the key structural devices in *The Rime of the Ancient Mariner* is the reference to the Albatross that ends the first six parts, and is also present in the seventh part. Here are the endings to each part:

- Part the First: 'with my cross bow / I shot the Albatross'

- Part the Second: 'Instead of the cross, the Albatross / About my neck was hung'

- Part the Third: 'And every soul it pass'd me by. / Like the whiz of my Cross-bow'

- Part the Fourth: 'The Albatross fell off, and sank / Like lead into the sea'

- Part the Fifth: this ends with the debate about the Albatross and reference to penance.

- Part the Sixth: 'He'll shrieve my soul, he'll wash away / The Albatross's blood'

- Part the Seventh: this echoes references to the Albatross made earlier. 'The Ship went down like lead' echoes the end of Part the Fourth, which in turn echoes the words describing the bird as it 'Went down' at the beginning of Part the Second, and also the account of the crew as they too 'dropp'd down'.

## ACTIVITY 6

- Why might these references be made at the end of each part?

- How might these references help to reveal the structure of the poem?

- What do you think the Albatross might represent? (You might find it helpful to read other perspectives on the poem and then come back to this question.)

## *Mankind and nature in* The Rime of the Ancient Mariner

### *AO4*

Critics disagree over Coleridge's attitude to nature in this poem. Some suggest that in it nature may be seen to have restorative qualities and may offer support to mankind. Others think that nature is presented as amoral and indifferent to the wellbeing of mankind. For yet others, nature in this poem may be seen as only partly curative, at times supportive at other times terrifying.

### *AO3*

One of the difficulties in seeing nature as kindly is that although the Mariner blessed the sea-snakes, this didn't satisfy the Polar Spirit. So perhaps whilst a Christian God was happy, the other, mythological figure, was not, and doomed the Mariner to penance:

> He lov'd the bird that lov'd the man
> Who shot him with his bow.

When the ship is becalmed, the water is terrifying:

> Water water, every where,
> Ne any drop to drink

Elsewhere nature is shown as ugly:

> The very deep did rot

## ACTIVITY 7

- What qualities can you see in nature here?

- Might there be a suggestion of a need to co-operate with nature?

To assess Coleridge's attitude to nature you could consider his relationship with his friend William Wordsworth, the great poet of nature. Wordsworth believed that nature was kindly and revealed God's workings, as part of a Divine Universe, so that if people become part of nature they will find emotional, spiritual and physical completeness. Many critics think that the Hermit represents Wordsworth:

> He singeth loud his godly hymns
> That he makes in the wood.

He seems at peace with nature. But the Hermit has his limitations, as he thinks that the Mariner's ship is 'skeletons of leaves'.

## ACTIVITY 8

- What do you make of the Hermit?

- Is he able to help the Mariner?

- Is his knowledge limited to what he can perceive through nature?

- May his sort of natural knowledge be the best sort? Better, perhaps than the formal religion of the Wedding-Guest at the Kirk?

- Do you think that overall Coleridge had an ambiguous attitude to nature?

## A religious reading of The Rime of the Ancient Mariner

### AO4

'The Rime of the Ancient Mariner is a parable of guilt and redemption.'

In response to this comment you could look at three areas:

- the poem as a parable (a story with a moral)

- mankind's guilt

- mankind's redemption.

You may agree with this comment, disagree, or agree with a part of it.

### AO3

You could consider the poem in terms of three areas:

- the **sacramental** aspects of the poem

- the Old Testament

- the New Testament.

Remember, when you consider readings of the poem, you should always bear in mind that these are interpretations by other readers: the author did not necessarily intend them. These suggested readings are applied to specific parts or specific incidents in this poem, rather than to the poem as a whole. You may agree or disagree with them.

## Sacramental aspects of the poem

The areas in the poem that can be termed sacramental are those which relate to religious practices and sacraments. These include the references to the cross, related to both the Albatross and the Hermit, who might be seen to administer the sacrament of Holy Confession. In order to receive Holy Confession, a person must feel contrite for his/her sins, confess them, and then perform a penance. The Hermit begins this process when he asks the Mariner, 'What manner of man art thou?' The Mariner tells the tale of his sins, and thus carries out his penance by telling his tale. The sacramental act of prayer is apparent:

He prayeth well, who loveth well
  Both man and bird and beast.

### ACTIVITY 9

* Do you think that the telling of the tale is the Mariner's atonement for his sins?

* What about the crew? What did they do, and what happened to them?

## The Old Testament

If you recall the biblical story of Cain and Abel, you will remember that Cain killed his own brother, the first sacrifice. But strangely, the killing became part of the route that led to mankind's salvation (you could consider it as prefiguring Christ's death). What about the Mariner? Did he commit a 'murder'? But was he also a victim of the unkindly Polar Spirit? Was he punished for the whole crew, who thought at one point that it was right to kill the bird? Do you think that the Mariner could be a mixture of both Cain (who was condemned to wander the earth as punishment for his crime) and Abel?

## The New Testament

This area is concerned with the biblical story of Christ's death on the cross in order to redeem mankind. When reading the poem, you can see a picture of the Mariner with the Albatross hung around his neck like a cross. The Mariner says that he suffers 'a woeful agony', and he repeats the word 'agony'. Perhaps he dies to atone for the sins of the whole crew.

## ACTIVITY 10

- Do you think that there are suggestions that the Mariner can be understood as both Cain and Abel?

- Do you think he might be seen as a Christ-like figure?

## A historical reading of The Rime of the Ancient Mariner I: the French Revolution

### AO4

'Referring to the French Revolution, Coleridge said that he felt guilt for believing that "mankind could improve itself by its own actions without grace".'

In this comment you are told of Coleridge's views on the French Revolution. He felt that without the Grace and help of God, mankind was helpless. You may agree that there is a reading of the poem which refers to the French Revolution, or disagree and offer an alternative reading.

### AO3

Originally the French Revolution had many supporters because of its aim of overthrowing a corrupt monarchy in order to establish 'Liberty, Equality and Fraternity' for all. But the revolutionaries became as corrupt as the old monarchy, massacring many thousands of innocent people in a reign of terror. Some critics see this later stage represented in *The Rime of the Ancient Mariner*. To consider this perspective you might think about the questions in the next activity.

## ACTIVITY 11

- When, where and why does the community on the ship seem to have broken down?

- Did the crew, and especially the Ancient Mariner, have any freedom?

- The nature of the justice you see in the poem. You might think about whether the crew deserve to die, and whether the Ancient Mariner's punishment is just or too harsh.  Might the justice meted out to him seem random or arbitrary, given that the Spirits don't agree over his case?

- What degree of violence is evident in the events of the poem? You could list all the physical and mental violence that occurs to human and non-human beings.

## A historical reading of The Rime of the Ancient Mariner II: the slave trade

### AO4

'Coleridge felt that the slave trade implicated all of his countrymen in "a shameful commerce". This is what *The Rime of the Ancient Mariner* is about.'

In this comment you are told of Coleridge's response to the slave trade as carried on by Britain, as well as by other nations. He thought that this sort of trade was 'shameful'. You might agree that the poem refers to the slave trade, or disagree and offer an alternative reading.

### AO3

To consider this aspect you might think about the questions in Activity 12 below.

### ACTIVITY 12

- Is the spectral ship a slave ship, rotted with the diseased slaves it carried?

- Might the Mariner with the Albatross around his neck be seen to carry the chains of a slave?

- Might the Mariner, in his loss of home and freedom, his forced penance, and his physical and mental suffering, be like a slave?

## A literary reading: Coleridge's use of the ballad form

### AO4

'Coleridge uses a simple ballad form in *The Rime of the Ancient Mariner*.'

Here you are offered a comment about the sort of poem that Coleridge wrote. You are invited to agree or disagree about whether he used the ballad form, and whether his use of it was simple.

### AO3

To respond to this perspective you might consider whether certain characteristics of the ballad form are evident in this poem. These are reviewed in Activity 13 below.

## ACTIVITY 13

Which of the following characteristics of the ballad form do you find in *The Rime of the Ancient Mariner*:

- A vividly told story?

- A tale of heroism and suffering?

- Certain stock characters (such as the Spirits)?

- Certain stock events (such as battles)?

- The use of simple, brief dialogue?

- The use of some sort of refrain?

- A simple four-stressed rhythm (which may be complicated at times)?

- As a ballad in the Romantic tradition, a stress upon the importance of the imagination?

## Conclusion

This completes your study of seven critical perspectives on Coleridge's *The Rime of the Ancient Mariner* (remember that this list is not exhaustive). Using this model framework, you can go on to explore other critical perspectives on your own, perhaps looking at the **socialist** reading of the poem, based on the idea of the ship as a community.

## Prescribed Poems – Alfred Lord Tennyson

Tennyson published poetry for sixty-five years of his long life, and the selection in *Prescribed Poems* covers a span of fifty-nine of those years. He was appointed Poet Laureate when he was 41, and was initially much loved by his readers, although his poetry became less popular in the later years of his life. Critics generally praise the musical and lyrical qualities of his poetry; they also point to an inner conflict in Tennyson's mind. This conflict may have been a reflection of the tensions inherent in the robust industrial world of Victorian England; in particular, he struggled with the poets' sense of isolation in such a society.

Six critical perspectives are offered on the *Prescribed Poems* by Alfred Lord Tennyson:

- Landscape in Tennyson's poetry: 'Mariana'

- The relationship of the poet to society: 'The Lady of Shalott'

- The conflict between freedom and duty: 'Ulysses'

- The use of the **dramatic monologue**: 'Tithonus'

- Social commentary: 'Godiva'

- The acceptance of death and the perfection of form: 'Crossing the Bar'

Quotations are taken from *Poems of Tennyson*, ed. Christopher Ricks, Longman.


## Landscape in Tennyson's poetry: 'Mariana'
### AO4

'In his poetry Tennyson presents landscape as a mood or state of mind.'

Here it is suggested that Tennyson uses landscape in his poetry to create a mood, but also a state of mind. You could respond in one of three ways:

- agree, demonstrating how Tennyson uses landscape for both purposes

- partly agree, showing how he uses landscape for only one of these purposes, or

- disagree, suggesting completely different uses for landscape (such as creating a vivid picture).


### AO3

In this area you might consider how Tennyson uses landscape to present a situation in which there is no possibility of action. Some critics claim that the subject matter of 'Mariana' is inaction and isolation. Might Tennyson feel that this is the situation of the poet in the modern world?

In the first stanza of the poem, Tennyson emphasises sadness and decay. He first describes the house, concluding:

> Weeded and worn the ancient thatch
> Upon the lonely moated grange.

## ACTIVITY 1

- What sort of a picture does Tennyson present here?

- How does he present a picture of decay?

- How is the isolation conveyed?

- How is this conveyed by sound effects? (Consider for example the use of soft consonants such as 'w', and internal **half-rhymes**, such as 'moated' and 'lonely'.)

Tennyson then moves from a description of the house to a description of the landscape around the house:

> Hard by a poplar shook alway,
>     All silver-green with gnarled bark:
>     For leagues no other tree did mark
>     The level waste, the rounding grey.

## ACTIVITY 2

- How is the isolation conveyed here?

- Why do you think that the colours are dark or drab?

- What might the shaking poplar represent?

- Consider his use of sound effects (such as the soft 's' and 'd' sounds, and the rhymes). How might such effects help to convey a mood?

You might think that in Mariana's refrain 'I am aweary, aweary' Tennyson emphasises her unhappiness and isolation. Why do you think that the second line of the refrain changes in the last verse? In this presentation of an isolated, lonely individual who cannot help her situation, do you think that the poet could be using this female character from a different period to suggest certain conditions of his own mind? Do you think that he succeeds in presenting such conditions?

To discuss this issue, you might also refer to 'The Lady of Shalott' and 'St. Agnes' Eve'; and to discuss his use of landscape, you might study 'To Virgil' and 'The Brook'.

## The relationship of the poet to society: 'The Lady of Shalott'

### AO4

'Tennyson makes melancholy the subject of his poetry.'

### AO3

One of the questions often asked about 'The Lady of Shalott' is whether it is a mirror of Tennyson's own experience – his use of a mirror may certainly suggest as much. As in 'Mariana', you might also find evidence of a lack of harmony within the poet and in his relationship with nature and society. In 'The Lady of Shalott', Tennyson describes the island as follows:

> Four grey walls, and four grey towers,
> Overlook a space of flowers,
> And the silent isle imbowers
>     The Lady of Shalott.

## ACTIVITY 3

- Why are the words 'four' and 'grey' repeated?

- Why is there emphasis on space and silence?

- What might be the force of the word 'imbowers'?

Tennyson then describes the lonely and repetitive life of the Lady:

> But in her web she still delights
> To weave the mirror's magic sights,
> For often thro' the silent nights
> A funeral, with plumes and lights,

## ACTIVITY 4

- Does she have any part in social life?

- What is the function of the mirror?

- Might there be a reference here to the role of women at the time?

Tennyson goes on to describe the effects of the 'meteor' that disturbs her life when Lancelot rides by:

> Thick-jewell'd shone the saddle leather,
> The helmet and the helmet-feather
> Burn'd like one burning flame together,

## ACTIVITY 5

- How does Tennyson convey the masculine image of Lancelot here?

- How does he create vitality and texture?

- Why is there a double stress on 'burning'? Might it be sexual?

- Might the lady be destroyed for feeling such emotions?

To take the idea a little further, you could consider what Tennyson suggests about society, and how he presents the mirror. Society appears in the references to the funeral pageantry and lovers. But the Lady is apart from them. Might there be a suggestion that such things will not concern an isolated poet? Might her state of mind again be that of the poet in disguise? Tennyson writes:

> The mirror crack'd from side to side:
> 'The curse is come upon me,' cried
>     The Lady of Shalott.

## ACTIVITY 6

- Might the mirror represent the poet's relationship with society?

- Might there be a suggestion that art mirrors life?

- Might there be a suggestion that though the poet observes society, he is not a part of it?

- Might the poem be seen as an expression of the poet's alienation from society?

You might also consider 'Mariana' and 'St. Agnes' Eve' here.

## The conflict between freedom and duty: 'Ulysses'

### AO4

'Tennyson uses mythology to discuss contemporary matters, and matters concerning his inner feelings.'

In this comment two uses of mythology are suggested: Tennyson may wish to discuss matters concerning the society in which he lives, or matters that concern himself. Here you may agree:

- that myth is used for either or both of these purposes; or

- think of other purposes that would allow you to disagree in part with this opinion.

### AO3

Perhaps Tennyson allows the character Ulysses to present his own ideas about loss of identity.

You can identify four stages in the poem. In the first few lines (1–5), Ulysses explains the situation that forced him to make the decision to travel; in the following lines (6–32), he justifies his need for travel and experience; in the third part (lines 33–43), he thinks about his son, Telemachus; and in the fourth and final part (line 44 to the end) he makes heroic claims about what he intends to achieve. Critics have suggested that this is an exploration of the role and trials of the poet in society.

Having justified his need to travel ('It little profits that an idle king'), and having rejected his wife, family and responsibilities, Ulysses describes how it is vile:

For some three suns to store and hoard myself,
And this gray spirit yearning in desire
To follow knowledge like a sinking star,
Beyond the utmost bound of human thought.

## ACTIVITY 7

- What is the tone of the conclusion to this part of the poem?

- Is there any sense of spiritual fulfilment here?

- Might the 'fading margin' be death?

- Is it enough just to *experience* things? Or are the feelings important, too?

In the third part, the poem seems to change tone: here Ulysses thinks of his son, Telemachus, recalling his virtues and his rule 'by slow prudence':

Most blameless is he, centred in the sphere
Of common duties, decent not to fail
In offices of tenderness, [. . .]

## ACTIVITY 8

- Is Ulysses wholly blameless in leaving these responsibilities behind?

- Are these social and religious virtues necessary to society?

- Is Ulysses therefore alienated, unable to move away from a heroic past to a more ordinary life in society?

- Again, might this be the situation of the poet?

The conclusion to the last part of the poem might seem ambiguous. Again, it could be that Tennyson sounds a note of heroic challenge as Ulysses urges his band 'to seek a newer world', to gain experience until death. Tennyson concludes the poem with a bold-sounding statement:

One equal temper of heroic hearts,
Made weak by time and fate, but strong in will
To strive, to seek, to find and not to yield.

| ACTIVITY 9 |
| --- |

- Which do you think is important in the poem – the striving or the achievement?

- Might this refer to a sense of duty in the face of difficulties?

- Might it refer to the courage to carry on the ancient tradition of being a poet?

- Might it refer to the fact that the poet has to live in contemporary society, but finds it hard to do so?

You might also consider 'Tithonus' or 'The Lotos-Eaters' here.

## The use of the dramatic monologue: 'Tithonus'

### AO4

'Life involves maintaining oneself between contradictions that can't be solved by analysis.'

This critic offers the opinion that in life there are contradictions which we are forced to accept and live with. They cannot be resolved by analysing them. You are asked if this line of thought is evident in Tennyson's poetry. You may either:

- agree, showing that there are conflicts in the poetry which cannot be resolved, or

- disagree, showing that in certain poems contradictory situations or ideas are resolved.

### AO3

You could consider here whether Tennyson uses the dramatic monologue to re-create certain types of personal experiences, but by using the persona of the speaker is able to *distance* himself from what that persona says. Again, you may feel that Tennyson explores a state of mind which reveals his own attitudes, feelings and thoughts.

As in 'Ulysses', Tennyson here uses classical mythology: in this case, the myth of Tithonus, who was granted immortality by the goddess Aurora, but not eternal youth. Tithonus looks around him as he ages, and wishes that he were part of the natural cycle and so able to die:

> The woods decay, the woods decay and fall,
> The vapours weep their burthen to the ground,
> Man comes and tills the field and lies beneath,
> And after many a summer dies the swan.
> Me only cruel immortality
> Consumes: I wither slowly in thine arms,
> Here at the quiet limit of the world,
> A white-hair'd shadow roaming like a dream.

## ACTIVITY 10

- How does Tennyson present the natural cycle of life and death here?

- How does Tennyson present the unnaturalness of Tithonus' situation?

- What might be the effect of the word-order of line 4 of this extract?

- What might the 'quiet limits of the world' represent?

- Who might the 'white-hair'd shadow' be? Might this also represent the poet?

Tennyson presents the effects of ageing in Tithonus' responses and increasing lack of vigour. At first, the landscape is presented with great beauty as Tennyson describes the time when Tithonus felt his blood

> Glow with the glow that slowly crimson'd all
> Thy presence and thy portals, [. . .]

Then Tennyson shows how the aged Tithonus later feels:

> Coldly thy rosy shadows bathe me, cold
> Are all thy lights, and cold my wrinkled feet

## ACTIVITY 11

Compare the language in the two brief extracts above: how is vitality conveyed in the first extract? You might look at:

- the use of colour

- the use of active verbs

- the sound patterns, in particular **assonance** (such as 'glow', 'slowly')

- the use of repetition.

Now look at the second brief extract:

## ACTIVITY 12

- What has happened in this extract? How is it conveyed?

- What has happened to the colours?

- What is the effect of repetition here?

- What are the effects of the use of the hard consonant 'c'?

- Where do the stresses fall in the second line?

- Might Tennyson be reflecting on his own loss of poetic energy?

At the end of the poem Tithonus expresses a tragic outlook: he wishes to die, and not to be cut off from the rest of nature by his immortality:

Of happy men that have the power to die,
And grassy barrows of the happier dead.

## ACTIVITY 13

- How does Tennyson present Tithonus and his state of mind now?

- How might the loss of energy and life be a goal worth achieving?

- Might this be the presentation of a nightmare for the poet: weak and not able to be what he was, but forced to continue writing?

You might also consider 'Ulysses' and 'The Lady of Shalott' here.

## Social commentary: 'Godiva'

### AO4

'Tennyson avoids the discussion of views related to the society of his age.'

Here you are asked to consider whether Tennyson ignores social matters in his poetry. You could either:

- disagree, and discuss poems which you think demonstrate his concern with society, or

- agree, and suggest that Tennyson has other reasons for writing his poetry.

## AO3

Tennyson cleverly uses historical perspectives when he looks at a past episode from the perspective of his own age. You might consider four places in this poem where Tennyson seems to be making social comments:

### ACTIVITY 14

- Why does Tennyson use the setting of a Victorian railway station, but talk about the past? Might he be trying to avoid criticism himself for criticising certain aspects of his own age?

- Lines 1–23: might the taxes refer to aspects of policy in his own society?

- Lines 24–25: might the husband's patronising attitude to his young wife say something about the treatment of women in Victorian society?

- When Tennyson refers to the 'blind walls', and 'Chinks' and 'holes', might he be mocking Victorian prudishness or hypocrisy?

You might also consider 'Locksley Hall' here.

## The acceptance of death and the perfection of form: 'Crossing the Bar'

### AO4

'Tennyson requested that in any edition of his poems 'Crosssing the Bar' should be the last poem. How appropriate do you think this is?'

Here you are asked to consider Tennyson's own request about this poem, and think about:

- why he felt this poem should be placed last

- what the particular qualities of this poem are

- whether you agree with his judgement.

Tennyson's request seems to say a lot about his own feelings about this poem; perhaps he felt that he has achieved peace in his life and so was resigned about death.

### AO3

The perfect form of the poem might suggest this harmony. You might consider here both the ideas, and also the language and form of the poem.

## ACTIVITY 15

- Compare the tone and mood of this poem to those of poems you have looked at already: how is it different?

- How would you describe the mood of this poem?

- What might the image of crossing the bar suggest?

- Look at the use of language: quiet words, perfect rhymes – how does this help to present the meaning?

- Look also at the line lengths: why is the long line always checked by the shorter following line? Might this remind you of the movement of the waves?

## Conclusion

This completes your study of six critical perspectives on the *Prescribed Poems* by Tennyson (remember that this list is not exhaustive). Using this model framework, you can go on to explore other critical perspective on your own, perhaps beginning with a consideration of the role of women in society as presented in 'St. Agnes' Eve'.

## Prescribed Poems – Emily Dickinson

The American poet Emily Dickinson is something of a puzzle for biographers, as she never revealed the facts behind two key events in her life. The first of these is what she called in a letter 'the terror of September 1861'. Some critics have guessed that it might be linked to the illness of her brother between 1856 and 1860; others think that it may have been a failed love-affair, heterosexual or gay; and others suggest that she may have had a nervous breakdown. Whatever the cause, in many of the poems written after that date, which includes those in this selection, there is a sense of terror at something unspecified.

The second notable event of her life was her withdrawal from society, which she admitted herself in a letter of 1866: 'I do not cross my father's ground to any House or Town.' Again there are uncertainties about the cause, possibly a breakdown, rejection in love, the death of a friend, the serious problems she had with her eyesight, or perhaps boredom with society. This sense of isolation is evident in many of her poems.

Six critical perspectives are offered on the *Prescribed Poems* by Emily Dickinson:

- Poems that may be interpreted as dramatic monologues

- Poems written from the perspective of the dead or of death

- Poems about nature

- Poems that move from outward observation to inner contemplation

- Poems with biographical concerns

- Poems that present common experiences

Quotations are from *Poems and Letters of Emily Dickinson*, ed. Robert N. Linscott, Anchor Books.

You will see that for the purpose of these activities, the *Prescribed Poems* have been divided into six groups. But remember that these groupings are not authoritative: you may choose to place the poems in totally different groupings, or place individual poems in several groups.

## Poems that may be interpreted as dramatic monologues
### AO4

*What are Emily Dickinson's 'dramatic monologue' poems?*

In this type of poem Emily Dickinson imagines a specific voice, and often a specific situation. Elizabeth Philips, for example, suggests that Emily Dickinson 'created not one, but many persona whose voices enlarge our visions of life – and of death'. In this category you could consider the poem 'Because I would not stop for Death', in which a 'gentleman' takes a younger person, presumably a lady, for a coach ride:

> Because I could not stop for Death,
> He kindly stopped for me;
> The carriage held but just ourselves
> And Immortality.

## ACTIVITY 1

- What does Dickinson imagine here? Might it be both a voice and a situation?

- Is it an individual experience or one that is shared with the reader – 'ourselves'?

The poem continues with some narrative:

> We passed the school where children played
> Their lessons scarcely done;
> …
> We paused before a house that seemed
> A swelling on the ground;

And then the conclusion of the poem is reached:

> I first surmised the horses' heads
> Were toward eternity.

## ACTIVITY 2

- What sort of description of the early evening ride are offered?

- What might the house with the 'swelling ground' suggest?

- Why might the horses' heads turn towards eternity?

### AO3

*How Dickinson presents this dramatic monologue*

Looking at the first quotation above, you might ask yourself:

## ACTIVITY 3

- Might the poet be using the image of a young lady seduced by a lover?

- What is the tone at the beginning of the poem? Does it change?

Then you might look again at the second and third extracts above, asking yourself questions such as:

## ACTIVITY 4

- How does Dickinson create the suggestion of human activities?

- How does she introduce the thoughts of death?

- How is the image of the journey used overall?

- How would you define the tone of the poem? Is there any change from the casual opening? Is it shocking? Or menacing? Or dramatic?

These characteristics seem to typify Emily Dickinson's style in these dramatic monologues. The reader is first drawn into the poem by a deceptively casual tone; there are then changes of tone, pace and language; and finally the poem moves from the outer human world to an inward contemplation of death.

You might also consider under this heading 'I dreaded that first Robin, so' and 'The only ghost I ever saw'.

## Poems written from the perspective of the dead or of death
### AO4

Emily Dickinson often wrote about death and about what happens after death.

Several critics – such as Yvor Winters, believe that she was wholly successful in conveying the sense of what is left behind at death.

To explore this type of poem, you might consider ''Twas just this time last year I died':

'Twas just this time last year I died.
    I know I heard the corn,
When I was carried by the farms, –
    It had the tassels on.

ACTIVITY 5

- Can you tell that this is written from the viewpoint of a child?

- What does the dead person recall about life? Is this a country person?

You can now read the whole poem. You will see that the first three verses describe country life, and then the focus changes to family life:

If father'd multiply the plates
    To make an even sum.

And if my stocking hung too high,
    Would it blur the Christmas glee,

ACTIVITY 6

- Are there other family members presented in the poem now?

- How might they be seen to react to the absence of the dead child?

At the end of the poem the perspective seems to be adjusted again, where the 'I' persona says that 'this sort' of memory is hurtful, so thinks about:

When just this time, some perfect year,
    Themselves could come to me.

ACTIVITY 7

- What sort of comfort does the child-persona find?

- Is there any sense that death is the end of everything?

- Alternatively, is some sort of life after death suggested?

## AO3

*How Dickinson presents these ideas*

### ACTIVITY 8

You might consider the way the world of nature is presented. What senses are used? Is it like a painting of a country scene?

- What about family life? Is this presented through actions and feelings?

- What might these reactions tell us about the family members?

- Might the poem again move from concrete description to abstract ideas?

You might also consider under this heading 'Ample make this bed' and 'Though I get home how late, how late!'

## Poems about nature

When Emily Dickinson wrote her poem 'A light exists in spring', she acknowledged her debt to Wordsworth in her efforts to achieve a clarity of vision in her account of nature, and in her attitude to it. The poem begins:

A light exists in spring
      Not present on the year
At any other period.
      When March is scarcely here

A color stands abroad
      On solitary hills

## AO4

It would be useful when assessing Emily Dickinson's response to nature to bear in mind Robert Frost's comment about some of his own poems: 'it is realism with the dirt washed off.' You might look at this opening verse and think about what it is in nature that interests Dickinson.

In responding to Robert Frost's comment, you could consider how Emily Dickinson presents nature. Is it a 'prettified' sort of nature, or is there some realism, with the presentation of some of the more negative aspects of nature?

## ACTIVITY 9

- Is Emily Dickinson specific about the time-frame of the poem?

- How much concrete detail is there? Is the scene fully described?

- Do you think that she is more concerned with depicting a mood?

The poem continues:

It waits upon the lawn;
    It shows the furthest tree
Upon the furthest slope we know;
    It almost speaks to me.

*AO3*

*How Dickinson presents her response to nature*

## ACTIVITY 10

- How does Dickinson suggest distance here? Might it be through the use of single words?

- What is the tone of the poem?

- How does Dickinson create this tone? You could consider: the use of alliteration, of sibilance, and of 'quiet' consonants; and the use of a regular alternate rhyme scheme.

In the last five lines of the poem, the range of enquiry again broadens, as Dickinson introduces the question of our relationship to nature. Here she uses the word 'sacrament'. What might this suggest about her attitude?

Dickinson's descriptions of nature have been extended to include some philosophical themes, so to suggest that she writes about nature only may be very misleading. Perhaps it is more accurate to say that natural description is a platform for a deeper contemplation, as may be seen in the next group of poems.

## Poems that move from outward observation to inner contemplation

Here you are asked about what Emily Dickinson prioritises in her poetry. Is it nature? Or is it human nature? It is up to you to decide which, offering evidence to support your choice.

### AO4

Emily Dickinson wrote in a letter: 'Of all nature, *human* nature is the most interesting and quickening to me.' How do you interpret her response to nature?

You may perhaps conclude that in the course of her nature poems the interest in nature gives way to Dickinson's interest in human concerns. You may see this in the first and last verses of her poem 'There's a certain slant of light':

> There's a certain slant of light
> On winter afternoons,
> That oppresses, like the weight
> Of cathedral tunes.
>
> …
>
> When it comes, the landscape listens,
> Shadows hold their breath;
> When it goes, 'tis like the distance
> On the look of death.

### AO3

*How Dickinson represents her response to nature*

## ACTIVITY 11

- How might the words 'slant' and 'weight' suggest the poet's feeling?

- Might you conclude that the poet feels oppressed or isolated in the quiet world?

- Why might the shadows 'hold their breath'? What might they anticipate?

- Why might Dickinson use religious language?

- Is there any sense in this poem of a life after death?

You might also consider the religious imagery and the ideas of a life after death in the poems 'As imperceptibly as grief' and 'I started early, took my dog'. In this second poem you may see a sense of nature becoming menacing in a non-specific way.

## Poems with biographical concerns

In some of her poems Emily Dickinson offers a brief amount of important experiences in somebody's life. Is this sort of poem evident in the *Prescribed Poems*?

- If there are such poems, how do they work?

- If you think there are no such poems, how would you define the range of her poetry?

In such poems, men or women are given voices in a short biography. Examples include 'Safe in their alabaster chambers' and 'She rose to his requirement', which begins:

She rose to his requirement, dropped
The playthings of her life
To take the honorable work
Of woman and of wife.

## ACTIVITY 12

- What do you make of the two opposite directions described in the first line?

- How important are the words 'rose' and 'dropped'?

- Might the word 'honorable' be ironical?

If you continue to study this poem, you will find the outline biography of a woman who keeps everything to herself ('it lay unmentioned'). But you might also find that the 'downward movement' of the poem continues. It is up to you to decide whether this movement is towards the inner heart of the woman, or downwards towards darkness and death. Are the pearl and the weed of equal value, of different values, or are they opposed? The poet seems to leave this open, but critics such as Vivian Pollack see her as a 'psychological realist'.

This open-endedness and reticence seem to be one of the poet's characteristics, as the critic William Shurr commented: 'The reader feels that some essential information is missing.' Why might Emily Dickinson withhold personal information?

## Poems that present common experiences

Emily Dickinson is seen by many critics, including Elizabeth Philips, as offering a 'gratifying and haunting record of human experience'. Philips suggests three things: (1) that Emily Dickinson writes about human experience; (2) that she does so in a way which is pleasing; and (3) that she does so in a way that is so moving that the poetry is haunting. You have to ask yourself whether:

- she *does* in fact write about human experience, or about something else

- you agree or disagree that her poetry is pleasing

- you agree or disagree that her poetry is haunting.

As you saw in 'Because I could not stop for death', Dickinson's poems often require the reader to explore personal experiences. Similar poems include 'It can't be summer, – that got through', 'Victory comes late', and 'The last night that she lived', a poem in which she describes the experience of tending to the dying. Read through this poem and ask yourself:

## ACTIVITY 13

- How might the poet make the use of a little imagery effective?

- Might this both relieve and intensify emotions? If so, how?

- Are the 'we' figures seen as united in experience and in grief?

## Conclusion

This completes your study of six critical perspectives on the *Prescribed Poems* by Emily Dickinson. Using this model framework, you can go on to explore other critical perspectives on your own, perhaps beginning with a consideration of her attitude to religion in 'Safe in their alabaster chambers'.

# Section B: Drama before 1770

The dominant Assessment Objective in this section is AO5ii. In other words candidates are expected to evaluate the significance of cultural, historical and other contextual influences on literary texts and study.

This Assessment Objective has been outlined in the Introduction (page iv), but here is a reminder of the seven central types of context mentioned in the Specification:

- the context of period or era, including significant social, historical, political and cultural processes

- the context of the work in terms of a writer's biography and/or **milieu** (milieu refers to the particular environment in which the writer lived and worked, such as social, academic or professional environments)

- the context of other works, including other works by the same author

- the different contexts for a work established by its reception over time, including the recognition that works have different meanings and effects upon readers in different periods; this could overlap with AO4 in consideration of the different critical responses

- the context of a given or specific passage in terms of the work from which it is taken (a part-to-whole context)

- the literary context, including **generic** factors and period- specific styles

- the language context, including relevant and significant episodes in the use and development of literary language: this includes imagery (for example, the use of certain common images in a **Revenge Tragedy**) and matters of style, the use of colloquial, dialect or demotic language.

You will see the different contexts embodied in the questions in all of the texts in this section. It would therefore be worth looking at the questions relating to texts you are not studying in order to see how the different contexts may be tested.

The difference between Advanced Subsidiary Level and A2 Level is that you are now required to 'evaluate the significance' of the context. In other words, you are required to consider the *context* as well as the *text*. This is not the same as saying that you must spend excessive time studying the actual context. But it is essential that you understand the links between the context and the text in terms of a writer's ideas and manner of expression.

## An example of 'evaluating the significance' of a given context

The genre of Revenge Tragedy provides a literary context for Middleton's play *Women Beware Women* and Webster's play *The White Devil*. Later in this section you will look at the characteristics of Revenge Tragedy generally, and then assess how an individual play fits into this pattern (see Activity 6, page 129). In this way, you will 'evaluate the significance' of the Revenge Tragedy genre in your response to an individual play.

## Exploring contexts for Section B

For each drama text, you are offered six contexts to explore. You will see how the context becomes apparent in the ideas of the drama, and how an individual context relates to a contextual frame. The word 'primary' is used to describe the particular context explored in each of the six sub-sections because, as you will see, there is very often overlap between contexts.

## *Edward II* – Christopher Marlowe

Compared to Marlowe's earlier plays, *Edward II* is written in a style that is much plainer and much more muted in tone. His drama had moved from the presentation of powerful heroic characters to the depiction of the personal struggle of a rather weak individual who is subjected to intense pressures by the inheritance of the crown.

The six contexts considered for the study of *Edward II* are:

- The historical context: kingship in *Edward II*

- The moral context

- The literary context I: *Edward II* as a **Morality Play**

- The religious context

- The literary context II: *Edward II* as a tragedy

- The language context

Quotations are from *Edward II*, ed. R. Gill, Oxford Paperbacks.

## *Evaluating the significance of the contexts*

One way of evaluating the significance of the contexts treated below is to compare what you would gain from them.

For example, an Elizabethan audience would probably have seen many plays that dealt with the subject of kingship. They would probably have known, for example, Shakespeare's *Richard II*, which was performed at about the same time. They would also have been aware that Elizabeth I had no heir and that the issue of who would succeed her was beginning to preoccupy the Court. So a consideration of the *historical context* can bring you close to some of the issues which may seem remote at the beginning of the twenty-first century, but which were of passionate interest to people of all social classes at the time the play was written and first performed.

Consideration of the *moral context* of the play could make you aware of the ethical issues that are important in any period – those of justice, loyalty, dishonesty, judging character against behaviour, and so on. But ideas, attitudes and values about crucial moral issues are often very different now from what they were in the sixteenth century; important examples include attitudes to homosexuality and the role and status of wives. In many Western cultures now, homosexuality is accepted and arranged marriages are frowned upon. But there are still many countries and cultures where arranged marriages are the norm and homosexuality is severely punished. A consideration of moral issues in *Edward II*, therefore, alerts us to the fact that while some issues are universal, attitudes and values relating to them may change profoundly during time and across cultures.

It also raises specific questions about the extent to which you think Marlowe might be arguing for change, and about what kinds of things he wanted to change.

A consideration of the two *literary contexts* – both of which raise questions relating to genre – will alert you to very different aspects of the play. Comparison with Morality Plays, for example, encourages you to think about good and evil, particularly in a religious context. By contrast, consideration of the play as a tragedy allows you to compare this play with quite different ones and so focus instead on what happens to the main character at the end of the play and also on how different audiences and different individuals might respond to the main character. Although there are aspects of *Edward II* that are episodic (as in a Morality Play), there are other aspects which correspond more to the concerns and structure of a tragedy.

Different contexts, therefore, draw our attention to different features of the play. They might also lead to different interpretations of the play. Which context you find the most helpful or useful will, therefore, depend upon what you see as the most interesting and significant features of the play. However, remember that AO5ii asks you to consider a range of different contexts, to think about how each of them might be important, and to assess how far each of them illuminates your interpretation.

## The historical context: kingship in Edward II

Marlowe's consideration of kingship differs in many ways from that of other Elizabethan writers. Generally, the Elizabethans accepted the theory of the **divine right of kings**, according to which God chose the king independently of the wishes of the nation's subjects, this right to rule being passed down through generations.

In *Edward II*, Marlowe seems to explore what it is that gives a king the right to rule, but the ideas he offers may not be concerned with divine right.

### What sort of a king is Edward II?

At the start of the play Edward is introduced through Gaveston's words:

> 'My father is deceas'd, come Gaveston,
> And share the kingdom with thy dearest friend.'
> Ah, words that make me surfeit with delight!
> What greater bliss can hap to Gaveston
> Than live and be the favourite of a king?

## ACTIVITY 1

- What might Edward's priorities be when he takes over the kingdom?

- Do you think that a king should have favourites?

- What do you make of Gaveston's attitude here?

The Barons believe that Edward neglects his kingdom because of his relationship with Gaveston, and demand that he renounce his friend. Edward replies:

I cannot brook these haughty menaces:
Am I a king and must be overrul'd?

## ACTIVITY 2

- What is Edward's attitude to the Barons and to his own powers?

Shortly afterwards (Act 1, Scene 4), Mortimer makes a clear threat that if the king does not give up his favourite, the Pope will have to:

Curse him if he refuse; and then may we
Depose him, and elect another king.

## ACTIVITY 3

- Why should the Pope oppose Edward's wishes?

- Who is now seen to have the right to elect the King?

Edward, however, is seen to be reconciled with the Barons when he appears to make peace with his queen, Isabella, and most of the Barons offer loyalty:

EDWARD:     Once more receive my hand; and let this be
            A second marriage 'twixt thyself and me.
            . . .
LANCASTER:  This salutation overjoys my heart.
            . . . .
WARWICK:    Slay me, my lord, when I offend your grace.

## ACTIVITY 4

- Why do you think that Edward makes peace with Isabella?

- Do you think he has 'won over' the Barons at this point?

In the course of the ensuing battles, Edward, supported by the Spencers, crowns himself afresh in what is a very dramatic moment, saying (Act 3, Scene 2):

By earth, the common mother of us all,
By heaven, and all the moving orbs thereof,
By this right hand and by my father's sword,
And all the honours 'longing to my crown,
I will have heads and lives for him ...

## ACTIVITY 5

- This is like Edward's coronation service; what are his motives in repeating this service here?

- Why might Marlowe use such noble language, and refer to 'heaven'?

- Are Edward's motives here worthy of a king?

### The decline of Edward II as a king

In Act 4, Scene 4, Isabella explains how Edward might be regarded:

Misgovern'd kings are cause of all this rack;
And Edward, thou art one among them all
Whose looseness hath betray'd thy land to spoil,
And made the channels overflow with blood;

## ACTIVITY 6

- What problems might a weak king cause?

- Do you think that the description 'a weak king' might apply to Edward?

- Do you trust Isabella?

Edward cannot help his affections for his favourites. In the course of the play you see Edward arrested, imprisoned, degraded, tortured and finally killed. He therefore sees the reversal of his ideas about kingship and of his earlier hopes. When Lightborn comes to kill him (Act 5, Scene 5), Edward says:

> Know that I am a king – O, at that name
> I feel a hell of grief! Where is my crown?
> Gone, gone; and do I remain alive?

## ACTIVITY 7

- Do you see a reversal in Edward's language from that quoted before (Activity 5)?

- Why might Marlowe use the word 'hell'?

- Is there anything in life left for Edward if he is not a king?

Here are some questions you might consider in order to evaluate the significance of this context:

- Who is seen to have a right to elect kings? Is it God?

- What do you think might be the qualities of a good ruler?

- How does Edward match up to these qualities?

## The moral context

To consider this context you could look at two areas:

- the moral framework of the play

- how other characters fit into the moral scheme of the play.

### The moral framework of the play

You have already seen in the discussion of kingship how the right of electing a king shifted from being the responsibility of God to being that of man.

At the end of the play (Act 5, Scene 6), Mortimer speaks what might be considered the 'moral' of the play:

Base Fortune, now I see, that in thy wheel
There is a point, to which when men aspire,
They tumble headlong down; [. . .]

## ACTIVITY 8

- Is there any reference to God or morality here?

- Does Mortimer suggest that life is ruled by fate and chance?

The new king, Edward III, makes reference to 'grief and innocence', but probably does not draw any further moral conclusion. Marlowe often made comments about his own atheism, such as 'The only beginning of religion was to keep men in awe'. Do you think that it is possible that he deliberately offered a play in which there are no moral rules stemming from divine law?

### How other characters fit into the moral scheme of the play

The characters to be considered here are Gaveston, Mortimer and Isabella (but you could consider others for your own study).

#### Gaveston

You have already looked at Gaveston's words when he asked what 'greater bliss' there could be than to be a king's 'favourite' (Activity 1).

Later in Act 1, Scene 1, Gaveston arranges entertainment for the king, saying that he:

May draw the pliant King which way I please;
Music and poetry is his delight:

## ACTIVITY 9

- What do these words suggest about Gaveston? Might he be cunning?

- Might he be seen as manipulative, aware of the king's weaknesses?

- Is he governed by any concern for the king's wellbeing?

- Do you think that Gaveston is a manipulator? A **Machiavellian** figure?

- Remember the king's words about why he loves Gaveston: 'Because he loves me more than all the world' (Act 1, Scene 4)

- Do you think Gaveston is rather shrewd in his analysis of the king?

### Mortimer

Mortimer might have some justification for being angry with the king. But does this anger justifies his ambition to plot with Isabella and overthrow the king? In Act 4, Scene 5, his feelings are made clear:

> [*Aside to the* QUEEN] I like not this relenting mood in Edmund,
>
> …
>
> Your king hath wrong'd your country and himself,
> And we must seek to right it as we may.

## ACTIVITY 10

- What do you make of Mortimer's aside to the queen?

- Is he interested in reaching a peaceful solution?

When you consider his final words (which you looked at in Activity 8), you might consider whether Mortimer had any moral purposes at all, or whether ultimately he, like Gaveston, was just out to better himself.

### Isabella

In the scene where Edward makes peace with Isabella (Activity 4), you might feel sorry for her. But think about what happens in Act 2, Scene 5, where Isabella and Mortimer join forces:

> MORTIMER:    Madam, I cannot stay to answer you,
> But think of Mortimer as he deserves.
> QUEEN:    So well hast thou deserv'd, sweet Mortimer,
> As Isabel could live with thee for ever.

## ACTIVITY 11

- How do you respond to Isabella now? Do you still feel sympathy?

- Do you think that she, too, might be self-interested?

- Might she be out for revenge?

To evaluate the significance of this context, you might consider if there are any moral rules established in the play. You could ask yourself whether any of them think of anything other than themselves. Do you think there might be some real love shown by Edward and his two lovers, who are both finally willing to die for him?

## The literary context I: Edward II *as a Morality Play*

Morality Plays were popular in the Middle Ages, dramatising mankind's journey through life with all its temptations. Moral qualities of evil and goodness were presented on stage, and there were 'good' and 'bad' angels. The **Mystery Plays** developed a similar theme using stories from the Bible, playing out the whole of mankind's story from the fall to redemption through the birth of Jesus Christ.

There might be echoes of the Morality and Mystery Plays in the presentation of Lightborn in *Edward II*. When the audience first sees Lightborn (Act 5, Scene 4), he describes his 'apprenticeship':

'Tis not the first time I have kill'd a man.
I learn'd in Naples how to poison flowers;
To strangle with a lawn thrust through the throat;
To pierce the windpipe with a needle's point;

### A C T I V I T Y   1 2

• Read through the discussion of the genre of Revenge Tragedies in Activity 6 on page 129. How might Lightborn be seen as a Machiavellian figure?

This speech might establish Lightborn as a villain, but there are references that link him, as a character, with Morality Plays. His name is taken from the name of a Devil in the Chester Cycle of Mystery Plays. The name 'Lightborn' is Lucifer, the name of the Devil, anglicised. In his scenes in the dungeon with Edward, certain significant references are made (Act 5, Scene 5):

This dungeon where they keep me is the sink
Wherein the filth of all the castle falls.

…

My mind's distemper'd and my body's numb'd,
And whether I have limbs, or no, I know not.

### A C T I V I T Y   1 3

• Look at the language register here and in the dungeon scenes – darkness, rats, damp, dungeon, deprivation of the senses, Lightborn as Lucifer: might Marlowe be suggesting that Edward is in hell on earth?

To evaluate the significance of this context you might consider whether Marlowe created a drama with some suggestion of a Christian framework, but without drawing a Christian moral.

## The religious context

To assess this context you could re-order material assembled in Activities 12 and 13 above, and interweave the material for the second context, the moral context.

### ACTIVITY 14

- Might the Morality Play elements imply a religious context?

- Are there the suggestions of Lightborn as a devil, and of damnation?

- Might Edward be seen to endure the tortures of hell on earth?

- Do you think Marlowe suggests that there are consequences for mankind's wrongdoing, other than punishment here on earth?

- Is there in the play any sense of reward or punishment in an afterlife?

- Are there any 'judges' for Edward, other than his fellow men?

- What might Mortimer's words about the 'Wheel of Fortune', at the end of the play, suggest about certain views of mankind's destiny?

- Is the 'Wheel of Fortune' a Christian concept?

## The literary context II: Edward II *as a tragedy*

To assess this context you could consider three types of tragedy:

- the tragedy of a king's fall from grace: Edward

- the tragedy implicit in the concept of the 'Wheel of Fortune': how a person may apparently achieve wealth or fame, and then suddenly lose everything

- the personal tragedy of Edward himself.

### ACTIVITY 15

To consider a king's fall from grace, think about the following:

- What does Marlowe suggest about the divine right of kings?

- Should a man be entitled to rule because he is from a certain family?

- Alternatively, should he have particular qualities that entitle him to rule?

To consider the tragedy of the Wheel of Fortune, think about the following:

- What kind of men are Mortimer and Gaveston?

- Do they reach a certain pinnacle of success, only to be thrown down again as the Wheel of Fortune turns?

- Might this also be true of Edward?

To consider the personal tragedy of Edward, think about his personal qualities:

- Has he the wrong sort of temperament to become a king?

- There seems to be genuine love between Edward and his male lovers: might Marlowe be commenting on the contemporary social injustice of the impossibility of such a love being allowed to find fulfilment?

- Does Marlowe manipulate your sympathies towards Edward?

- Might Marlowe be creating hostility towards characters such as Isabella and Mortimer, for example, to enlist your sympathies for Edward?

## The language context

To assess this context, think about the plainness of the language of this play, unusual for a drama of its time. There is a limited use of 'elevated' language, so when it appears in this play, you need to consider Marlowe's reasons for including it. You have seen the use of noble language in Activity 5 above (page 106).

- Why does Marlowe make Edward speak in this noble way here? How does this language affect your response to Edward?

- Why do you think that the language is generally so plain? (You might think about what Marlowe could be suggesting about a 'new' sort of king.)

- Is he a king in an age that is less heroic than that presented in other dramas of the period?

- Might he be a non-heroic king for a non-heroic age?

You might also consider Isabella's lofty speech to the troops (Act 4, Scene 4). Mortimer cuts the speech down:

Nay Madam, if you be a warrior,
You must not grow so passionate in speeches.

## ACTIVITY 16

- How does this language affect your response to Isabella? Does it change your sympathies for her?

- What might Marlowe be implying in Mortimer's rebuff to Isabella?

- Might Mortimer be a better politician and tactician than she is, aware of the needs of troops? Aware of how language must be adapted to suit situations?

## Conclusion

You have now worked through six contexts relating to *Edward II*. Using this model framework, you can go on to address other contexts on your own, perhaps beginning by considering *Edward II* as a history play, exploring Edward's conflict with the Barons.

## *Measure For Measure* – William Shakespeare

In the development of *Measure for Measure* and in its conclusion – when a reformed society based on sound principles of law and justice is established after a period of chaos – the play may be classed as a comedy. However, some critics label *Measure for Measure* one of Shakespeare's 'problem plays'. This may be partly because of the extreme cruelty evident at times, which could put the play in the genre of tragicomedy, and partly because the play varies in its methods of presentation between realistic and non-realistic methods. You should not quibble if certain events or situations seem unlikely, but rather accept that they are there for specific dramatic purposes. If you accept the conventions of the play and 'suspend your disbelief', you can see many possible areas to explore, including that of the nature of just government. These three contexts – of comedy, of a 'problem play', and of an enquiry into the nature of just government – will be explored in the following pages.

The six contexts considered for the study of *Measure for Measure* are:

- The social context: an enquiry into the nature of just government

- The moral context: the development of self-knowledge

- The context of genre I: *Measure for Measure* as a comedy

- The dramatic context: the interlinking of two social classes

- The language context

- The context of genre II: *Measure for Measure* as one of the 'problem plays'

Quotations are taken from *Measure for Measure*, ed. J. W. Lever, Arden Edition, Methuen.

## Evaluating the significance of the contexts

One way of evaluating the significance of the contexts treated below is to compare what you would gain from them.

For example, enquiring into the *social context* of the play will enable you to think about issues relevant both to the time when the play was written and also, more broadly, to any society. More specifically, it might help you to consider the way society is organised and to reflect on the limits of legal justice.

But Shakespeare is not writing a tract about the way the law operates; he is also interested in that uncertain line between legal justice and moral justice. Evaluating the significance of this social context, therefore, might lead you to the conclusion that a consideration of the social context alone does not really get to the heart of the moral issues that Shakespeare was exploring in *Measure for Measure*. Similarly, whereas a consideration of the laws about pregnancy outside marriage gives some idea about the nature of the society Shakespeare chose to write about, a study of the *moral context* might show more about the issues that people are faced with in their daily lives.

Contemporary audiences would probably have been thinking about similar plays they had seen, and would thus have been particularly alert to what Shakespeare was doing in his play. So a consideration of the play as a comedy – its *literary context* – would enable you to highlight some of those things in *Measure for Measure* that an audience would find particularly striking. The audiences of Shakespeare's day would be well aware that a comedy was a play in which no one died, and so they would have been prompted to think especially hard about the cruelty surrounding the report that Claudio had been killed.

A modern audience, perhaps brought up on twentieth-century feminist ideas, would react strongly to the ending of the play; a consideration of the play as a comedy would allow you to think in particular about whether the ending is a happy one. But there is no clear answer to this; Shakespeare leaves the audience to decide for themselves whether Isabella and the Duke are going to live 'happily ever after'. Thinking about *Measure for Measure* as one of Shakespeare's 'problem plays' (again a *literary context*) means that you can compare it with 'darker' plays, such as *Hamlet*, or *The Merchant of Venice,* and therefore concentrate on features very different from those you might have looked at had you been comparing it with other comedies.

The different contexts, therefore, draw our attention to different features of the play. They might also lead to very different interpretations of the play. Which context you find the most helpful or useful will therefore depend on what you see as the most interesting and significant features of the play. However, remember that AO5ii asks you to consider a range of different contexts, to think about how each of them might be important, and to assess how far each of them illuminates your interpretation of the play.

## The social context: an enquiry into the nature of just government

You could consider three characters here: Angelo, Escalus, and the Duke. You might discover that each character has a different view of how to govern.

### Angelo

The Duke makes Angelo his deputy in his absence, and Angelo starts off by reviving an old law relating to fornication. The result of this is that Claudio is condemned to die. The Duke knows Angelo's character (Act 1, Scene 4):

> … Lord Angelo is precise;
> Stands at guard with Envy; scarce confesses
> That his blood flows; or that his appetite
> Is more to bread than stone. . . .

## ACTIVITY 1

- What sort of a person is Angelo? What are his attitudes?

- What might be the significance of the word 'precise', both here and in Act 3, Scene 1?

- Might it suggest that Angelo is an absolutist, seeing things in black and white, and not allowing for grey areas?

It would be helpful here to read through the two dramatic confrontations between Angelo and Isabella in Act 2, Scenes 2 and 4. You might ask yourself whether Angelo has fallen into a trap through his view of justice.

## ACTIVITY 2

- Should Angelo take into account an individual case, such as Claudio's?

- If he were to give in to Isabella, and pardon Claudio, would he still be impartial in carrying out the law?

- If he were to go ahead and execute Claudio, would he be inhumane?

- Does this suggest that there is a problem in his type of justice?

### Escalus

Escalus is exactly the opposite. In Act 2, Scene 2, he is asked by his constable, Elbow, to arrest Pompey for being a bawd. Angelo leaves him to take the case, and Escalus comments to Elbow:

Truly, officer, because he hath some offences in him that thou wouldst discover if thou couldst, let him continue in his courses

...

So for this time, Pompey, fare you well.

## ACTIVITY 3

- What do you make of Escalus's view of justice?

- Might he take too much notice of the individual?

- Might he undermine the idea of the necessity of rigorous laws?

### The Duke

Perhaps the Duke is not completely blameless in his rule of Vienna. Perhaps he has let the law drift, and not made his presence strongly felt? Do you think this may be the reason why Lucio refers to him twice as the 'dark' Duke (Act 2, Scene 2; and Act 4, Scene 3)? Might there be another reason?

He has seen the lawlessness of Vienna: '. . . I have seen corruption boil and bubble / Till it o'errun the stew' (Act 5, Scene 1). Perhaps he has let the law drift because he knows that it may be too harsh if applied to the letter. Perhaps he wishes to establish a *balanced* form of justice tempered by mercy.

Overall, the Duke might be seen to represent both justice and mercy in the sentences he hands out in Act 5, Scene 1, where he 'punishes' Angelo, Claudio and Lucio.

## ACTIVITY 4

- What are these punishments? Are they 'negative' punishments, or are they designed to reform the 'sinners'?

- Was Pompey's earlier punishment negative or redemptive?

Perhaps there is a justice in which the law works through wisdom and mercy, to reform and not just to punish. To evaluate the significance of this context you could compare the sort of justice meted out by Angelo and Escalus to that of the *balanced* judgement of the Duke.

## The moral context: the development of self-knowledge

To assess this context, consider the moral character of Angelo, Isabella and Claudio.

### Angelo

You read in Activity 1 (page 116) a description of Angelo by the Duke. Other characters in this play, such as Justice, think that Angelo is 'severe' (Act 2, Scene 1). Angelo himself thinks that he is faultless:

When I that censure him do so offend,
Let mine own judgement pattern out my death.

## ACTIVITY 5

- What do you think of Angelo's attitude here? Is it rather smug?

- Would you know at this stage that he himself has had a love affair?

To consider the ways in which Angelo gains self-knowledge, and therefore can improve himself, you could consider two areas:

- his 'espousal' to Mariana

- his dealings with Isabella.

## Angelo's 'espousal' to Mariana

The Duke is aware of this relationship, which he reveals in his plan to Mariana – 'he is your husband on a pre-contract' (Act 4, Scene 1) – so legally and morally he sees that Angelo is flawed. In Act 3, Scene 1, the Duke explains why she was abandoned by Angelo before the marriage agreement was finalised:

> Between which time of the contract and limit of the solemnity, her brother Frederick was wracked at sea, having in that perished vessel the dowry of his sister.

## ACTIVITY 6

- Angelo was *legally* entitled to break his espousal, but do you think he acted morally?

- What do you think his motives were? What might this suggest?

- When you compare Angelo's actions to those of Claudio, who was also 'espoused', who do you think is the better man? Is there any irony here?

## Angelo's dealings with Isabella.

But Angelo is presented as more than just a hypocrite, as you can see in his dealings with Isabella. In Act 2, Scene 4, he offers to waive Claudio's death penalty on condition that she:

> ... to redeem him,
> Give up your body to such sweet uncleanness
> As she that he hath stain'd?
> ...
> Might there not be a charity in sin

## ACTIVITY 7

- What do you think of Angelo now?

- Why do you think Shakespeare uses words such as 'redeem', 'charity', and 'sin'?

Then Angelo gives the matter another twist. He plans to deceive Isabella after he has slept with her by ordering her brother's execution – in case Claudio might 'have ta'en revenge' (Act 4, Scene 4).

## Isabella

When you first see Isabella she is about to become a novice nun. Even at this stage you can see that she is an extremist, who wishes 'a more strict restraint' on nuns (Act 1, Scene 4).

Shakespeare ensures that, as with Escalus and Angelo, the moral principles of Isabella are put to the test. You may see this in her two confrontations with Angelo in Act 2, Scenes 2 and 4, where she too faces an impossible choice. In the first confrontation, she works through four stages:

1. that Claudio should condemn the fault but not her brother (from line 34)

2. she then makes a plea for tolerance for all sinners (from line 88)

3. she now moves to the idea of mercy in law, asking Angelo to 'show some pity' (from line 100)

4. when all these pleas fail, she attacks all human authority: 'man . . . like an angry ape plays such fantastic tricks before high heaven.'

### ACTIVITY 8

- Pick out the different stages of Isabella's argument, and Angelo's counter-arguments, as you read through the scene.

In the second confrontation, in Act 2, Scene 4, Isabella responds to the deadly choice of either sleeping with Angelo and so saving her brother's life, or keeping her virtue and letting him die:

Th'impression of keen whips I'd wear as rubies,
And strip myself to death as to a bed
That longing have been sick for, ere I'd yield
My body up to shame.

### ACTIVITY 9

- Why might Shakespeare give Isabella such very sensuous language here?

- What do you make of her choices: that she must let her brother die or give up her virginity?

- Is that choice consistent with the Christian ideas of love and sacrifice to which she claims she wishes to adhere as a nun?

- Should she break her own pledge as a nun and lose her chastity?

### Claudio

Claudio has rather different weaknesses. Technically, he has offended state and moral law by sleeping with Juliet before they were married, but Claudio has other moral difficulties, as you may see in the scene with the Duke in prison (Act 3, Scene 1). Claudio may be seen to veer wildly in his responses to the Duke. When the Duke offers the advice 'Be absolute for death', Claudio seems heartened and resolute:

> I humbly thank you.
> To sue to live, I find I seek to die,
> And seeking death, find life. Let it come on.

But then Isabella reveals Angelo's offer, and in Act 2, Scene 1, when Claudio thinks about the terrors of death, his resolution fails:

> Death is a fearful thing.
> …
> Ay, but to die, and go we know not where;

## ACTIVITY 10

- How do you respond to Claudio at this point?

- Might it be thought that just as Angelo was too absolute in his morality, so here Claudio wavers too much? That he is not resolute enough?

The Duke may be seen as the moral ideal, with the themes of morality and justice being drawn together in one of his speeches (Act 3, Scene 2):

> He who the sword of heaven will bear
> Should be as holy as severe:
> …
> Twice treble shame on Angelo.

## ACTIVITY 11

- How does Shakespeare link morality and justice here?

- Why might the Duke be made to refer to 'the sword of heaven'?

To evaluate the significance of this context, you could:

- assess how each character has gained moral self-knowledge through experiencing 'new' and difficult situations, and

- measure each character against the 'ideal' standard of the Duke.

## The context of genre I: Measure for Measure *as a comedy*

It has been suggested in one distinctive form of social comedy there are three stages: (1) it opens with an unsettled society governed by a harsh or irrational law; (2) there is then a temporary loss of identity; and (3) finally there is the discovery of a new identity and a reconciliation. This structure seems to suit the development of *Measure for Measure*.

### An unsettled society governed by a harsh or irrational law

At the beginning of the play, you can see the result of reviving the old law about fornication in Claudio's arrest. In Act 1, Scene 2, the Duke says:

> We have strict statutes and most biting laws,
> The needful bits and curbs to headstrong jades,
> Which for this fourteen years we have let slip.

## ACTIVITY 12

- Do you think that this society is unsettled? Why might this be?

### A temporary loss of identity

In exploring the first two contexts you have already identified the confusion in both events and moral attitudes.

### The discovery of a new identity and a reconciliation

You could explore the ending of the play to see how the processes of self-discovery and reconciliation are achieved. You have already discussed 'punishment' and reconciliation in Activity 4 above (page 117), so to complete the exploration of this context, you might 'flesh out' the full evidence under these three headings in your own time.

## The dramatic context: the interlinking of two social classes

To assess this context you could consider how the lower-class characters counterpoint or illuminate the issues related to the higher-class characters. You can look at Pompey, Lucio and Barnardine.

## ACTIVITY 13

### Pompey and his attitude to law

- Does Pompey seem to talk good sense at times, for example when he points out the folly of closing all the brothels in the Dukedom?

- Might he be seen as a character of common sense?

- Why is he made to make Escalus look foolish?

- How is his behaviour reflected by those of a higher class?

- Does he provide humour in the play?

- How does his punishment fit into the final mood of the play?

### Lucio

- Does Lucio seem at first to represent and parallel the Duke?

- Does he too seem to exhibit common sense? What effects does this have?

- Does he seem to be treated more harshly as the play goes on?

- How does this affect the mood of the play?

- How does his punishment fit into the final moral scheme of the play?

### Barnardine

- Does Barnardine deny the Duke's right of dispensing law to every citizen when he refuses to be executed?

- What effect does this have on your perception of the Duke?

## The language context

To assess this context you could explore two of the different **registers** evident in *Measure for Measure*. There are two central registers operating in the play, each carrying certain values:

- the register linked to moral virtue, established by such words as 'redeem, grace, charity'; this register introduces the theme of morality and virtue

- the register linked to the title of the play, *Measure for Measure*, in other words language linked to weighing, testing, balancing; this register brings together the ideas of morality and justice.

## ACTIVITY 14

- How might the register to do with grace and Christian virtue interlink with that of testing?

- Might they come together in the idea of Christian mercy?

- Might this be part of the exploration of the nature of justice in the play?

- Might the Old Testament idea of justice – of testing and weighing a person's deserts and then meting out punishment – need to be balanced with a New Testament concept of Christian grace in order to achieve a new sort of justice based also on mercy?

*The context of genre II:* Measure for Measure *as one of the 'problem plays'*

## ACTIVITY 15

- Which issues are too serious for comedy?

- Is Duke right to abuse Isabella and pretend that her brother is dead?

- Is Angelo's seduction of Isabella – a nun – appropriate for comedy?

- Is Claudio's attempt to prostitute Isabella in order to save his own life a proper subject for comedy?

- Does the constant threat of death which hangs over several characters seem right for comedy?

- Is the ending of the play completely convincing?

- Might this play, with its dark and complex themes and its threats of death, be best defined as a tragicomedy – a blend of two genres?

Do you think that the different types of characterisation might cause an audience some difficulty? To answer this, work through the next activity:

## ACTIVITY 16

- Does Shakespeare present some characters, such as Angelo, Isabella and Claudio, with any psychological realism?

- Is the Duke a difficult character to assess because he is not fully rounded, but indeed part realistic and part a stock 'type' issuing moral statements?

- Does he hold up the pace of the play with his long speeches?

You might think about whether you are being asked to suspend disbelief and accept these presentations of character and situation without quibbling too much about the way in which Shakespeare has chosen to present certain ideas.

## Conclusion

You have now worked through six contexts relating to *Measure for Measure*. Using this model framework, you can now go on to address other contexts on your own, such as the links Shakespeare makes between self-knowledge, mercy, compassion, morality and justice.

## *The White Devil* – John Webster

*The White Devil* is an example of the genre of Revenge Tragedy, but Webster creates a very complex type of drama out of this form. As the title of the play suggests, he is exploring ambiguities in human nature: Vittoria is seen to be a devil, and therefore morally black, but she also displays strength of character and courage that may gain the respect of an audience, and so she is also seen as 'white'.

In Webster's plays it is not easy to establish a clear understanding of the characters because we usually see them only in brief flashes. He shows the disparity between words and deeds, and makes his characters comment on each other to give us a range of contrasted viewpoints. The result is that there is no one certain viewpoint to adopt, no certainty about how to find meaning or discern a moral law. At the end of his plays there is usually a sense of distance from, but also some pity for, the characters who inhabit the dark world he created.

As some of the contexts related to this play overlap with those in Middleton's Revenge Tragedy *Women Beware Women*, you may find it helpful to look through the next section also.

The six contexts considered for the study of *The White Devil* are:

- The dramatic context

- *The White Devil* as a Revenge Tragedy

- The moral context

- The language context: imagery and register

- The social, historical, and cultural context of court life

- The religious context

Quotations are from *The Revels Plays*, ed. John Russell-Browne.

## *Evaluating the significance of the contexts*

One way of evaluating the significance of the contexts treated below is to compare what you would gain from them.

A consideration of the *moral context* might make you aware of the relationships between the characters, their morality and their motivation. It will alert you to the codes that the characters do or do not live by, and encourage you to think about a world where many live their lives outside any kind of moral law.

By taking a cardinal as one of his characters, Webster gives the moral context a religious dimenssion. Consideration of this *religious context* will in turn raise questions about Webster's purposes in choosing a setting in Roman Catholic Italy. Was this because he wanted to say something about Catholicism at a time when the Puritans were gaining strength in England? Or was it because he could say things about contemporary society in England by setting the play at one remove? The *social, historical and cultural context* of court life would have encouraged contemporary audiences to think about the court that they knew, that of James I, and about changes that had occurred since the death of Elizabeth I in 1603.

Consideration of the *dramatic* and *generic contexts* – *The White Devil* as a Revenge Tragedy – draws attention to very different features. The elements of the play that you look at in terms of the dramatic context concern the ways in which Webster provides spectacle and variety for his audience. In terms of dramatic context, the play can be seen both as a structure and as an entertainment. The generic context of the Revenge Tragedy invites a comparison with other Revenge Tragedies, perhaps *The Spanish Tragedy* by Thomas Kyd or Shakespeare's *Hamlet*. You do not necessarily have to read any other Revenge Tragedies, but you do need to be aware of the central features of the genre.

The different contexts, therefore, draw our attention to different features of the play. They might also lead to other interpretations of the play. Which context you find the most helpful or useful will, therefore, depend upon what you see as the most interesting and significant features of the play. However, remember that AO5ii asks you to consider a range of different contexts, to think about how each of them might be important, and assess how far each of them illuminates your interpretation of the play.

## The dramatic context

Three features of Webster's dramatic style will be considered here:

- his use of fables

- his use of dumb shows

- his use of commentators.

Remember that this list is not exhaustive; these are just some examples of Webster's dramatic technique.

### The use of fables

Vittoria tells a fable when she explains to the Duke her dream about the yew tree (Act 1, Scene 2). She goes on to explain her feelings:

> They told me my intent was to root up
> That well-grown yew, and plant i'th'stead of it
> A withered blackthorn, . . .

## ACTIVITY 1

- Who does Vittoria mean when she says 'that well-grown yew'? Is there a pun on the word 'you'? Is it Camillo or the Duke?

- Similarly the 'withered blackthorn': do you think she referring to Camillo or the Duke?

- Might Webster have deliberately provided two alternative readings here?

- Might this tie in with the ambiguity of the whole play? Are you ever sure what may be taken as the truth in this play?

- Why might Webster repeat the image of the yew in Act 4, Scene 3?

You could refer to other fables in the play, such as Francisco's fable about Pheobus (Act 2, Scene 1), or Flamineo's fable of the crocodile and the tooth-picking bird (Act 5, Scene 2).

## ACTIVITY 2

- Analyse these fables as you did Vittoria's reference to the 'yew tree'.

- How do these fables create ambiguity?

### Webster's use of dumb shows

The first example of this is the account of Isabella's death in Act 2, Scene 2, when she dies after kissing the Duke's poisoned picture. After watching it the Duke says: 'Excellent, then she's dead.'

## ACTIVITY 3

- Why do you think that Webster presented Isabella's death like this?

- Might this be a way of letting the audience know about events?

- Might it serve to remind the audience about Bracciano's crimes?

- Might it be a way of keeping the audience at a distance, so that no sympathetic bond is created with Isabella?

- What do you think of the Duke's words? Might they too distance you from the grim spectacle?

The second dumb show, that of Camillo's death, is also in Act 2, Scene 2.

## ACTIVITY 4

- Explore this second dumb show in the same way you looked at the first.

## Webster's use of commentators

Throughout the play Webster's characters offer running commentaries on the action of which they are a part. Here are some examples:

- Francisco watches the sprinkling of Bracciano's helmet with poison (Act 5, Scene 2); Flamineo is with him to watch the Duke die

- Lodovico watches Zanche make love to Francisco (Act 5, Scene 2)

- Flamineo describes Vittoria's death and his own (Act 5, Scene 6)

- The assassin's comment on the killing of Zanche, Vittoria and Flamineo, as when Lodovico says (Act 5, Scene 6):

> Nought grieves but that you are too few to feed
> The famine of our vengeance. What dost think on?

## ACTIVITY 5

- Why might Webster have the assassin comment on his own actions?

- Why does the assassin ask Flamineo a question?

- Could Webster again be using a device to distance the audience?

- Flamineo talks of 'spectacles fashion'd with such perspective art'. Might this be one of the main purposes of the commentaries as a whole? Might Webster be offering multiple perspectives in order to confuse an audience?

To evaluate the significance of each of these techniques, you could continue to discuss how each contributes to the effectiveness of the play.

## The White Devil *as a Revenge Tragedy*

This play has many of the characteristics of a Revenge Tragedy. The Elizabethan and Jacobean audiences had mixed views about revenge, and an ambiguous attitude towards those seeking revenge. Whilst it was acceptable to avenge the murder of a blood relative, or a very brutal murder, or a murder in circumstances where the victim could not get legal redress, nevertheless it was an offence in the eyes of God to kill another human being.

The genre of Revenge Tragedy has certain characteristics that you could apply to *The White Devil*:

## ACTIVITY 6

- There will be one or more revengers. Who are they, and what are their motives?

- There is usually an Italian or Spanish setting. Where is *The White Devil* set? Could this be England in disguise?

- There is usually a discontented central character who comments on the action. This is often a Machiavellian figure, who cynically manipulates events for his own ends. Who is this in *The White Devil*? Might there be more than one?

- There is intrigue, violence, poisoning, death. Are there any of these in *The White Devil*?

- Disguise is often used to create confusion. Is this evident in *The White Devil*?

To evaluate the significance of this context, you might ask yourself how Webster uses the Revenge genre, for example:

## ACTIVITY 7

- Does (do) the revenger(s) retain your sympathy? Is a better society established after revenge has been taken?

- Might Webster use this genre to address contemporary problems, including: (a) Questions of personal honour and morality? (b) Political problems related to the use and abuse of power? (c) Questions of divine law in society? (d) Questions relating to human frailty or evil?

## The moral context

In the society of the play there would seem to be moral anarchy; characters generally behave according to their own desires, without apparent reference to a governing moral law. In exploring this theme you could consider both individual and social morality.

### Individual morality

You have seen Bracciano's response to Isabella's murder in Activity 3 above. Preparing for Camillo's death, the conjurer says (Act 2, Scene 2):

And view Camillo's far more politic fate, –
Strike louder music from the charmed ground,
To yield, as fits the act, a tragic sound.

## ACTIVITY 8

- Why might the conjurer use the word 'politic'?

- Is there any indication that murdering another person is a sin?

In Act 4, Scene 1, Francisco dismisses Isabella's ghost with: 'remove this object.' This may suggest that for him there is no such thing as conscience or an afterlife.

Cornelia appears to observe some moral principles, but when one son, Flamineo, murders the other, Marcello, she falls first into fit of grief, and then into madness. Marcello seems to have a conscience, for example in Act 5, Scene 1, when he says to Flamineo:

Why does this devil haunt you? say.

…

She is your shame.

But what has happened to him now? In the same Act (Scene 4) Cornelia says:

This sheet
I have kept this twenty year, and every day
Hallow'd it with my prayers,

…

O reach me the flowers.

## ACTIVITY 9

- What might be the significance of the words 'Hallow'd' and 'prayers'?

- If the two people who had some sense of morality are either dead or mad, what might this suggest about the world of the play?

Giovanni may perhaps indicate some hope for the future, but think of Flamineo's words to him: 'thy uncle, / Which is a part of thee' (Act 5, Scene 6). Finally Giovanni leaves Lodovico to see 'What use you ought to make of their punishment' (Act 5, Scene 6).

## ACTIVITY 10

- Why might it matter if Giovanni were to resemble his uncle?

- Is there any clear sense of a guiding authority in him?

On the other hand, characters do have flashes of conscience. Look at Flamineo's words when, in Act 5, Scene 4, he observes his mother's madness, which he has caused:

> I have a strange thing in me, to th'which
> I cannot give a name, without it be
> Compassion, . . .

## ACTIVITY 11

- What might Webster be suggesting by the use of the word 'compassion'?

- For how long are these feelings evident in Flamineo? Do they last?

- Might this be one of Webster's 'Flashes of light' in a dark world?

### Social morality

Society as a whole is seen to be corrupt, as is evident in the use of the Cardinal's black book of offenders. Its list of wrong-doers is huge, and as Francisco says (Act 4, Scene 1), if he wanted:

> Ten leash of courtezans, it would furnish me;
>
> ...
>
> See the corrupted use some make of books:

## ACTIVITY 12

- Why do you think that Webster uses the image of the black book?

- What might it tell you about the man who compiled it, the Cardinal?

To evaluate the significance of this context, you could measure individuals and society against a sound moral code based on virtue.

### The language context: imagery and register

There are at least three sets of key words used in *The White Devil*. Those in the first group relate to witchcraft, poison, and the devil; in the second, to politics and politicians; and in the third group, evident in the trial of Vittoria, to moral concepts such as charity and justice.

To evaluate the significance of this context, you could relate these sets of words to the themes and actions of the play.

You could, for example, look at the language related to witchcraft, poison, and the devil, as in the next activity:

## ACTIVITY 13

- How does the idea of witchcraft or poison improve your understanding of the motives and actions of certain characters? Does this register suggest evil and evil practices?

- Might references to the Devil suggest that all is not well in the moral state of this nation? If so, how and where?

You could also look at the words related to politics and politicians:

## ACTIVITY 14

- How might these words suggest something about motives and actions in this play?

- Might these words remind you of Machiavelli?

- How might this link affect your response to certain characters in the play?

## ACTIVITY 15

- You might look at the trial of Vittoria (Act 3, Scene 2) to explore how Webster may be seen to undermine the concepts of charity and justice.

## The social, historical and cultural context of court life

Here you might consider two aspects:

- the setting of an Italian court

- the theme of the uses and abuses of power.

### The setting of an Italian court

In dealing with this, you could think about the questions in the next activity:

## ACTIVITY 16

- What actual Italian elements are used, in characters and settings?

- Are the Italians seen as treacherous and malicious in character?

- Is there evidence of any characters who are Machiavellian?

- Is poisoning seen as a particularly Italian activity in the play?

- Is there evidence of corruption, intrigues and vengeance?

- Could Italy be seen as a hotbed of vice, corruption and villainy?

- Might there be any suspicion on the part of the Protestant English towards Roman Catholicism and Popery?

- How far is the landscape naturalistic, and how far is it in fact a 'moral landscape'?

- How far is Italy important because it represents certain ways of feeling and of behaving? What are these ways of feeling and behaving?

- Could the Italian court be that of England 'in disguise'?

### The theme of the uses and abuses of power

To address this context you could look at the words and deeds of the Duke throughout the play. You could also look at those of Vittoria, who gains power through the Duke. But this aspect is rather tricky, as at times both characters attract our sympathy; Vittoria at her trial, and both at the moment of death.

## ACTIVITY 17

Read through the scenes of their deaths again.

- Could it be claimed that both characters triumph in their very strong love for each other?

- Does this strength almost become a virtue, an 'integrity of life'?

### The religious context

In a way, this context overlaps with the moral context you have looked at above (page 129). You could develop this context by thinking about the points raised in the next activity.

## ACTIVITY 18

- Consider Vittoria's words to the Cardinal at her trial: 'O poor charity / thou art seldom found in scarlet' (Act 3, Scene 2).

- Is the Cardinal right in being simultaneously the representative of the Church, and also Judge and Juror?

- Might this combination undermine his religious role, and diminish your respect for him as a Churchman?

- Flamineo also scorns him, as he says (Act 3, Scene 3):

  ... A cardinal; – I would he would hear me, – there's nothing so holy but money will corrupt and putrify it, like victual under the line.

- What is the attitude towards the Cardinal and what he represents in these lines from Vittoria and Flamineo?

- What do you make of the assassins, who, dressed as Capuchin monks, pretend to give the Duke the last sacraments, but in fact murder him?

- What are the characters' attitudes towards death? Is there any idea of hell or heaven? Or do they believe that we have our rewards and punishments here on earth?

## Conclusion

You have now worked through six contexts relating to *The White Devil*. Using this model framework, you can now go on to address other contexts on your own, perhaps beginning with the psychological/social context of what moves characters in this play to act in the way they do.

## *Women Beware Women* – Thomas Middleton

This play was written about nine years after another Jacobean Revenge Tragedy, Webster's *The White Devil*. There may well be overlap between work on *Women Beware Women* and *The White Devil*, so you might find it helpful to look at Activity 6, page 129, where the typical elements of a Revenge Tragedy are set out. You could follow the same model to work out the ways in which *Women Beware Women* falls into the category.

There are two aspects of Thomas Middleton's life which may affect your reading of this play, and which therefore form part of the biographical context. First, Middleton was a Calvinist. Calvinists believed that each individual is sinful, and can be redeemed only by God's grace; and moreover that each individual is *predestined* to salvation or damnation. This could in part explain the apparent helplessness of individual characters in *Women Beware Women* as they drift into sin and damnation.

Second, Middleton lived at a time when there was a rapid growth of the middle classes. There was also a gradual movement towards a capitalist economy, so that money and material possessions were becoming very important. As a result, moral and economic values clashed, as you can see in the use of the money/value register through this play.

The six contexts offered for the study of *Women beware Women* are:

- The social context: women in society

- The moral context

- The dramatic context: Middleton's use of spectacular stage effects

- The cultural context: life at an Italian court

- The language context

- The religious context

Quotations are from *Women Beware Women*, New Mermaids Edition, ed. R. Gill.

## *Evaluating the significance of the contexts*

One way of evaluating the significance of the contexts treated below is to compare what you would gain from them.

A consideration of the *moral context* will make you aware of the relationships between the characters, their morality, and their motivations. It will alert you to the codes that the characters do or do not live by, and to a world where many live their lives outside any kind of moral law. By having a cardinal as one of his characters, Middleton gives the moral context a religious dimension. Consideration of this *religious context* will in turn raise questions about Middleton's purposes in choosing a setting of Roman Catholic Italy. Was this because he wanted to say something about Catholicism at the time when the Puritans were gaining strength in England? Or was it because he wanted to say things about contemporary society in England by setting the play at one remove? The *cultural context* of court life would have encouraged a contemporary audience to think about the court that they knew, that of James I, and about the changes that had occurred since the death of Elizabeth I in 1603.

Consideration of the *dramatic* and *generic contexts* – Women Beware Women as a Revenge Tragedy – draws attention to very different features. The elements of the play which you look at in terms of the dramatic context concern the ways in which Middleton provides spectacle and variety for the audience. The play can be seen both as a structure and as an entertainment. The generic context of the Revenge Tragedy invites a comparison with other Revenge Tragedies, such as *The Spanish Tragedy* by Thomas Kyd or Shakespeare's *Hamlet*. You do not necessarily have to read any other Revenge Tragedies, but you do need to be aware of the central features of the genre.

The different contexts, therefore, draw our attention to different features of the play. They might also lead to other interpretations of the play. Which context you find the most helpful or useful will, therefore, depend upon what you see as the most interesting and significant features of the play. However, remember that AO5ii asks you to consider a range of different contexts, to think about how each of them might be important, and to assess how far each of them illuminates your interpretation of the play.

## The social context: women in society

Women appear to have a generally subservient role in the society portrayed in *Women Beware Women*. There are several examples of this in the play.

- Leantio sees no harm in marrying above his social status, but expects his wife Bianca to be trapped in his poor home with his widowed mother.

- Bianca is, in the Duke's eyes, a thing to be bought for his pleasure.

- In the marriage which her father Fabritio wants to arrange with a fool of a man, Isabella is discussed as though she were a piece of property. Sordido and the Ward inspect her as though she were an animal.

- Livia outrages her brother when she takes the much younger Leantio as her lover. It is perfectly all right for older men such as Hippolito or the Duke to do this, but when the situation is reversed, Livia is seen to offend the social laws.

### Leantio and Bianca

Here is part of the opening speech by Leantio to his mother (Act 1, Scene 1):

And here's my masterpiece. Do you now behold her!
Look at her well, she's mine; . . .

He then goes on to plead with his mother not to spoil her:

I pray do not you teach her to rebel,
When she's in a good way to obedience;

## ACTIVITY 1

In considering Leantio's attitude here to Bianca, and so to women, you might want to think about the following:

- Leantio's attitude – does he treat Bianca as if she were a possession?

- Does he think of her in material terms?

- Do you think that he is aware of the needs of a young wife?

- Look at Leantio's speeches elsewhere in this opening scene: do you think that he could be considered to be crude or smug or vulgar?

### The Duke's attitude to Bianca

Here is part of the speech in which the Duke tries to persuade Bianca to be his mistress (Act 2, Scene 2):

But I give better in exchange – wealth, honour.
She that is fortunate in a duke's favour
Lights on a tree that bears all women's wishes:

## ACTIVITY 2

In considering the Duke's attitude here to Bianca, and so to other women, you might want to think about the following:

- Does he have any doubts about what is best for Bianca?

- What are the most important things which he thinks he can give?

- Is there any concern for morality here?

- What does he think is the role of a mother?

- What does he think that women may achieve socially?

Using these model frameworks, you could go on to look at how Isabella is regarded. You could analyse her speech in Act 1, Scene 2, and the scene with the Ward and Sordido (Act 3, Scene 3). To consider Livia, you might look at Hippolito's response to the discovery that Leantio is her lover (Act 4, Scene 2).

To evaluate the significance of this context, you could contrast the position and role of women with those of the male members of their society.

## The moral context

This context is in some regards related to the context of women in society. In the discussion above you have looked at male attitudes to women; but in a way these male attitudes have been made possible by the responses of the female characters. Consider, for example, the changes in both Bianca and Isabella. After the Duke has courted her, Bianca speaks to the widow (Act 3, Scene 1):

> ... Must I live in want,
> Because my fortune matched me with your son?
> Wives do not give away themselves to husbands
> To the end to be quite cast away; they look
> To be the better used and tendered rather,
>
> ...
> They're well rewarded

## ACTIVITY 3

- What does Bianca now seem to demand from a marriage?

- How does this compare to her earlier speeches to the widow in Act 1, Scene 1?

- How does Bianca's character change after she has taken the Duke as her lover and husband?

- Critics see Bianca as initially immature, naive and sensuous, but also as weak enough to be easily swayed into evil ways. Do you agree?

- How far do you think that Bianca's weakness or naivety make her unable to resist the pressures of a corrupt society?

Isabella seems to be similar. At the beginning of the play she is horrified at the thought of being 'sold' in marriage, but remains obedient to her father (Act 2, Scene 1). She also seems horrified at the thought that her uncle loves her (Act 1, Scene 3). But read through her speech to Livia soon afterwards (Act 2, Scene 1), beginning 'Troth, I begin . . .').

## ACTIVITY 4

- What sort of changes can you see here in Isabella's attitude and her language?

- Do you think that, like Bianca, she is rather weak and naive? Does she too give in to social pressures in having an affair with Hippolito?

Livia is very different. She seems to be manipulative, but she also seems concerned for her brother's welfare. Consider her plan to ensnare Isabella (Act 2, Scene 1):

That I shall venture much to keep a change from you
So fearful as this grief will bring upon you –

…

And I can bring forth
As pleasant fruits as sensuality wishes

## ACTIVITY 5

- What is Livia's main concern here? Is it for morality?

- What might be the significance of the imagery related to fruit?

Elsewhere Livia entraps the widow and Bianca (Act 2, Scene 2).

## ACTIVITY 6

- What do you think Livia's motives are in this scene?

- Is there any concern for morality?

With the exception of the Cardinal, the men, like the women, seem not to have any moral sense. In Activity 2 above (page 137) you considered the Duke's attitude to Bianca. Leantio also seems to live by financial rather than moral considerations – you can see his attitude in response to Livia's approaches to him (Act 3, Scene 3):

| LIVIA: | Do but you love enough, I'll give enough. |
| LEANTINO: | Troth then, I'll love enough and take enough. |
| LIVIA: | Then we are both pleased enough. |

## ACTIVITY 7

- Why does Leantio make his decision about Livia? Does he really love her?

- Do you think that perhaps he may now see life in purely mercenary terms?

- Why are the words 'give' and 'take' used?

- Why do you think that the word 'enough' is repeated five times?

- Could it relate to an idea of bargaining and of self-interest?

You could continue developing this context by exploring the morality of all the main characters in the play. You may well find that with the exception of the Cardinal, they all operate on terms of self-interest rather than moral consideration; and that all the characters (including the Cardinal) appear to be motivated by greed. Activities 13 and 14 (pages 143–144) will look at the language context, and you will see that imagery of food and money also work throughout the play to develop this central idea.

To evaluate the significance of this context, you could measure the words and actions of the characters against moral norm based on virtue.

### The dramatic context: Middleton's use of spectacular stage effects

When he wrote this play, Middleton was 'Chronologer to the City of London', responsible for writing and directing official entertainments (this is an example of the biographical context). There are two spectacular staging effects in *Women Beware Women*: the chess scene (Act 2, Scene 2), and the masque (Act 5, Scene 2). Both illustrate Middleton's dramatic skills.

**The chess scene.** In performance, Livia entertains the widow with a game of chess on the stage, while Bianca is entertained, or rather seduced, by the Duke off stage. You do not see the seduction, but you hear Livia's commentary (Act 2, Scene 2):

| | |
|---|---|
| LIVIA: | Did I not say my duke would fetch you over, widow? |
| MOTHER: | I think you spoke in earnest when you said it, madam. |
| LIVIA: | And my black king makes all the haste he can, too. |
| MOTHER: | Well, madam, we may meet with him in time yet. |
| LIVIA: | I have given thee blind mate twice. |
| MOTHER: | You may see, madam, My eyes begin to fail. |
| LIVIA: | I'll swear they do, wench. |

## ACTIVITY 8

- Why does Middleton give these words to Livia?

- How might the chess game relate to Bianca's seduction? Is she a pawn?

- What is the key characteristic of Middleton's method here?

- Could you use the word 'ironical' to describe his method?

- Do you feel distanced from events because you do not see the seduction?

- What effects does this distancing have on you? Does it play down the horror of what is going on? Does it lessen your sympathy for Bianca? Does it make you feel a spectator of other people's tragedies?

- Could all this be one of the reasons why Middleton's tone is often called 'cool'?

**The masque.** Read through the masque scene (Act 5, Scene 2) and then ask yourself the questions in the next activity.

## ACTIVITY 9

- Does the nature of the deaths seem appropriate to the characters?

- Do you find the events here rather confusing?

- Do certain characters such as the Duke also find events confusing?

- Does this confusion again distance you from any emotional response?

- Does it force you into making other sorts of judgements on both the characters and the events?

To assess the significance of this context you might consider how these scenes contribute to the dramatic effectiveness of the play. But remember, this is only one aspect of Middleton's dramatic art; you may want to explore other aspects.

## The cultural context: life at an Italian court

To assess this context you could consider the presentation of, and the purposes behind, Middleton's setting, which is the court of an Italian duke. Italian and Spanish settings were often used in Revenge Tragedies. To assess why this might be, consider questions in the next activity.

## ACTIVITY 10

- What actual Italian elements are used, in characters and settings?

- Are Italians seen as treacherous and malicious in character?

- Is there evidence of any characters who are Machiavellian?

- Is poisoning seen as a particularly Italian activity?

- Is there evidence of corruption, intrigue and vengeance?

- Could Italy be seen as a hotbed of vice, corruption and villainy?

- Might there be any suspicion on the part of the Protestant English towards Roman Catholicism and Popery?

- How far is the landscape naturalistic, and how far is it in fact a 'moral landscape'?

- How far is Italy important because it represents certain ways of feeling and of behaving? What are these ways of feeling and behaving?

- Could the Italian court be 'England in disguise'?

## The language context

This context draws attention to the fact that Middleton's language, especially his imagery, illuminates the themes of the play. You might decide that the imagery is used to point up the confusion of values in this corrupt society, which is dominated by the lust for power of money.

To explore this context, you could look at three areas, all of which are characteristic of Revenge Tragedies:

- imagery related to food and appetite

- imagery related to money and value

- imagery related to disease and sickness.

### Imagery related to food and appetite

As an example of language embodying such images, read Livia's words in Act 1, Scene 2, where she is talking about having casual love-affairs:

And if we lick a finger then, sometimes,
We are not too blame; your best cooks use it.

## ACTIVITY 11

- What does this suggest about the morality of the characters?

- Should they act in accordance with whims and appetites, without ideas of moral restraint?

- Is mankind reduced to some sort of animal status if people live just to indulge themselves in this way?

- Is this how other images in this group work?

### Imagery related to money and value

To consider such images you could look at the scene in Act 3, Scene 3 where the Ward inspects Isabella as though he were buying an animal at a cattle-sale. Or the scene where Bianca and Leantio talk of what they have gained materially through Bianca's seduction of the Duke, which ends with Bianca's words: 'Fair clothes by foul means, come to rail and show 'em.' (Act 4, Scene 1)

## ACTIVITY 12

- What does this tell you about the motives and actions of the characters?

- Are there any moral considerations involved?

### Imagery related to disease and sickness

Consider the Mother's words to Bianca in Act 1, Scene 3:

>                         you take the course
> To make him an ill husband, troth you do,
> And that disease is catching, . . .

## ACTIVITY 13

- How might the idea of sickness and disease say something about the state of society?

### The religious context

To address this context you could consider the Cardinal. Most critics accept that he is the sole moral voice of the play. Others comment that his religious preaching is ineffectual, generally ignored by all. How do you respond to him? Begin by working through his speeches in Act 4, Scenes 1 and 3; and Act 5, Scene 2.

## ACTIVITY 14

In the first speech the Cardinal is appealing to the Duke to give up Bianca, and thinks he has persuaded him to do so: 'here's a conversion.'

- What does the Duke decide to do? Has he followed the Cardinal's advice?

In the second speech, the Cardinal realises the effects of his appeal and thunders at the Duke. Why?

In the last speech, at the end of the play, he expresses the moral of the play, concluding: 'So where lust reigns, that prince cannot reign long.'

- Might the Cardinal be the mouthpiece for traditional religious views?

- Does anybody in the play take any notice of him?

- Whose side are you on when Bianca criticises him for lack of charity at her wedding (Act 4, Scene 3)?

- What might this suggest about the importance of religion in this court?

## Conclusion

You have now worked through six contexts relating to *Women Beware Women* (remember that this list is not exhaustive). Using this model framework, you can go on to address other contexts on your own, perhaps beginning with the literary context of *Women Beware Women* as a play within the genre of the Revenge Tragedy. You could also explore, for example, the relationship of the main plot to the sub-plot (a dramatic context).

## The Rover – Aphra Behn

Restoration Drama is so called because theatres that had been closed by the Puritan Oliver Cromwell were re-opened to the public in 1660 after the restoration of Charles II to the throne. However, although public performances had been banned, plays had still been performed privately and read. So the Restoration dramatists had no sharp break with past traditions, and in the re-opened theatres older plays, such as the Revenge Tragedies, were very popular. It is no surprise, therefore, that Aphra Behn may then have used some of the conventions of the Revenge Tragedy in her play *The Rover*. But *The Rover* has been described in many ways: as a comedy, a tragicomedy, a drama of intrigue, a farce, and a history play, to name but a few.

Aphra Behn was vilified over the publication of *The Rover*, apparently because she was a woman who dared to enter a man's field. She was unmarried, and supported herself by her own writing. Concern for women and their roles and rights are therefore very important in this play.

As Aphra Behn's *The Rover* is a **Restoration Comedy**, you might find it helpful to look at the characteristic features of the genre listed on page 153.

The six contexts considered for the study for the study of *The Rover* are:

- The literary and social contexts of comedy

- The social context: the female perspective

- The social context: the male perspective

- The literary context: the Revenge Tragedy

- The dramatic context: the carnival setting

- The psychological/dramatic context

Quotations are from *The Rover*, Methuen Student Edition.


## Evaluating the significance of the contexts

One way of evaluating the significance of the contexts treated below is to compare what you would gain from them.

Aphra Behn wrote her play at a time when women were just emerging as playwrights, and so it might well be assumed that she would have something to say about gender and the roles and behaviour of men and women. Consideration of the *social context* from both the female and the male perspective might well draw attention to issues the dramatist was particularly interested in. It would still have been something of a novelty for audiences to see a play written by a woman. Gender is also a major issue for audiences today, and so consideration of these contexts allows modern readers and audiences to draw some conclusions as to the similarities and differences between their own attitudes and values and those of Restoration society.

Consideration of the *literary context* of comedy, however, will draw your attention to those elements of *The Rover* that were conventional at the time it was written. It could indicate which aspects of Aphra Behn's craft might have seemed novel to an audience and which would have been familiar. But Aphra Behn is also mixing genres in this play, and consideration of the play in the context of the Revenge tradition would draw attention to its darker and more sinister aspects.

Similarly, consideration of the carnival setting draws attention to the stagecraft employed by Aphra Behn and to those aspects of 'entertainment' that a contemporary audience might particularly have enjoyed (this is a *dramatic context*). Disguise was a common feature of plays of the period and so contemporary audiences would have been able to think about the treatment of disguises in *The Rover* by comparing it with the use of disguises in other contemporary plays.

Consideration of the *psychological/dramatic context* can focus attention on two main areas of the play – the extent to which the characters are fully rounded or mere 'types', and the extent to which Aphra Behn is concerned to show us the thought processes of the characters. This will allow you to identify which characters appear to be most fully developed, in other words those to whom she wanted the audience to pay particular attention. You could go on to think about what aspects of motivation and behaviour she wanted the audience to consider.

The different contexts, therefore, draw our attention to different features of the play. They might also lead to different interpretations of the play. Which context you find the most helpful or useful will, therefore, depend on what you see as the most interesting and significant features of the play. However, AO5ii asks you to consider a range of different contexts, to think about how each of them might be important, and to assess how far each of them illuminates your interpretation of the play.

## The literary and social context of comedy

As you saw when looking at Shakespeare's *Measure for Measure* (see page 121), it has been suggested that there are three successive stages in a social comedy: (1) first, an unsettled society governed by a harsh or irrational law; (2) then a temporary loss of identity; and (3) and finally the discovery of a new identity and a reconciliation. This structure seems to suit the development of *The Rover*.

### An unsettled society governed by a harsh or irrational law

You can see immediately that the members of society shown in *The Rover* are very unsettled. It has been decided that for the sake of family honour, Hellena must become a nun. She gives her view on this in Act 1, Scene 1:

And dost thou think that ever I'll be a Nun? Or at least til I'm so old, I'm fit for nothing else. Faith no, Sister; . . . nay, I'm resolv'd to Provide my self this Carnival,

## ACTIVITY 1

- What is Hellena's attitude towards her intended life?

- What sort of person does she seem to be?

Florinda is no happier. She has had one fiancé, Don Vincentio, selected for her by her father without consultation. She talks about him to Hellena (Act 1, Scene 1):

. . . and how near so ever my Father thinks I am to marrying that hated Object, I shall let him see I understand better what's due to my Beauty, Birth and Fortune, and more to my Soul, than to obey those unjust Commands.

## ACTIVITY 2

- What might be the reasons behind Florinda's rejection of this proposed marriage?

Her brother, Don Pedro, hears her complaints, and suggests another fiancé instead, his friend Antonio. Florinda explains why she will find it difficult to get out of this second match (Act 1, Scene 1):

I've no Defence against Antonio's Love,
For he has all the Advantages of nature,
The moving arguments of Youth and Fortune.

These words may explain the harsh or irrational law governing this society.

## ACTIVITY 3

- Why has Florinda 'no Defence' in refusing Antonio's courtship?

- Why might the family be pleased with this marriage?

Florinda also talks to her brother, who will:

follow the ill Customs of our Country, and make a Slave of his Sister.

## ACTIVITY 4

- Is Don Pedro's attitude towards his sister the same as his father's?

- What does this tell us about the role of women in society, and how they are perceived by men? Is this treatment of women just, or 'an ill custom'?

### A temporary loss of identity

Dominated as they are by disguise and confusion, the carnival scenes establish this period of lost identity.

## ACTIVITY 5

Remind yourself of the scene in Act 3, where Florinda, hoping to elope with Belvile, is accosted by Willmore, who is drunk.

- Might the drunkenness suggest confusion? Is it a form of 'disguise'?

- Is there a serious issue here about attitudes to women?

In Act 4, Scene 1, Florinda is again chased by Willmore, but she is captured by Ned Blunt, who is joined by Frederick. Later (Act 4, Scene 3) Blunt says:

. . . we must be better acquainted – we'll both lie with her, and then let me alone to bang her.

In Act 5, Scene 1, Willmore suggests that they 'draw cuts' for her.

## ACTIVITY 6

- Do you think that this is a serious situation for Florinda?

- What might be the implications of the idea of disguise here?

- Could there be a suggestion that Florinda is, to the men, a mere animal-like convenience, and not a woman? Women 'disguised' as animals?

- Might the men seem to behave as though they were animals also, unconcerned with the rights of a woman? Men 'disguised' as animals?

### The discovery of a new identity and a reconciliation

After the disguise and confusion of the carnival, Act 5 presents reconciliations and the foundation of a new and better society. In keeping with the traditions of comedy, this is achieved through marriage: Florinda and Belvile, the idealised 'Romantic' lovers, finally wed, as do Hellena and Willmore. But here Aphra Behn may present a realistic view when Willmore says (Act 5, Scene 1):

> . . . I adore thy Humour and will marry thee, and we are so of one Humour, it must be a Bargain – give me thy Hand –

Hellena later adds that she would rather spend her inheritance of three hundred thousand crowns 'in Love than in Religion'.

## ACTIVITY 7

- Do you think that their relationship will be smooth or stormy?

- Has Aphra Behn been honest in showing that marriage requires courage?

- Has she been honest in showing that in this society money helps to achieve independence?

There are tragic tones at the end, related to Angelica and Moretta, which are considered in the next context. The significance of this context has been evaluated by considering *The Rover* within the genre of comedy.

### The social context: the female perspective

This context was touched on above in Activities 1–4 (pages 147–148), when you assessed Florinda's and Hellena's reactions to the marriages proposed by their father and their brother. It is seen to be a patriarchal society, dominated by men and ruled by men's laws. Activities 5 and 6 explored the lack of value placed on women, and another perspective was touched on in the assessment of the comic outcome of the play, while also noting the tragic element introduced by Angelica, Moretta and Lucetta.

The problem for these three women may be that in this harsh society, a woman needed financial independence in order to live as she wanted to. It may have been all right for wealthy young women of powerful families, but what about women of a different social order? In Act 2, Scene 1, the men discuss Angelica's picture and her price as a prostitute. Belvile thinks she 'has rais'd the Price too high', but Willmore says:

> How wondrous fair she is – a Thousand Crowns a Month – by Heaven as many Kingdoms were too little.

## ACTIVITY 8

- Why do you think that Angelica has set such a high price?

- Do you think that she might have some pride in herself?

- How do you respond when Willmore has sex with her without payment?

Moretta, Angelica's assistant, is quite realistic about the future for women such as them. As she is dependent upon Angelica, she is dismayed when Angelica falls for Willmore (Act 2, Scene 1):

Oh Madam we're undone, a pox upon that rude Fellow, he's set on to ruin us:

## ACTIVITY 9

- Why do you think that Moretta is so concerned for Angelica's actions?

- Do you think that she might be talking sense financially?

To consider the outcome of Angelica's love for Willmore, ask yourself the questions in the next activity.

## ACTIVITY 10

- Do such women have a hope of improving their situations in Restoration society?

- Angelica and Moretta 'sell' their favours. Can you see any similarity to the ways in which wealthy fathers 'sell' their daughters in marriage?

- Is the difference social or moral? Willmore says about the carnival "tis a kind of legal authoriz'd Fornication' (Act 1, Scene 2). Might this be the truth?

- Might the situation of the prostitutes be seen as tragic?

- Might the audience, through Angelica's moving speeches in Act 5, Scene 1, warm to her?

To evaluate the significance of this context, you could assess the situation of the women in the society in which they lived; you could carry out the opposite exercise when you consider the male characters in the next context.

## The social context: the male perspective

The men, in contrast, seem to have complete sexual freedom. Pedro offers to buy Angelica (Act 2, Scene 1); Ned Blunt tries to use Lucetta (Act 2, Scene 2); and Ned and Frederick both abuse Florinda (Act 4, Scene 3). Belvile seems to be unique in his faithfulness to Florinda. The central character of the play, Willmore, is 'the rover'. He is almost pathological in his need to pursue and conquer women. Belvile recognises this in Act 3, Scene 4:

> ... if it had not been Florinda, must you be a Beast? – a Brute, a senseless Swine?

## ACTIVITY 11

- Why is Belvile so enraged with Willmore?

- Might he be making a point about Willmore's attitude to women generally?

But Willmore is a complex character who may well charm an audience. In Act 5, Scene 1, he is honest about his fault to Angelica:

> I wish I were that dull, that constant thing,
> Which thou woud'st have, and Nature never meant me:

## ACTIVITY 12

- How do you respond to Willmore's honesty here? Is he disarming?

- Do you find the honest Belvile or the wild Willmore the more attractive?

Willmore is 'reformed' to some extent by marriage, but Aphra Behn seems to indicate that married life will not be easy. Many critics point out the political context of the men. They are exiled Cavaliers, noblemen or upper-class gentlemen who fought on the side of the King in the English Civil War; they were defeated, made penniless for their efforts, and exiled by the new ruler, the Lord Protector of England, Oliver Cromwell. They are attractive and spirited, and accept the social climber Blunt because he is rich, 'his Purse be secure', which will provide the Cavaliers' 'whole Estate' (Act 2, Scene 1). Might Blunt be somewhat resented because, by avoiding fighting in the Civil War, he risked nothing? Might Aphra Behn feel some nostalgia for the glamorous past in a new, rather dull, less heroic England?

To evaluate the significance of this context, you could assess the situation of the men in the society presented in the play.

### The literary context: the Revenge Tragedy

To consider this aspect, it might be helpful to think about the characteristic features of plays in the Revenge genre, such as:

- How many revengers are there in *The Rover*?

- Is there the usually foreign setting, such as Italy or Spain?

- Is there intrigue, violence, a poisoning, death?

- Is there a disguise to create confusion?

- Is there a bloodbath at the end?

- Is there a central character who can act as a commentator?

Now consider the questions in the next activity.

## ACTIVITY 13

- Who are the revengers? Might Angelica and Blunt be considered as such?

- Is the need for revenge justified?

- Is the ending that of a Revenge Tragedy or that of a comedy?

- If any component parts of a Revenge Tragedy are omitted or altered, why might Aphra Behn have made that particular choice?

- What is it that she wishes to say about the society portrayed in the play?

## The dramatic context: the carnival setting

Aphra Behn makes much use of this setting, and you can assess its implications by considering the questions in the next activity.

## ACTIVITY 14

- Might the disguise help to create humorous situations for the audience?

- Does it allow for multiple action on stage?

- How does it allow the different layers of the plot to come together?

- Does the Naples setting allow for the introduction of characters such as Angelica, Moretta or Lucetta?

- What effects does the introduction of characters such as these women have on the breadth of the play's action and themes?

- Might this setting allow the sexual double standards of the society to be made clear? What are the differences in the rules of behaviour for men and for women?

- How does Aphra Behn undermine these codes of behaviour, and what does she achieve by this?

- Does the carnival allow for the reversal of the usual social situation, so that the sisters may become the pursuers instead of the pursued?

## The psychological/dramatic context

To address this context you could consider the different types of character presented in *The Rover*. For example, you could distinguish between characters who have psychological motivation, and those who remain largely undeveloped. Examples here might be:

### ACTIVITY 15

- Belvile: how much variety or development is created for him?

- Willmore: is he the central protagonist whom we see as a Restoration 'rake' or philanderer reformed?

- Are Hellena, Florinda and Angelica presented 'from the inside'?

- To what extent is Blunt a realistic character, and to what extent is he the stock 'country bumpkin' of Restoration Comedy?

- Might he be used as the main source of broad humour in the play?

- Are Lucetta and Moretta anything more than two-dimensional?

- Might they act as ciphers to allow Aphra Behn to develop her ideas?

## Conclusion

You have now worked through six contexts relating to *The Rover* (remember that this list is not exhaustive). Using this model framework, you can go on to address other contexts on your own, perhaps beginning with a consideration of the play as a Restoration Comedy. The following checklist identifies some of the typical features of Restoration Comedy.

- What classes of society are presented in this play?

- How far is the play concerned with the issue of 'manners', of how to behave properly in society?

- Is the author interested in something that might seem rather more serious?

- Is there sexual intrigue?

- Are there attractive, high-spirited, noble gentlemen?

- Is there a character outside this charmed circle (from the country, for example) who is mocked or used as a source of humour?

- Might this 'gull' be mocked because he tries to be fashionable and wise like the hero, but becomes a fool in doing so?

- Is there a central hero who develops during the course of the play?

- How do you respond to the idea that the audience of the day saw in the hero a reflection of themselves, and in the fop or bumpkin a reflection of their neighbour?

- Do you think that the author has a serious moral purpose in writing the play?

## *The Way of the World* – **William Congreve**

*The Way of the World*, like *The Rover* by Aphra Behn, belongs to the genre of Restoration Comedy, and it would be helpful to read through the discussion of this genre on page 153 above. Congreve's play is considered by many critics to be the peak of Restoration Comedy, and this context is the sixth context discussed below.

First staged in 1700, *The Way of the World* is concerned with the nature of society, and relationships within society. Congreve's interest, as he explains in the dedication, is with the 'affected' and 'false' **wit** that damages society. True 'wit' implies an intelligent and well-judged understanding of how to behave properly and elegantly in society. 'False wit' is characterised by affection and pretence. Congreve may be seen to extend this criticism to include 'false' people who are not really what they appear to be, such as Fainall and Mrs Marwood. At first such people seem to thrive in the society of *The Way of the World*; but after the 'Proviso scene' between Millamant and Mirabell in Act 4, Scene 1, a new society, based on social justice and fairness, is established.

Because the concerns of Restoration Comedy are finally centred on the individual as a member of society, drama became secular; that is to say, religious themes such as sin and punishment are not included. This marks a major break with pre-Restoration drama.

The six contexts considered for the study of *The Way of the World* are:

- The philosophical context

- The social context

- The biographical context: the influence of Congreve's training as a lawyer

- The dramatic context: 'patterning' within the play

- The context of genre I: the play as a **Comedy of Manners**

- The context of genre II: the play as a Restoration Comedy

Quotations are from *The Way of the World*, ed. Brian Gibbons, New Mermaids Edition.

## *Evaluating the significance of the contexts*

One way of evaluating the significance of the contexts treated below is to compare what you would gain from them.

Consideration of the *social context* might lead you to think about the ways in which society is organised. This context in particular will allow you to compare attitudes and values as depicted in the play with the attitudes and values of the author's own time and society. It therefore leads you to think about the extent to which Congreve's play needs to be understood in terms of the time in which it was written, and the extent to which it deals with matters that transcend time. By looking at this context, characters' attitudes and values are identified and compared and some conclusions can be drawn about matters such as marriage and inheritance, as well as the laws which govern the passing of property from one person to another, particularly to a woman.

An understanding of the *philosophical context* places this exploration of different kinds of people in a wider context of ideas – those of Thomas Hobbes and John Locke – and so make you aware that the play is part of a much wider concern in the period about reason, sensation and society.

The *context of genre* allows you to make comparison not so much with the ideas prevalent in the Restoration period as with the kind of plays that were popular at the time. An exploration of the genre of Restoration Comedy will make you aware of *The Way of the World* within the context of what contemporary audiences would be familiar with, and what they might be expecting from a new play. The more these contexts are explored the more it becomes apparent that in this play Congreve introduced new elements into the comedy genre. A contemporary audience would have been particularly fascinated by Mrs Marwood, by the Proviso scene, and by the character of Millamant, and they would have been intrigued by how matters of inheritance are sorted out.

The context of *patterning* within the play allows us to appreciate more fully Congreve's craftsmanship. His skilful use of such patterning allowed him to construct what was thought at the time, and by many critics since, to be a 'well-made play'.

The different contexts, therefore, draw our attention to different features of the play. They might also lead to different interpretations of the play. Which context you find the most helpful or useful will, therefore, depend on what you see as the most interesting and significant features of the play. However, AO5ii asks you to consider a range of different contexts, to think about how each of them might be important, and to assess how far each of them illuminates your interpretation of the play.

## The philosophical context

This context is made apparent in the contrast between Fainall and Mirabell. The character of Fainall may be evident in the opening scene, where he has won the card game, and says to Mirabell:

> … I'd no more play with a man that slighted his ill fortune than I'd make love to a woman who undervalued the loss of her reputation.

### ACTIVITY 1

- What is Fainall's attitude here?

- Does he seem to care for anybody other than himself?

Throughout the play Fainall can be seen to treat life as he treats the card game, as a game of chance and opportunity. His response to other people is seen in his words about his wife, Mrs Marwood (Act 2, Scene 1):

... and wherefore did I marry, but to make lawful prize of a rich widow's wealth, and squander it on love and you?

### ACTIVITY 2

- What do you think of his attitude here? What about the word 'squander'?

- Does he appear to think of anything but satisfying his own desires?

Mirabell can be seen as a contrast. He appears to think about other people, as you can see in the Proviso scene (Act 4, Scene 1). But he isn't perfect: he has arranged a marriage for a pregnant mistress and deceived Lady Wishfort, though at several points in the play he appears to feel sorrow for his past actions. He tries to make amends to Mrs Fainall (Act 2, Scene 1):

In justice to you, I have made you privy to my whole design, and put it in your power to ruin or advance my fortune.

And in Act 5, Scene 1, he apologies to Lady Wishfort with 'a sincere remorse and a hearty contrition'.

### ACTIVITY 3

- How is his attitude towards other people different from that of Fainall?

- Which attitude do you think is the best as a basis for society?

What is the difference between these two sets of attitudes? Behind the presentation of these two characters, Mirabell and Fainall, there probably lie two contrasting seventeenth-century philosophies, those of Thomas Hobbes and John Locke. Hobbes believed we learn from experience and sensation, and that our 'appetites' let us gather experience through our own activities (Mrs Marwood refers to 'appetites' in Act 3, Scene 1). Does Fainall live to experience different sorts of pleasure entirely for his own satisfaction?

On the other hand, Locke suggested that we learn to work out our situation in society and the world as a whole through the application of our reason. Mirabell might be seen to represent a way of thinking drawn from the philosophy of Locke. In his *Essay Concerning Human Understanding* (1690), Locke argues that we can make sound judgements by using reason. In *The Way of the World*, Mirabell works through reason, through applying his judgement, so that his actions will no longer damage other people, as you saw in Activity 3 above. His responses to other people seem to be based on an idea of social justice, namely that people should think about others around them as well as of themselves.

## ACTIVITY 4

- Which set of ideas do you think provides the best basis for society?

- Do you think Congreve believed in Hobbes or Locke?

- Which rules do you think govern the new society at the end of the play?

## The social context

This context is related to the philosophical context, as the female characters in the play generally follow the same categories as the men. You may see Mrs Fainall and Millamant as characters in the Lockean sense, and Mrs Marwood as a Hobbesian character. Mrs Fainall seems to be a generous and caring character, as you can see when she replies to Millamant's question about marrying Mirabell (Act 4, Scene 1):

Ay, ay, take him, take him, what should you do?

…

Fie, fie, have him, have him, and tell him so in plain terms;

## ACTIVITY 5

- How might Mrs Fainall have damaged Millamant's happiness here?

- What do you think of her as a person here? Is she generous? Forgiving?

Throughout the play, Millamant seems to be a sensible person, and she seems aware of the foolishness of those around her. Congreve might be thought to use Mirabell to point up Millamant's character, as in Act 2, Scene 1:

You would affect a cruelty which is not in your nature; your true vanity is in the power of pleasing.

## ACTIVITY 6

- What sort of a character sketch of Millamant is presented here?

- Do you think that it is a fair judgement of Millamant overall?

- Do you see her hurt people?

Mrs Marwood is a different kettle of fish. She plots with Fainall (Act 3, Scene 1):

You married her to keep you; and if you can contrive to have her keep you better than you expected, why should you not keep her longer than you intended?

## ACTIVITY 7

- What sort of a person do you think that Mrs Marwood is?

- Does she care about the wellbeing of anyone else?

- Is she interested in anything more than money, and her own desires?

You could then consider the observations Congreve is making about society. You might ask yourself questions such as those in the next activity.

## ACTIVITY 8

- What attitudes towards marriage are evident in this play?

- Are the rules of marriage re-written in the Proviso scene?

- What are the attitudes towards money and love?

- Are money and love linked?

- Is the society represented in most of the play caring or just?

- What happens at the end of the play? Are any social rules reformed?

## *The biographical context: the influence of Congreve's training as a lawyer*

Congreve had some training in law, having entered the Middle Temple to study law in 1691. This legal knowledge is evident in the Proviso scene in Act 4, when Mirabell and Millamant discuss what marriage means. Millamant begins, and Mirabell comments:

Have you any more conditions to offer? Hitherto your demands are pretty reasonable.

Millamant continues her demands and says:

… These articles subscribed, if I continue to endure you a little longer, I may by degrees dwindle into a wife.

## ACTIVITY 9

- How is the legal metaphor presented in these exchanges?

- Is there a serious message beneath the playful tone?

- Would you say that it is sensible to think like this before marriage?

- Might there be a suggestion that, in using a reasoned approach to marriage, the marriage will be fairer for both people? Is this a right basis for marriage?

You might analyse the rest of the scene by exploring its legal imagery, such as 'imprimis', 'item', and the 'sealing of the deed'.

To evaluate the significance of this context, you could consider whether Congreve suggests that law and justice are as important in society as good manners, decorum, wit or social graces.

## The dramatic context: 'patterning' within the play

Remember that this is just one part of the dramatic context of the play, but it is significant in evaluating the nature of Congreve's *The Way of the World*. There are five aspects of the patterning to be considered here:

- the implications of the idea of a card game

- the sequenced introduction of characters

- the echoes of the central Proviso scene

- the use of suspense and a cliff-hanger ending

- the repetition of the phrase 'the way of the world'.

### The implications of the idea of a card game

References to the playing of a chance game of cards are to be found throughout the play. Consider the following examples: in the opening scene, when plotting about his wife, Fainall thinks that 'she might throw up her cards'; in the last scene (Act 5, Scene 1), Fainall's gamble has failed, and Petulant says 'how now, what's the matter? Whose hand's out?'

## ACTIVITY 10

- To whom do most of the gaming images relate?

- How do these images suggest a certain view of the world?

- Do you think that it is a sensible or just viewpoint?

### The sequenced introduction of characters

Congreve introduces his characters in a specific order. If you look at the introduction of both male and female characters into the play, you will notice a set pattern:

## ACTIVITY 11

- The men: Mirabell, Fainall, Witwould, for example, are introduced in that order. Do you think this has something to do with the intelligence of each character?

- The women: Mrs Marwood, Mrs Fainall, Millamant: might this be in reverse order to the males? Why do you think Congreve does this?

### The echoes of the central Proviso scene

The key scene between Mirabell and Millamant is echoed twice afterwards. First, there is the scene between Fainall, Mrs Marwood and Lady Wishfort (Act 5, Scene 1), in which Fainall lays down her terms.

## ACTIVITY 12

- How might this scene echo that between Millamant and Mirabell?

- What are the similarities and what are the differences?

Second, there is a final echo in the last scene of the play, when Lady Wishfort says to Mirabell:

… but on proviso that you resign the contract with my niece immediately.

These words begin the unravelling of Fainall's plots, and thus lead to the satisfying conclusion of the play.

## ACTIVITY 13

- Might the echo be of a different nature here?

- Might the justice seen in the first Proviso scene now be extended?

### The use of suspense and a cliff-hanger ending

The ending comes as a shock to some of the play's characters, and often also to some of the audience. But Congreve has laid down clues for his ending. You might look at Mirabell's words to Mrs Fainall in Activity 5 above (page 158). Are any other clues offered?

### The repetition of the phrase 'the way of the world'

In Act 3, Scene 1, Fainall thinks of Foible, of his wife, and of himself as a husband, as all 'rank', adding 'all in the way of the world'. But in Act 5, Scene 1, when Mirabell reveals the legal deed which will be Fainall's downfall, Mirabell throws this back at him: ''tis the way of the world, sir.'

## ACTIVITY 14

- What is the difference between Fainall's and Mirabell's ways?

- Which 'way of the world' has finally prevailed?

## The context of genre I: the play as a Comedy of Manners

In a Comedy of Manners, the dramatist presents mankind in relationship to society, so that individuals are examined as a product of the existing fashion, of birth, of custom and of existing codes of behaviour. You might look at the range of characters and think about the various levels in society which they represent.

## ACTIVITY 15

- Place the characters in their different social levels.

- Does Congreve give each a particular way of speaking (look at Mincing, for example)?

- Might this be one of the sources of humour in the play?

You could take this enquiry further, and think about why manners are important and how they have a role in society. You might ask yourself questions such as those in the next activity.

## ACTIVITY 16

According to the new eighteenth-century philosophy, society is a 'man-made machine'.

- What might the role of manners be in this view of society?

- Might the observations of manners be a way of making sure that this sort of society runs smoothly?

- Might good manners therefore be a new virtue for a new society?

- How does the idea of 'manners' relate to the idea of social morality?

- Do you think that Congreve is concerned to establish a link between manners and morality? Could he be suggesting that manners must not be merely skin-deep?

- Do you think that he succeeds in doing this?

### The context of genre II: The Way of the World as a Restoration Comedy

Many critics agree that Restoration Comedy 'holds a mirror up to society', and the 'world' of the title is the world of society. Here again are some of the characteristic features of this genre. How do they relate to *The Way of the World*?

- What classes of society are presented in this play?

- How far is the play concerned with the usual Restoration Comedy issue of 'manners', that is, of how to behave properly in society?

- Is the author interested in something that might seem rather more serious?

- Is there sexual intrigue?

- Are there attractive, high-spirited, noble gentlemen?

- Might these qualities have appealed to the audience of the period?

- Is there a character outside this charmed circle (from the country, for example) who is mocked or used as a source of humour?

- Might this 'gull' be mocked because he tries to be fashionable and wise like the hero, but appears to be a fool in doing so?

- Is there a central hero who develops during the source of the play?

- How do you respond to the idea that the audience of the day saw in the hero a reflection of themselves, and in the fop or fool a reflection of their neighbour?

- Do you think that the author had a serious moral purpose in writing the play?

## Conclusion

You have now worked through six contexts relating to *The Way of the World*. Using this model framework, you can go on to address other contexts on your own, for example the social context of marriage in *The Way of the World*.

# Internet resources and select bibliography

## INTERNET SITES

British Literature.com
http://www.britishliterature.com/

English Teaching in the United Kingdom
http://ourworld.compuserve.com/homepages/harry_dodds/

Literary Resources on the Net
http://ww.andromeda.rutgers.edu/-jlynch/Lit

## CD-ROMS

The following are available from Headstrong Interactive, Magdale House, Lea Lane, Netherton, Huddersfield, HD4 7DL

*Silver Hooks and Golden Sands* (an introduction to poetry and prose in English from 1360 to 1900)

*The English Romantic Poets* (for Coleridge)

## BIBLIOGRAPHY

### General Textbooks

*Cambridge Companion to English Literature*

*The New Pelican Guide to English Literature*, ed. Boris Ford

## POETRY

### The General Prologue – Geoffrey Chaucer

*The Canterbury Tales*, ed. J. J. Anderson, Macmillan, 1974

*The Poet Chaucer*, Neville Coghill, OUP, 1949

*Chaucer and Chaucerians*, ed. D. S. Brewer, Nelson, 1970

*A Reading of the Canterbury Tales*, T. Whittock. CUP, 1968

### Prescribed Sonnets – William Shakespeare

*Shakespeare's Sonnets*, ed. Harold Bloom, Chelsea House, 1987

*Shakespeare's Living Art*, Rosalie Colie, Princeton University Press, 1974

*Captive Victors: Shakespeare's Narrative Poems and Sonnets*, Heather Dubrow, Cornell University Press, 1987

*All in War with Time: Love Poetry of Shakespeare, Donne, Jonson, Marvell*, Anne Ferry, Harvard University Press, 1975

*The Mutual Flame: on Shakespeare's Sonnets and 'The Phoenix and the Turtle'*, G. Wilson Knight, Methuen, 1955

*Shakespeare: The Sonnets*, ed. Peter Jones, Macmillan, 1977

*Themes and Variations in Shakespeare's Sonnets*, J. B. Leishman, Hutchinson, 1967

## Prescribed Poems – George Herbert

*The Metaphysical Poets*, Helen Gardner, OUP, 1967

*George Herbert, his Religion and Art*, J. H. Summers 1981

*Theory and Theology in George Herbert's Poetry: 'Divinity, and Poesie, Met'*, Elizabeth Clarke, OUP, 1997

*The Oxford History of English Literature, vol. 7, The Early Seventeenth Century*, Douglas Bush, Clarendon Press, 1990

*The Poetry of Meditation*, L. I. Martz, Yale University Press, 1962

## The Rime of the Ancient Mariner – Samuel Taylor Coleridge

*The Rime of the Ancient Mariner*, ed. Paul H. Fry, Macmillan, 1989

*Samuel Taylor Coleridge's The Rime of the Ancient Mariner*, ed. Harold Bloom, Chelsea House, 1986

*Coleridge's Submerged Politics: The Ancient Mariner and Robinson Crusoe*, Patrick. J. Keane, University of Missouri Press, 1994

## Prescribed Poems – Alfred Lord Tennyson

*Tennyson: The Critical Heritage*, ed. J. D. Jump, Routledge & Kegan Paul, 1967

*Critical Essays on the Poetry of Tennyson*, ed. John Killham, Routledge & Kegan Paul, 1967

*Tennyson*, Roger Ebbatson, Penguin, 1988

*A Tennyson Companion*, F. B. Pinion, Macmillan, 1984

*Tennyson*, Christopher Ricks, University of California Press, 1989

## Prescribed Poems – Emily Dickinson

*Emily Dickinson, Personae and Performance,* Elizabeth Phillips, Pennsylvania State University Press, 1988

*The Years and Hours of Emily Dickinson*, Jay Leyda, Yale University Press, 1960

*The Poetry of American Women*, Emily Stipes Watts, University of Texas Press, 1978

*Literary Women*, Ellen Moers, W. H. Allen, 1977

*The Undiscovered Continent: Emily Dickinson and the Space of the Mind*, Suzanne Juhasz, Indiana University Press, 1983

## DRAMA

### *Edward II* – **Christopher Marlowe**

*Themes and Conventions of Elizabethan Tragedy*, M. C. Bradbrook, CUP, 1980

*Marlowe: 'Tambourlaine the Great', 'Edward II' and 'The Jew of Malta'*, ed. J. R. Brown, Macmillan, 1982

*Christopher Marlowe: A Study of his Thought, Learning, and Character*, P. H. Kocher, Russel & Russell, 1962

*The Overreacher*, H. Levin, Faber & Faber, 1965

*Marlowe: A Critical Study*, J. B. Steane, CUP, 1970

### *Measure for Measure* – **William Shakespeare**

*Measure for Measure*, ed. C. K. Stead, Macmillan, 1971

*The Problem of Measure for Measure*, R. Myles, Vision Press, 1976

*Themes and Conventions of Elizabethan Tragedy*, M. C. Bradbrook, CUP, 1980

*The Problem Plays of Shakespeare,* Ernest Schanzer, Routledge, 1965

*The Wheel of Fire*, G. Wilson Knight, University Paperbacks, 1960

### *The White Devil* – **John Webster**

*The White Devil and The Duchess of Malfi*, ed. R. V. Holdsworth, Macmillan, 1975

*The White Devil and The Duchess of Malfi,* John. D. Jump, Blackwell, 1966

*John Webster: A Critical Study*, Clifford Leech, Hogarth Press, 1951

Chapter on Webster in *Second Thoughts More Studies in Literature*, M. R. Ridley, Dent, 1965

*Themes and Conventions of Elizabethan Tragedy*, M. C. Bradbrook

### *Women Beware Women* – **Thomas Middleton**

*Three Revenge Tragedies*, ed. R. V. Holdsworth, Macmillan, 1990

*Horrid Laughter in Jacobean Tragedy*, Nicholas Brooke, Open Books, 1979

*English Drama to 1710*, ed. Christopher Ricks, Sphere Books, 1971

*Puritanism and Theatre: Thomas Middleton and Opposition Drama under the Early Stuarts*, Margot Heinemann, CUP, 1980

*Themes and Conventions of Elizabethan Tragedy*, M. C. Bradbrook, CUP, 1980

### *The Rover* – **Aphra Behn**

*Feminist Theatre and Theory*, ed. H, Keyssar, Macmillan, 1996

*The Passionate Shepherdess: Aphra Behn: 1640-89*, Maureen Duffy, Methuen, 1989

*Reconstructing Aphra*, Angeline Goreau, Dial Press, 1980

*Aphra Behn*, F. M. Link, Twayre Publishers, 1968

### *The Way of the World* – **William Congreve**

*William Congreve,* Mermaid Critical Commentaries, ed. Brian Morris, Benn, 1972

*Congreve's Plays on the Eighteenth-Century Stage*, E. L. Avery, New York, 1951

*The Cultivated Stance. The designer of Congreve's Plays*, W. H. Van Voris, Dolmen Press, 1965

*Restoration Theatre Production*, Jocelyn Powell, Routledge & Kegan Paul, 1984

# MODULE 6 Exploring Texts

The aim of this final module is to test what you have learned during the course. It therefore tests all the Assessment Objectives, which are set out below.

---

## ASSESSMENT OBJECTIVES

AO1    communicate clearly the knowledge, understanding and insight appropriate to literary study, using appropriate terminology and accurate and coherent written expression
(5% of the final A2 mark; 2$^1$/$_2$% of the final A Level mark.)

AO2ii respond with knowledge and understanding to literary texts of different types and periods, exploring and commenting on relationships and comparisons between literary texts
(10% of the final A2 mark; 5% of the final A Level mark)

AO3    show detailed understanding of the ways in which writers' choices of form, structure and language shape meanings
(10% of the final A2 mark; 5% of the final A Level mark)

AO4    articulate independent opinions and judgements, informed by different interpretations of literary texts by other readers
(10% of the final A2 mark; 5% of the final A Level mark)

AO5ii evaluate the significance of cultural, historical and other contextual influences on literary texts and study
(5% of the final A2 mark; 2$^1$/$_2$% of the final A Level mark)

---

## Introduction

These Assessment Objectives embody the skills that you use in reading and studying literary texts. In this module you have to show your ability to use these skills by working on (a) a set of pre-release materials, which you will receive three days before the examination, and (b) an unseen text, which will be in the examination paper itself. The key text might be prose, poetry or drama, and the other materials will relate to it: they might be articles or reviews, biography or autobiography, historical information or interpretation – in other words, materials relating to contexts and interpretations. The unseen text will bear some relation to the key text, too, and is most likely to be used as a comparative piece, to test AO2ii. On the examination paper, the Assessment Objectives will be tested discretely, that is, each one separately. The format could look like this, for instance:

- **Question 1** might focus on the key text and on the unseen text, and test AOs 1, 2ii and 3

- **Question 2** might focus on the material relating to interpretations, and test AO4

- **Question 3** might focus on the materials relating to contexts, and test AO5ii.

Most of this module will deal with how to look at the pre-release materials and at how to approach the examination questions. It ends with two sample examination papers that you can attempt; Paper 1 has sample responses for you to study.

## Preparing for Module 6

The real preparation for this module is the rest of the course. When you sit this examination, you will have prepared for and taken five other modules in AS and Advanced Level, and in the course of that work you will have gained skills and experience in applying the Assessment Objectives to the texts that you have studied. The focus of any revision you might want to do, therefore, should be on the Assessment Objectives. If you haven't already attempted it, the activity on page ooo of *AS English Literature for AQA B* in this series might be a useful reminder, as might the activity on page vii of the Introduction to this book. The activities in Module 5 cover the full range of Assessment Objectives, while focusing chiefly on AO2ii, and further work on AOs 4 and 5ii can be found in Module 4.

## What to do with the materials

You will receive the pre-release materials approximately three days before the examination. This gives you plenty of time to read the texts thoroughly, but it is important to keep in mind the reason for doing so – you have to look for the features which relate directly to the Assessment Objectives being tested in the three questions you will be asked. It is a good idea to make some notes as you read, but remember that you can make only brief marginal annotations on the material itself, as you'll be taking this into the examination room with you. Here are the rules from the Specification:

> Such annotation should amount to no more than cross-references and/or the glossing of individual words or phrases. Highlighting and underlining is permitted. Annotations going beyond individual words or phrases, or amounting to *aides-mémoire* or notes towards the planning of essays are not permitted. Insertions of pages, loose sheets, 'post-its' or any other form of notes or additional material is not permitted.

You must stick to these rules. If you don't, you risk disqualification – but apart from that, it is best practice anyway. You don't know what the questions will be, so it would be foolish to try to write the answers in advance. There's the unseen element, too – the second text will be given in the examination itself, and so you can't know what the points of comparison with the first passage will be until you see it.

Here are the Assessment Objectives tested on each question, together with comments on what to look for as you work on the materials.

## Question 1

This question will ask you to compare an extract from a text (Item 1 of the pre-release materials) with an unseen extract, which will be printed on the examination paper.

The Assessment Objectives tested here will be AO1, AO2ii, and AO3. As stated above, you won't know what you have got to compare (AO2ii) until the day of the examination, but you can work on AO3 with the pre-release extract. In other words, you can identify the features of 'form, structure and language' that 'shape meanings'. As this isn't a text that you've worked on before, you need to think about what the writer's meanings seem to be, and how the writer has shaped them. Underlining, highlighting or writing brief marginal annotations will allow you to provide reminders for yourself of what you've seen, so that you can quickly find similar or contrasting features in the second extract when you read it. Of course, reading the second extract might well lead you to look for different features in the first extract from those you have already identified – so don't make the mistake of limiting yourself to your annotations when you revisit the pre-release extract. You need to be familiar with the whole piece.

## Question 2

This question will ask you to look at some of the items of the pre-release material that offer interpretations, and to write about them in a way which demonstrates both your understanding and your judgement of them.

The Assessment Objective tested here is AO4. As you work through the relevant materials – the items featuring different interpretations of the key text, which question 2 will focus on – you need to identify the interpretations offered in the items, and mark where they appear. This will help to focus your work in the examination. You then need to think about the interpretations you have identified – what they are saying, how they relate to the text, and how they relate to, and differ from, the other interpretations. Perhaps this is a point where making some notes for yourself might be useful; you can then, by comparing interpretations, take an overview of the merits of each of them. This should go a long way towards equipping you for an answer to Question 2.

## Question 3

This question will ask you to look at some of the Items of the pre-release material which give contexts for the key text, and to write about them in a way which demonstrates your understanding of them and your ability to assess their significance.

The Assessment Objective tested here is AO5ii. As you work through the relevant materials – the items about contexts, which Question 3 will focus on – you need to identify the contexts offered in the items, and to mark where they appear. This will help to focus your work in the examination. Remember to look for as wide a range of contexts as possible – your work in previous modules should help you to do this – and to indicate them by highlighting or underlining, perhaps with a brief marginal annotation. AO5ii asks you to 'evaluate the significance' of 'cultural, historical and other contextual influences on literary texts', so when you have identified the contexts you might gather them together in notes, and consider which might be significant, given the information that you have. This should go a long way towards equipping you for an answer to Question 3.

## A Sample Paper

On the following pages you will find the first Sample Paper for this module, followed by suggestions about how you could shape responses to the questions.

## Sample Paper I

Time allowed: 3 hours (including 30 minutes' reading time).

You should spend about $1\frac{1}{4}$ hours on Question 1 and about 35 minutes each on Questions 2 and 3.

The Assessment Objectives will be printed on the paper.

## ITEM 1

This is an extract from *The Color Purple* by Alice Walker, published in 1982. This is the first of Celie's letters in the novel which is not written to God, but to her sister Nettie, who is in Africa. Celie has discovered that her real father was lynched. Her step-father, who she thought of as Pa, abused her and married her to Mr. _____, who does not love her. Mr._____'s old lover, Shug, a blues singer, has come to live in their house, and she and Celie have formed a relationship.

Dear Nettie,

I don't write to God no more, I write to you.

What happen to God? ast Shug.

Who that? I say.

She look at me serious.

Big a devil as you is, I say, you not worried bout no God, surely.

She say, Wait a minute. Hold on just a minute here. Just because I don't harass it like some peoples us know don't mean I ain't got religion.

What God do for me? I ast.

She say, Celie! Like she shock. He gave you life, good health, and a good woman that love you to death.

Yeah, I say, and he give me a lynched daddy, a crazy mama, a lowdown dog of a step pa and a sister I probably won't ever see again. Anyhow, I say, the God I been praying and writing to is a man. And act just like all the other mens I know. Trifling, forgitful and lowdown.

She say, Miss Celie. You better hush. God might hear you.

Let 'im hear me, I say. If he ever listened to poor colored women the world would be a different place, I can tell you.

She talk and she talk, trying to budge me way from blasphemy. But I blaspheme much as I want to.

All my life I never care what people thought bout nothing I did, I say. But deep in my heart I care about God. What he going to think. And come to find out, he don't think. Just sit up there glorying in being deef, I reckon. But it ain't easy, trying to do without God. Even if you know he ain't there, trying to do without him is a strain.

I is a sinner, say Shug. Cause I was born. I don't deny it. But once you find out what's out there waiting for us, what else can you be?

Sinners have more good times, I say.

You know why? she ast.

Cause you ain't all the time worrying bout God, I say.

Naw, that ain't it, she say. Us worry bout God a lot. But once us feel loved by God, us do the best us can to please him with what us like.

You telling me God love you, and you ain't never done nothing for him? I mean, not go to church, sing in the choir, feed the preacher and all like that?

But if God love me, Celie, I don't have to do all that. Unless I want to. There's a lot of other things I can do that I speck God likes.

Like what? I ast.

Oh, she say, I can lay back and just admire stuff. Be happy. Have a good time.

Well, this sound like blasphemy sure nuff.

She say, Celie, tell the truth, have you ever found God in church? I never did. I just found a bunch of folks hoping for him to show. Any God I ever felt in church I brought in with me. And I think all the other folks did too. They come to church to *share* God, not find God.

Some folks didn't have him to share, I said. They the ones didn't speak to me while I was there struggling with my big belly and Mr._____children.

Right, she say.

Then she say: Tell me what your God look like, Celie.

Aw naw, I say, I'm too shame. Nobody ever ast me this before, so I'm sort of took by surprise. Besides, when I think about it, it don't seem quite right. But it all I got. I decide to stick up for him, just to see what Shug say.

Okay, I say. He big and old and tall and graybearded and white. He wear white robes and go barefooted.

Blue eyes? she ast.

Sort of bluish-gray. Cool. Big though. White lashes, I say.

She laugh.

Why you laugh? I ast. I don't think it so funny. What you expect him to look like, Mr._____?

That wouldn't be no improvement, she say. Then she tell me this old white man is the same God she used to see when she prayed. If you wait to find God in church, Celie, she say, that's who is bound to show up, cause that's where he live.

How come? I ast.

Cause that's the one that's in the white folks' white bible.

Shug! I say. God wrote the bible, white folks had nothing to do with it.

How come he look just like them, then? she say. Only bigger? And a heap more hair. How come the bible just like everything else they make, all about them doing one thing and another, and all the colored folks doing is gitting cursed?

I never thought bout that.

Nettie say somewhere in the bible it say Jesus' hair was like lamb's wool, I say.

Well, say Shug, if he came to any of these churches we talking bout he'd have to have it conked before anybody paid him any attention. The last thing niggers want to think about they God is that his hair kinky.

That's the truth, I say.

Ain't no way to read the bible and not think God white, she say. Then she sigh. When I found out I thought God was white, and a man, I lost interest. You mad cause he don't seem to listen to your prayers. Humph! Do the mayor listen to anything colored say? Ask Sofia, she say.

But I don't have to ast Sofia. I know white people never listen to colored, period. If they do, they only listen long enough to be able to tell you what to do.

Here's the thing, say Shug. The thing I believe. God is inside you and inside everybody else. You come into the world with God. But only them that search for it inside find it. And sometimes it just manifest itself even if you not looking, or don't know what you looking for. Trouble do it for most folks, I think. Sorrow, lord. Feeling like shit.

It? I ast.

Yeah, It. God ain't a he or a she, but a It.

But what do it look like? I ast.

Don't look like nothing, she say. It ain't a picture show. It ain't something you can look at apart from anything else, including yourself. I believe God is everything, say Shug. Everything that is or ever was or ever will be. And when you can feel that, and be happy to feel that, you've found It.

Shug a beautiful something, let me tell you. She frown a little, look out cross the yard, lean back in her chair, look like a big rose.

She say, My first step from the old white man was trees. Then air. Then birds. Then other people. But one day when I was sitting quiet and feeling like a motherless child, which I was, it come to me: that feeling of being part of everything, not separate at all. I knew that if I cut a tree, my arm would bleed. And I laughed and I cried and I run all round the house. I knew just what it was. In fact, when it happen, you can't miss it. It sort of like you know what, she say, grinning and rubbing high up on my thigh.

*Shug!* I say.

Oh, she say. God love all them feelings. That's some of the best stuff God did. And when you know God loves 'em you enjoys 'em a lot more. You can just relax, go with everything that's going, and praise God by liking what you like.

God don't think it dirty? I ast.

Naw, she say. God made it. Listen, God love everything you love – and a mess of stuff you don't. But more than anything else, God love admiration.

You saying God vain? I ast.

Naw, she say. Not vain, just wanting to share a good thing. I think it pisses God off if you walk by the color purple in a field somewhere and don't notice it.

What it do when it pissed off? I ast.

Oh, it make something else. People think pleasing God is all God care about. But any fool living in the world can see it always trying to please us back.

Yeah? I say.

Yeah, she say. It always making little surprises and springing them on us when us least expect.

You mean it want to be loved, just like the bible say.

Yes, Celie, she say. Everything want to be loved. Us sing and dance, make faces and give flower bouquets, trying to be loved. You ever notice that trees do everything to git attention we do, except walk?

Well, us talk and talk bout God, but I'm still adrift. Trying to chase that old white man out of my head. I been so busy thinking bout him I never truly notice nothing God make. Not a blade of corn (how it do that?) not the color purple (where it come from?). Not the little wildflowers. Nothing.

Now that my eyes opening, I feels like a fool. Next to any little scrub of a bush in my yard, Mr._____'s evil sort of shrink. But not altogether. Still, it is like Shug say, You have to git man off your eyeball, before you can see anything a'tall.

Man corrupt everything, say Shug. He on your box of grits, in your head, and all over the radio. He try to make you think he everywhere. Soon as you think he everywhere, you think he God. But he ain't. Whenever you trying to pray, and man plop himself on the other end of it, tell him to git lost, say Shug. Conjure up flowers, wind, water, a big rock.

But this hard work, let me tell you. He been there so long, he don't want to budge. He threaten lightening, floods and earthquakes. Us fight, I hardly pray at all. Every time I conjure up a rock, I throw it.

Amen

## ITEM 2

This is an extract from notes about *The Color Purple* written for A Level students.

*The Color Purple* was published in June 1982. Its release was heralded by Gloria Steinem's interview with Alice Walker in the June issue of *Ms.* Steinem is a founding member of *Ms.* and a leading white woman activist. Her interview with Walker was placed next to a succinct piece by the black literary critic, Mary Helen Washington. The latter article concerned Walker's mother and her significance in the writer's work. A large picture of Walker's face, underlined by the caption, 'Alice Walker, a Major American Writer,' was featured on *Ms.*'s cover, a portent of the media attention she would receive once the novel was released.

In her assessment of Walker's earlier works, Gloria Steinem pointed out that 'a disproportionate number of people who seek out Walker's sparsely distributed books are black women,' and that a 'disproportionate number of her hurtful, negative reviews have been by black men.' ...

In the following months, the novel received high praise, particularly for its poetic language and its innovative form, from reviewers in national commercial magazines such as *Newsweek* and intellectual and political journals such as *The New Yorker* and *The Nation.* Mel Watkins, a black reviewer for *The New York Times*, called Walker 'a lavishly gifted writer.' He was taken with 'the density of subtle interactions among the characters,' and 'the authenticity of [the novel's] folk voice.' He noted, however, 'weaknesses in the novel,' what he called 'the pallid portraits of the males,' and that Nettie's letters seemed like 'mere monologues of African history.' These are points that would be made about the novel in other reviews. Watkins ended his review with a superlative comment: 'These are only quibbles however about a striking consummately well-written novel.'

During the rest of 1982, *The Color Purple* received similar praise in mainstream publications. But black feminist critic Barbara Smith, in her review for *Callaloo*, a respected black literary journal, wondered if many of the reviewers had actually read the work ... Smith focused on the womanist aspects of the novel. She called *The Color Purple* a classic because it does something new: 'what Walker has done for the first time is to create an extended literary work whose subject is the sexual politics of black life, as experienced by ordinary blacks.' Smith also pointed out that 'no black novelist until Alice Walker in *The Color Purple* has positively and fully depicted a lesbian relationship between two women, set in the familiar context of a traditional black community.' Smith ended her review with a provocative comment: '*The Color Purple* offers an inherent challenge to the Black community to consider fighting for the freedom of not just half but the entire race.'

Praise for *The Color Purple* as a womanist novel characterised reviews by other black women – Dorothy Randall-Tsuroto's review for *The Black Scholar* (published in

Summer 1983, but apparently written before the novel received the Pulitzer), and Yvonne Porter's review for *Colorlines*, written just as Walker was awarded the Pulitzer. Porter began her review with the statement that '*The Color Purple* is a woman's womanist book…' She did warn her readers that some of them may be disturbed by Celie and Shug's sexual relationship, and reminded them that 'lesbianism is an aspect of the black woman that has seldom been dealt with in any depth.'

These positive reviews by black women were followed by others during 1982–84, not all of which were entirely complimentary. Maryemma Graham in the Summer 1983 issues of *Freedomways* called *The Color Purple* Walker's 'most compelling and thought-provoking work to date.' But Ms. Graham thought that Walker identifies men as the sole source of female oppression, a view with which she disagrees. Graham also objected to the lesbian theme in the novel which she thought might 'muddy the waters' about female bonding. Her major objection to the novel was that it is bourgeois, that 'Walker has imbued her rural Georgia females with the strivings and potential for self-indulgence of the urban middle class.'

Another review by black woman critic Trudier Harris, in *Black American Literature Forum*, asked whether Walker hadn't reiterated white stereotypes of both black women and men. Ms. Harris, who had previously written essays on Walker's earlier work, was clearly disturbed by the characters of *The Color Purple*.

## ITEM 3

These two pieces are from a section about Alice Walker's work in *Writing Women*.

### Metaphors in *The Color Purple*

The sparingly used metaphors stand out against the dramatic simplicity of Walker's discourse. Two key metaphors are those of colour and quilting. They stress black artistry and link disparate episodes with patterning structures.

The title represents a complex symbol: at first Celie has no decent garment, only *drab* cast-offs; what she longs for is a sexy dress. When she is able to buy one, she chooses the bold, affirmative colour purple. The purple flowers in the field signify joy and freedom. In the Foreword Walker explicitly states that her womanism is to feminism what purple is to lavender: that black womanhood asserts strength and creativity.

When Celie inherits a house from her stepfather she decorates Shug's room in brilliant colour, symbolising her new economic choice and an intention of affirming her personality. When sewing trousers she selects materials and colours to suit diverse personalities. They bring beauty and colour into everyday design, for the use of friends and families.

The word 'coloured' had been used, like the word 'negro', to denigrate a whole race. Therefore the use of coloured metaphors signals a bold denial of humiliating associations. Morrison and Angelou both lovingly describe different shades of blackness; Walker makes the admired Shug very dark, and beautiful.

The symbol of quilt making links episodes and characters. It represents women coming together, sewing in sisterhood, as frequently quilt making was a group activity, for long winter evenings. Pieces discarded by others were used to make something new and beautiful. Alice Walker kept the quilt her mother made for her and still uses it 'for comfort'.

Quilt making begins the moment Celie has a few scraps of spare material and time, and wishes to make peace with her turbulent sister-in-law, Sofia: 'Let's make quilt pieces out of these messed up curtains, Sofia say. And I run git my pattern book. I sleeps like a baby now.' (p 39) Not only does the shared sewing bring peace to Celie, it helps the women make up. After this they no longer allow their men to divide them.

When Shug slowly recovers from her illness, Celie decides to sew for her, 'Shug gets out of bed, asks "How do you sew this damn thing?" I hand her the square I'm working on, start another one. She sew long crooked stitches, *remind me of that little crooked tune she sing'* (p 51), stressing the parallels between the two art forms allowed to women. Shug soon donates her old yellow dress: 'I call it Sister's Choice.' (p 53) This name, suddenly created by Celie, symbolises the emerging understanding and love which will help transform her from ugly to beautiful, in her own eyes and those of the world. Quilting transforms discarded pieces into beauty, as Walker's metaphors transfer her message into art.

## Men in *The Color Purple*

Walker presents a range of men, from the ideal Samuel to the violent, crass, irredeemable stepfather. The stepfather is irretrievably brutal, abusing Celie sexually and openly despising her. He feels no remorse, but turns his predatory eyes to the slightly more attractive younger sister Nettie. He gives no sexual pleasure in his frequent assaults, and finally, to get rid of Celie, gives her away to a violent lazy bully as husband. Till he died Celie did not even know that he was called Alphonso; he was a force, not a human being, to the violated girl. Celie discovers only from his will that he had made money, which she had never seen. He had bought some property, apeing white capitalists and their meanness, like Macon Dead in Morrison's *Song of Solomon*. At least when he dies, his house is left to the girls. Celie's first thought is to refuse to live in it but Shug's reactions are sensible, unsentimental and realistic: see the cruel as they are, and accept that some good may come from evil – 'Don't be a fool, Shug say. You got your own house now. That dog of a stepdaddy just a bad odor passing through.' (p 207)

Walker shows courage in not avoiding the topic of male brutality. Angelou and Morrison, aware of the racism of American society, are less trenchant, and recall a time when black men treated their women as equals, since all were equally exploited in the fields. Perhaps as she is younger, Walker can state publicly that there is no excuse for taking white racist violence into their homes. She depicts their interiorisation of white values in the desire to humiliate. Celie's husband insists that he should be called 'Mr. ____' precisely because white males call him 'boy' and deny his manhood publicly. However, he is represented as improving slowly once the economic situation improves. Above all his women teach him to respect them: first Shug by being herself and refusing sexual, emotional and intellectual domination; then Celie by rejecting his view of herself, and teaching him, against his will, to respect her. Respect earns love and love allows the possibility of self-love, which he attempts movingly to express: 'I start to wonder why us need love. Why us black. Why us suffer … I think us here to wonder … The more I wonder, the more I love.' (239) This resembles psychotherapy in teaching that love and respect for self are needed for us to be able to love others.

## ITEM 4

This is an extract from *The Female Gaze*, edited by Lorraine Gammon and Margaret Marshment (1988), a book about modern women writers.

The happy coincidences with which Celie's story concludes – the appearance of her long-lost children, the discovery that the man who raped her as a child was not her biological father, the return of her beloved sister – can be read as an improbable fairy-tale ending. In a sense, of course, it is. But it can be read as something other than a failure of the realist imagination. Folk tales and fairy tales traditionally reward the heroine/hero at the end, often in an excessive way (great wealth, marriage to the prince, sainthood). Celie's reward at the end of *The Color Purple* may seem equally excessive (at least by the criteria of the realist novel). But, in the manner of a folk-tale protagonist, she has earned it through her own subversive efforts; and, like the heroine of a morality tale, she deserves it. Seen within the context of the oral culture of American blacks, the happy ending is that of the folk tale or parable, and as such entirely appropriate in form and content.

For this is not just an optimistic book, but an optimistically didactic one. Black women must learn to respect themselves, it says, to be respected; learn to speak for themselves to be listened to; speak up for themselves to be recognised. They must not internalise oppression by responding with self-hatred and submission. They can, and must, look to themselves, and to those who can give them the support they need in this struggle – that is, other black women – and draw sustenance from them. Then they will realise that they have strength in community and can give as well as receive. Then they will find each other as sisters, discover that their past was worse than had been admitted, but not as bad as they'd feared (Celie's children are the product of rape, but not of incest), and thus forge their own future in autonomy and freedom. This would be a cruel message without the happy ending.

Despite the atrocities she suffers, Celie has the courage to speak of them. In giving voice to the unspeakable, she discovers that it can be spoken. She defies the taboos and thereby deprives them of their power to destroy her. In speaking to God she discovers herself and her own strength, because 'God' is not another powerful and potentially hostile force – 'God' is everything that lives:

> God is inside you and inside everybody else. You come into the world with
> God. But only them that search for it inside find it. And sometimes it just
> manifest itself even if you are not looking, or don't know what you are
> looking for … It ain't a picture show. It ain't something you can look at
> apart from anything else, including yourself. I believe God is everything,
> say Shug. Everything that is or ever was or ever will be. And when you feel
> that, and be happy to feel that, you've found it.

Celie learns to 'chase that old white man out of [her] head' and recognise her own 'divine' humanity – her own capacity for joy, freedom, control, autonomy and love. She learns to notice 'the color purple in the field', so that she can no longer dismiss her life as merely the sum of her oppression or accept suffering as her destiny. Here too is a message for black women generally – indeed for all oppressed people. Celie's redefinition of the meaning of her life is one that rescues oppressed people from the negative implications of their status as victims by pointing to ways of transcending it, without minimising either the intensity of their oppression or the difficulties of resistance.

This also gives her the strength to forgive. The capacity to forgive is much emphasised in black women's novels. It cannot, in *The Color Purple* at least, be read as a sentimental spirituality which aims to transcend the political, or as an act of Christian charity for the benefit of the individual's immortal soul. Rather, it is an essential mechanism in the black women's liberation, which allows her both to free herself from the self-destructive emotions of hatred and bitterness, and to shift her emotional focus back where it belongs – into the black community. For it is Mr. and his son Harpo who are forgiven; white people are not such much forgiven as excommunicated from consciousness.

## ITEM 5

This is an article by Alice Walker about the writing of *The Color Purple*.

I don't always know where the germ of a story comes from but with *The Color Purple* I knew it right away. I was hiking through the woods with my sister Ruth, talking about a lover's triangle of which we both knew. She said: *And you know, one day The Wife asked The Other Woman for a pair of her drawers.* Instantly the missing piece of the story I mentally was writing about two women who felt married to the same man – fell into place. And for months – through illnesses, divorce, several moves, travel abroad, all kinds of heartaches and revelations, I carried my sister's comment delicately balanced in the center of the novel's construction I was building in my head.

I also knew *The Color Purple* would be a historical novel, and thinking of this made me chuckle. In an interview discussing my work a black male critic said he'd heard I might write a historical novel some day, and I went on to say, in effect: Heaven Protect Us From It. The chuckle was because, woman-like (he would say) my 'history' starts not with the taking of lands, or the birth, battles and deaths of Great Men, but with one woman asking another for her underwear. Oh well, I thought, one function of critics is to be appalled by such behavior. But what woman (or sensuous man) could avoid being intrigued? As for me, I thought of little else for a year.

When I was sure the characters of my novel were trying to form (or, as I invariably thought of it, trying to contact me, to speak *through* me) I began to make plans to leave New York. Three months earlier I had bought a tiny house on a quiet Brooklyn street, assuming – because my desk overlooked the street and a maple tree in the yard representing garden and view – I would be able to write. I was not.

New York, whose people I love for their grace under almost continual unpredictable adversity, was a place the people in *The Color Purple* refused even to visit. The moment any of them started to form – on the subway, a dark street, and especially in the shadow of very tall buildings – they would start to complain.

*What is all this tall shit anyway?* they would say.

I disposed of the house, stored my furniture, packed my suitcases, and flew alone to San Francisco (it was my daughter's year to be with her father), where all the people in the novel promptly fell silent, I think, in awe. Not merely of the city's beauty, but of what they picked up about earthquakes.

*It's pretty*, they muttered, *but us ain't lost nothing in no place that has earthquakes.*

They also didn't like seeing buses, cars, or other people whenever they attempted to look out. *Us don't want to be seeing none of this*, they said, *it make us can't think.*

That was when I knew for sure that these were country people. So my lover and I started driving around the state looking for a country house to rent. Luckily I had found (with the help of friends) a fairly inexpensive place in the city. This too had been a decision forced by my characters. As long as there was any question about whether I could support them in the fashion they desired (basically in undisturbed silence) they declined to come out. And no wonder: it looked a lot like the town in Georgia most of them were from, only it was more beautiful, and the local swimming hole was not segregated. It also bore a slight resemblance to the African village in which one of them, Nettie, was a missionary.

Seeing the sheep, the cattle and the goats, smelling the apples and the hay, one of my characters, Celie, began, haltingly, to speak.

But there was still a problem.

Since I had quit my editing job at *Ms.* and my Guggenheim fellowship was running out, and my royalties did not quite cover expenses, and – let's face it – because it gives me a charge to see people who appreciate my work, historical novels or not, I was accepting invitations to speak. Sometimes on the long plane rides Celie or Shug would break through with a wonderful line or two (for instance, Celie said once that a self-pitying sick person she went to visit was 'laying up in the bed trying to look dead'. But even these vanished – if I didn't jot them down – by the time my contact with the audience was done.

What to do?

Celie and Shug answered without hesitation: *Give up all this travel. Give up all this talk. What is all this travel and talk shit anyway?* So, I gave it up for a year. Whenever I was invited to speak I explained I was taking a year off for Silence. (I also wore an imaginary bracelet on my left arm that spelled the word.) Everyone said Sure, they understood.

I was terrified.

Where was the money for our support coming from? My only steady income was a three hundred dollar a month retainer from *Ms.* for being a long distance editor. But even that was too much distraction for my characters.

*Tell them you can't do anything for the magazine,* said Celie and Shug. (You guessed it, the women of the drawers.) *Tell them you think about them later.* So, I did. *Ms.* was nonplussed. Supportive as ever (they continued the retainer). Which was nice.

Then I sold a book of stories. After taxes, inflation and my agent's fee of ten percent, I would still have enough for a frugal, no-frills year. And so, I bought some beautiful blue and red and purple fabric, and some funky old second hand furniture (and accepted donations of old odds and ends from friends) and a quilt pattern my mama swore was easy, and I headed for the hills.

There were days and weeks and even months when nothing happened. Nothing whatsoever. I worked on my quilt, took long walks with my lover, lay on an island we discovered in the middle of the river and dabbled my fingers in the water. I swam, explored the redwood forests all round us, lay out in the meadow, picked apples, talked (yes, of course) to trees. My quilt began to grow. And, of course, everything was happening. Celie and Shug and Albert were getting to know each other, coming to trust my determination to serve their entry (sometimes I felt *re*-entry) into the world to the best of my ability, and what is more – and felt so wonderful – we began to love one another. And, what is even more, to feel ommense [sic] thankfulness for our mutual good luck.

Just as summer was ending one or more of my characters: Celie, Shug. Albert, Sofia or Harpo, would come for a visit. We would sit wherever I was sitting, and talk. They were very obliging, engaging and jolly. They were, of course, at the end of their story but were telling it to me from the beginning. Things that made me sad, often made them laugh. *Oh, we got through that, don't pull such a long face, they'd say.* Or, *You think Reagan's bad, you ought've seen some of the rednecks us come up under.* The days passed in a blaze of happiness.

Then school started, and it was time for my daughter to stay with me – for two years.

Could I handle it?

Shug said, right out, that she didn't know. (Well, her mother raised *her* children.) Nobody else said anything. (At this point of the novel, Celie didn't even know where *her* children were.) They just quieted down, didn't visit as much, and took a firm, Well, let's wait and see, attitude.

My daughter arrived. Smart, sensitive, cheerful, at school most of the day, but quick with tea and sympathy on her return. My characters adored her. They saw she spoke her mind in no uncertain terms and would fight back when attacked. When she came home from school one day with bruises but said You should see the other guy. Celie (raped by her stepfather as a child and somewhat fearful of life) began to reappraise her own condition. Rebecca gave her courage (which she always gives me) – and Celie grew to like her so much she would wait until three-thirty to visit me. So, just when Rebecca would arrive home needing her mother and a hug, there'd be Celie, trying to give her both. Fortunately I was able to bring Celie's own children back to her (a unique power of a novelist), though it took me thirty years and a good bit of foreign travel. But this proved to be the largest single problem in writing the exact novel I wanted to write between about ten-thirty and three.

I had planned to give myself five years to write *The Color Purple* (teaching, speaking, or selling apples, as I ran out of money). But on the very day my daughter left for camp, less than a year after I started writing, I wrote the last page.

And what did I do that for?

It was like losing everybody I loved at once. First Rebecca (to whom everybody surged forth on the last page to say goodbye), then Celie, Shug, Nettie & Albert, Mary Agnes, Harpo and Sofia, Eleanor Jane, Adam and Tashi Omatangu. Olivia. Mercifully, my quilt and my lover remained.

## ITEM 6

This is an extract about Alice Walker from *Writing Women*.

### Alice Walker: The Color is Purple

Alice Walker is one of the younger pathbreaking black women novelists to come to prominence in the 1980s. Already she has produced thirteen remarkable volumes of poetry and prose. She was born in 1944 in Georgia, 'halfway between misery and the sun'. The South has provided Walker with spiritual balance and an ideological base, *despite* racist domination through sharecropping (giving half the crops to the landlord) or by wage labour. A southern writer also inherits a 'trust in the community. We must give voice not only to centuries of bitterness and hate but also of neighbourly kindness and sustaining love.'

Sustaining care came from her mother, who had married for love, running away from home to marry at 17. By the time she was 20 she had two children and was pregnant with a third.

> Five children later, I was born. And this is how I came to know my mother: she seemed a large soft, loving-eyed woman who was rarely impatient in our home. Her quick, violent temper was on view only a few times a year, when she battled with the white landlord who had the misfortune to suggest that her children did not need to go to school.

Her mother laboured beside – not behind – her father in the fields. Their working day began early, before sunrise, and did not end till late at night. There was seldom a moment for either to rest: they were sharecroppers, working for harsh white landlords. Yet they both found time to talk to their children, and encourage their talents. Though her father cared a great deal for her, she talks of him as being 'two fathers' and for a long time felt so shut off from him that they were unable to speak to each other. Alice Walker pays particular tribute to her mother's creativity, to the garden she planted lovingly, and watered before going off to the fields. Her flowers and her quilts become a symbol of black women's creativity, which found expression even in the hard daily work:

> She planted ambitious gardens, brilliant with colors, so original in design, so magnificent with life ... I notice it is only when my mother is working in her flowers that she is radiant ... Ordering the universe in the image of her personal conception of Beauty.

Indeed Alice Walker claims that a black southern writer has not an impoverished but a rich inheritance given by 'compassion for the earth. The heat is so intense and one is so very thirsty, as one moves across the dusty cotton fields, that one learns forever that water is the essence of all life.'

When she was eight Alice Walker lost one eye in a traumatic accident. This led her to believe she was ugly and made her shy and timid for years.

> It was from this period – from my solitary lonely position, the position of an outcast – that I began really to see people and things, really to notice relationships ... I retreated into solitude, read stories and began to write.

## ITEM 7

This is an extract from a critical commentary on *The Color Purple* for A Level students.

What Alice Walker has told us about her sources for *The Color Purple* is useful in understanding the novel. Her plans for her work in the 1970s, as discussed with critic Mary Helen Washington, suggested that her third novel would begin where *Meridian* had ended, that it would be contemporary in setting. Yet, *The Color Purple* is set in the early part of the twentieth century and could be called a historical novel. Walker has said that her third novel represented a detour; still it is a contemporary novel, in that it addresses contemporary issues with which Afro-American women's literature and the international women's movement have been intensely concerned: issues of men's violence against women, issues of sisterhood, women's eroticism and lesbianism, and issues of women's economic independence. These issues have been discussed more openly during the eighties than ever before and Walker's *The Color Purple* has been a significant contribution to that discussion.

Walker's description of the emergence of her characters' voices indicates how important the oneness of creation, as symbolised by the color purple, is to the novel's theme and to its title. For as she immersed herself in the countryside she realised that although one does not usually think of purple as a prominent color in nature, it is everywhere if one only takes the time to see it. As well, the language that her characters speak is related to the natural setting in which they live.

If we look at Walker's entire body of writing, we can also see how *The Color Purple* proceeds from her previous work. At the beginning of the novel, Celie resembles the Copeland women of Walker's first novel in that her body and spirit are battered, and she is seeking a language through which to articulate her condition. 'Burial,' and other poems in *Revolutionary Petunias*, are compressed narratives of rural Southern women and men that are developed in *The Color Purple*. Walker experiments with the letter/diary form as early as 'Really, Doesn't Crime Pay' in *In Love and Trouble* and as recently as '1955' in *You Can't Keep a Good Woman Down*. Like Roselily in *In Love & Trouble*, Celie wonders 'if she will ever know what it is to live,' and like Hannah, in 'The Revenge of Hannah Kemhuff,' Sofia is almost crushed by racism. Poems in *Good Night Willie Lee* relate directly to the image of woman as mule, a central motif in this first half of *The Color Purple*. And like Meridian, Celie is haunted by the loss of her children.

Perhaps the most significant precedents in Walker's previous work are her experimentation with the form of quilting, and the 'bodacious' spirit of the two publications that precede *The Color Purple*, a spirit arrived at only through the struggle so beautifully expressed in her early work. This spirit is embodied in the blues singer, Gracie Mae Stills, of '1955,' the singer who is a foreshadowing of Shug. *The Color Purple* is one of a few novels in the tradition of Afro-American literature which explores the female blues singer as heroine. Like Walker's other novels, it is intensely rooted in the history and creativity of back women even as it pushes that tradition to another level. And as in her other two novels, Walker uses that history to explore change in generations of one black Southern family. In contrast to the sharecropping Copeland family of her first novel, or the small town Hill family of her second novel, Celie's family is a middle-class land-owning black family, like many at the turn of the century. Walker explores in her novels the relationship of class to racism and patriarchy. *The Color Purple*, then, does not come out of nowhere. It is informed by Walker's own work, as well as by the tradition of Afro-American Literature.

One of the most arresting aspects of this novel is its form, a tour de force in that it is written entirely in letters. Letters are short units, each of which is complete in itself and, when stitched together with other letters, creates a series of patterns – a quilt. Just as important, letters tell us about the objective conditions of a person's life while being a subjective reflection on her life. The letter is a form of narrative that combines both the objective and the subjective. This dual quality may be one of the reasons why letters were written so consistently by women in the past, when their experience was considered trivial and was usually omitted from history. Through writing letters, women not only recorded their lives but also reflected upon them, a source of personal growth. Feminist historians have used women's letters as an important source of researching women's history in its concreteness as well as in its subjective ramifications. Walker has adopted this genre, so useful in history as a specifically female literary genre.

But letters can be arranged in many different ways as the European tradition of the epistolary novel indicates. Walker arranges the letters of *The Color Purple* in terms of the Afro-American literary tradition, specifically the genre of the slave's narrative, which usually traced the slave's growing awareness of her oppression, her increasing resistance, escape, and the final realisation of freedom in body and spirit. Like the slave in the nineteenth-century narratives, Celie's body and spirit are brutalised, a fate she accepts until she is confronted with other models, in this case Sofia's resistance through fighting, Shug's resistance through loving. Then there is a period of anger, followed by one of flight, her subsequent escape to Memphis where she develops her economic independence. Finally, there is a resolution of the spirit as she achieves independence of self, even from Shug, and effects the unification of her family and community. By ending her novel with a family reunion on the Fourth of July, Walker recalls Frederick Douglass, one of the finest writers of the slave's narrative, and the creator of the famous Fourth of July Speech that protested the institution of slavery.

In order to understand how typical and/or atypical Celie's experience is, we need to consider a few facts about woman's status at the turn of the century. In much of the world, as well as in the United States, woman was seen as inferior to man. She did not have many of the rights we now take for granted. As recently as the nineteenth century, many American women could not be legal agents and thus could not own property or negotiate contracts, except through their fathers, husbands or brothers. American women could not act as political agents; they could not vote or be elected to political office. They were not expected to speak in public or operate in the public domain and were to remain primarily within the family. They were not regarded as economically independent. 'Respectable' women were not expected to work, particularly if they were married and had children. And women's goal in life was supposed to be marriage and motherhood.

In effect, women, 'the weaker sex,' were under the control or 'protection' of their male relatives, and in many ways were conceived of as property. Husbands and fathers could not be prosecuted for physical or sexual abuse, and in many states, fathers, rather than mothers, had the right to children. Incest then, as now, existed although it was not often spoken about – young orphaned girls were considered particularly unfortunate since they had no access to power or even to protection. The Women's Rights Movement of the nineteenth century protested these conditions but it took some fifty years to achieve the vote for women.

Many people miss the fact that *The Color Purple* is not about a poverty-stricken black Southern family. Pa and Mister both are landowning blacks, of which there were many in Georgia at the turn of the century. In focusing on this class, Walker reminds us that many Southern blacks were economically successful during Reconstruction, though because of the Southern racist system, some were eventually dispossessed of their property.

In the case of *The Color Purple*, Walker does a critique of patrimony and how it is linked to the pursuit of power. Mister owns land that he has received from his father who, in turn, received land from his father, who was a white slaveowner. Mister's father objected to his relationship with Shug Avery, a woman who refuses to be owned. Mister doesn't marry Shug and complies with his father's wishes partly because his father determines whether or not he will inherit land. In a real sense, Celie's abuse is derived from that fact, for Mister gives up the woman he loves, and becomes a bully to his first.

One aspect of woman's condition critical to Celie's story was the denial of education. Ironically, it was the creation of The Freedman's Bureau, which taught one and one-half million blacks to read and write between 1864 and 1970, that resulted in general public school education for poor Southern whites and women. But because of the passage of segregationist laws, blacks did not have equal access to education. Being able to read and write was considered as valuable a prize as it had been for slaves.

Black women, of course, had an even lower status than white women, who were often placed on a pedestal, even as they lacked independence. In *Their Eyes Were Watching God*, Hurston characterises the status of black women as that of a mule, an animal bred to work; creating an image that comes out of slavery. Walker makes great use of this image in the first part of *The Color Purple* as well as in the section set in Africa.

This is not to say that black women did not oppose these conditions in many different ways. Walker presents three different ways in which black women resisted their lot. Sofia represents the strong black woman who does not accept the definition of woman as weak and helpless and resists whites' attempts to diminish her. Often women like her have been denigrated both in black and white society as Amazons, or matriarchs, and punished for their resistance. Nettie represents women who did not marry but became missionaries, leaders, etc., and who used education as a means to transcend the low status of the black woman. As well, Walker uses Nettie to demonstrate the long history of relationships between Afro-Americans and Africa. Often these women had to separate themselves from their families and become 'exceptional' women. Shug represents another avenue, that of the blues tradition, an area in which black women could express their creativity and eroticism, and be economically independent. Though maligned as immoral by the middle class, female blues singers were often seen by other blacks as queens. They were openly sexual, often bisexual, and explored pleasure as a woman's right. They, too, risked the possibility of separation from their children and experienced volatile economic changes in the music business as well as intense racism from the white world. That few novels, until recently, have used female blues singers as central figures indicates the ambivalence with which particularly the black middle class has related to these women. Their economic independence, overt eroticism, and spiritedness subverted the society's definition of the good woman.

# The Color Purple

Answer **all three** questions.

Read Item 8, printed after the questions.

30 minutes are allocated in the examination to the reading and consideration of this Item.

Question 1 will ask you to compare Item 8 with the passage from *The Color Purple* in your pre-release material, Item 1.

1. Compare the ways these two writers deal with the situation of black women in America in the early twentieth century by examining:

   • the attitudes of women to men, and to their own situation

   • the relationships between women and men

   • the attitudes of women to authority figures

   • the concept and presentation of religion

   • the writers' uses of form

   • the effects achieved by the choices of language.

   (40 marks)

2. Compare and contrast some of the different interpretations offered in Items 2, 3 and 4. Which do you find the most persuasive, and why?

   (20 marks)

3. Using Items 5, 6 and 7, explain what sources and values, in your view, most influenced Alice Walker in her writing of *The Color Purple*.

   (20 marks)

*This is the unseen extract, printed on the examination paper and not seen before the examination itself.*

## ITEM 8

This is an extract from *Jazz* by Toni Morrison.

Other women, however, had not surrendered. All over the country they were armed. Alice worked once with a Swedish tailor who had a scar from his earlobe to the corner of his mouth. 'Negress,' he said. 'She cut me to the teeth, to the teeth.' He smiled his wonder and shook his head. 'To the teeth.' The iceman in Springfield had four evenly spaced holes in the side of his neck from four evenly spaced jabs by something thin, round and sharp. Men ran through the streets of Springfield, East St. Louis and the City holding one red wet hand in the other, a flap of skin on the face. Sometimes they got to a hospital safely, alive only because they left the razor where it lodged.

Black women were armed, black women were dangerous and the less money they had the deadlier the weapon they chose.

Who were the unarmed ones? Those who found protection in church and the judging, angry God whose wrath in their behalf was too terrible to bear contemplation. He was not just on His way, coming, coming to right the wrongs done to them, He was here. Already. See? See? What the world had done to them it was now doing to itself. Did the world mess over them? Yes but look were the mess originated. Were they berated and cursed? Oh yes but look how the world cursed and berated itself. Were the women fondled in kitchens and the back of stores. Uh huh. Did police put their fists in women's faces so the husbands' spirits would break along with the women's jaws? Did men (those who knew them as well as strangers sitting in motor cars) call them out of their names every single day of their lives? Uh huh. But in God's eyes and theirs, every hateful word and gesture was the Beast's desire for its own filth. The Beast did not do what was done to it, but what it wished done to itself: raped because it wanted to be raped itself. Slaughtered children because it yearned to be slaughtered children. Built jails to dwell on and hold on to its own private decay. God's wrath, so beautiful, so simple. Their enemies got what they wanted, became what they visited on others.

Who else were the unarmed ones? The ones who thought they did not need folded blades, packets of lye, shards of glass taped to their hands. Those who bought houses and hoarded money as protection and the means to purchase it. Those attached to armed men. Those who did not carry pistols because they became pistols; did not carry switchblades because they were switchblades cutting through gatherings, shooting down statutes and pointing out the blood and abused flesh. Those who swelled their little unarmed strength into the reckoning one of leagues, clubs, societies, sisterhoods designed to hold or withhold, move or stay put, make a way, solicit, comfort and ease. Bail out, dress the dead, pay the rent, find new rooms, start a school, storm an office, take up collections, rout the block and keep their eyes on all the children. Any other kind of unarmed black woman in 1926 was silent or crazy or dead.

## Question 1

### Deconstructing the question

You need to look at the question carefully in order (a) to identify the Assessment Objectives you were expecting, and (b) to focus your reading and thinking on the terms of the task.

In Sample Paper 1, Question 1, 'Compare' is what you will have been expecting, as it focuses on the second part of AO2ii. 'The ways these two writers deal with' targets AO3. 'The situation of women in America' is the 'knowledge and understanding' part of AO2ii, which is then made more precise by the first four bullet points – though 'presentation' in the fourth bullet is a pointer to AO3. The last two bullets firmly target AO3, as you can see by 'form' and 'choices of language'.

You have probably already made some notes and underlinings on Item 1 which will be useful, but read it again with these specific questions in mind, making more notes if necessary. Then read Item 8 through once without making notes – remember you have not seen it before, so you need to get the whole thing clear in your mind – and then again, reading carefully and adding notes relevant to the task. You might even need to read it a third time. This may seem a lengthy process when you're anxious to start writing, but remember that the examination allows 30 minutes for reading.

There are a number of ways you might plan your response, but a key element is comparison – it's far better to keep comparing across texts than to write about one Item then the other. An obvious way is to work through the Assessment Objectives – in this case dealing first with attitudes, relationships and concepts in the two Items as indicated in the bullets, and then with form and language.

There are of course many possible responses to this question. The response below illustrates some – it is not an attempt to be definitive, and many other things could be said. The order in which the response is given is also just one possible way of framing it.

### Sample response

The attitudes of these two female writers to men are similar. Celie regards 'mens' as 'trifling, forgetful and lowdown', and Shug rejects God not only because he is white, but also because he is male. Man is an oppressive shadow, blocking thought: 'You have to git man off your eyeball, before you can see anything a'tall', and he 'corrupt everything'. Celie is so ingrained in her attitude to men that even Shug's advice about telling men to 'get lost' is difficult to follow. Celie cannot help her violent instincts – she wants to throw rocks at men. In this at least, her attitude is directly comparable to the more generalised attitudes of women to men offered in Item 8. The conflict here is 'armed', and violent instances and trends are given, not just imagined. Violence is a response both to men and to poverty. Like Celie's oppression at the hands of 'Mr.___', who she sees as evil, male abuse is partly sexual, as shown by the references to rape and to 'strangers sitting in motor cars'. The struggle here is general, though, not just in the individual lives of women such as Celie and Shug, as indicated by the mention of 'leagues, clubs, societies, sisterhoods'. In both extracts, relationships between women and women are seen as stronger, on an individual and communal basis, than between women and men. Though Item 8 tends more to aggression and violence, neither Item depicts a positive relationship between men and women, or a positive view of any single male.

In both Items, women are aware of their poverty, and their colour, and want to redress the injustices of their situations. Although referring to God – perhaps the most significant authority figure in either Item – Celie's comment that 'if he ever listened to poor colored women the world would be a different place' is a comment about earthly injustice. In Item 1, it is clear that one of the main authority sources responsible for black women's situation, and for black men's too, is the black community. In the white Bible, 'all the colored folks is doing is getting cursed'. This is echoed directly in the language of Item 8, where black women are shown not only as 'messed over', but also 'berated and cursed'. The mayor, who clearly doesn't 'listen to anything colored say', is probably both male and white. The police in Item 8, similar authority figures, not only oppress women with violence, but through this seek to break the spirits of their husbands. In this Item, women respond to their situation either with violence, by speaking out, or by combining in collective organisations with other women to 'solicit, comfort and ease'.

The concept of God, and its presentation, are quite different in the two Items. Item 1 actually presents two concepts: Celie's 'traditional' view not only pictures god as white and male, with beard and robes, but also as a Being, in the sense that he 'might hear you' or is 'deef'. Celie, unlike Shug, sees organised religion as a way of pleasing God. Indeed, she seems to see religion as a reflection of God, as the folks who didn't speak to her when she was in distress, 'didn't have him to share'. Shug challenges all of Celie's perceptions, though some elements of her belief are traditional. She sees God as a provider, who 'gave you life, good health, and a good woman that love you to death', and clearly has a notion of original sin: 'I is a sinner, say Shug. Cause I was born.' Shug's concept of pleasing God by being happy, 'admiring stuff', and having a good time, is so alien to Celie that she sees it as 'blasphemy, sure nuff'.  Shug has rejected the traditional concept of God because of colour and gender – 'When I found out I thought God was white, and a man, I lost interest.' Her concept of God is internal, 'inside you and inside everybody else', but also 'everything', so that a human being is 'part of everything'. Shug presents God not as a human 'he or she, but a It'. The idea is presented graphically, with the thought that 'if I cut a tree, my arm would bleed', and Celie is shocked that God's love extends to sexual feelings.

A God that loves, shares, is pleased by people admiring its creations and tries to 'please us back' is far removed from the concept and presentation of God in Item 8. Here God is seen as 'judging' and 'angry', exercising a wrath 'too terrible to bear contemplation'. This Old Testament concept of a vengeful being is further demonstrated by the reference to God's opponent, 'the Beast'. The aggression of men and police is presented as the work of the Devil, in effect, punished internally because its acts of 'filth' are 'what it wished done to itself'. Perhaps the starkest contrast in the tones of the two passages lies in the concepts and presentation of God offered.

Although both Items are from prose texts, the uses of form are very different. The letter form of Item 1, marked by the opening and ending, allow Celie's viewpoint to be aired in her 'voice'. This includes pronunciation, conveyed by phonetic spelling, as in the frequent use of the word 'ast', and dialect words, phrases and grammar. Celie's conversation with Shug is presented as dialogue rather than reported speech, giving an immediacy and a sense of drama to the scene presented. At the same time, her viewpoint is presented through her comments on the dialogue: 'I decide to stick up for him, just to see what Shug say.' This appears to be a moment of transition in the novel, echoed by the form: 'Amen' as a religious ending has now presumably changed its significance.

The form of Item 8 is a more conventional third-person narrative, though the third paragraph has items of spoken form, with the repetition of 'Uh huh', and 'see, see'. Here the religious context, combined with the elements of form, suggests the language of black gospel meetings. Compared to the looser, organic development of the conversation in Item 1, this Item has a much stronger sense of logical exposition, marked by the paragraph beginnings, which set the agenda, and the summative final sentence.

Although the direct language of the first Item makes it seem more casual, the writer uses devices to heighten effect. For example, the key moment of Shug's explanation of God employs the rhetoric of religion to echo and reinforce the sense she strives for: 'I believe God is everything,' say Shug. Everything that is or ever was or ever will be.' Celie's admiration of Shug is captured in a simile, 'look like a big rose', and her resentment of her treatment at the hands of men is presented through her clever use of the idea of the rock. Shug intends her to 'conjure up' a rock as a form of prayer, but Celie can't help using it to fight — 'Every time I conjure up a rock, I throw it.'

Fight characterises the language of Item 8, which is laced with the words of conflict and aggression. Despite the obvious differences, though, some of the writer's resources are similar to those employed in Item 1. A rhetorical repetition of form for emphasis appears in 'Black women were armed; black women were dangerous', and rhetorical questions are used too, though to very different effect. 'Did the world mess over them? Yes,' and the other questions in Item 8, reinforce oppression, whereas Celie's questioning ('How it do that?') captures her admiration of creation. The upper case 'H' in 'His' and 'B' in 'Beast' reflect an older concept of God, similar to Celie's, especially as 'His' identifies God as male. Shug's use of upper case 'I' for 'a It', presumably marked in her voice, is perhaps a playful mockery of this convention — again, far removed from the tone of Item 8.

## Question 2

### Thinking about the question and organising the material

The first task is to look through each of the Items for the interpretations being offered – you will probably do this as part of your work on the pre-release materials before the examination itself begins. Of course, you'll find some details of form, structure and language, and also of contexts, which can be used to give evidence for interpretations, but your primary task here is to look for an opinion or judgement about the text.

In this question you are asked to 'Compare and contrast', so you need to think about grouping together similar views and opposing views, or views about the same aspect of the text, before you start to write. There are only half as many marks as for Question 1, and only 35 minutes allowed to write your response, so you will need to do much of the work before the examination. In the sample response below, the writer has decided, after looking at some of the general views for and against the novel, to group the interpretations loosely around three topics. These topics are: (1) the position of women, (2) the text as a novel about the black community, and (3) some interpretations of literary contexts and devices. You are also asked for your view about interpretations you find 'persuasive', and in this case the writer has chosen to tackle this at the end of the response.

There are of course many possible responses to this question. The response below illustrates some – it is not an attempt to be definitive, and many other things could be said. The order in which the response is given is also just one possible way of framing it.

### Sample response

Items 2 and 3 offer some general judgements about The Color Purple. Some early reviewers saw it as compelling and thought provoking, and it was widely read by black women. It was praised for being 'optimistically didactic', and for the density of the subtle interaction between characters. Others, however, felt that the portraits of males were 'pallid', and there were some negative reviews by black males. Critics have attacked it as reiterating white stereotypes, and for the bourgeois aspirations of these rural characters, showing the 'strivings and potential for self-indulgence of urban middle class'. The African letters were seen by one critic as 'mere monologues of African history'.

Item 2 mentions the 'womanist aspects' of 'a woman's womanist book', and Item 4 uses Alice Walker's definition of the difference between feminism and womanism. This definition is seen as relating to the significance of colour in the novel, representing joy and freedom. Item 3 suggests that the novel shows women learning to respect themselves and to speak, both to themselves and to other black women, and sees the novel as affirmative, with life not being merely the sum of oppression. Suffering is not necessarily the destiny of black women, and the capacity to forgive is seen here as a mechanism in their liberation.

There are mixed responses to the lesbian relationship in the novel. One critic in Item 2 sees is as a 'positive, full depiction of a lesbian relationship in the black community', but another thinks that some readers may be disturbed by 'an aspect of the black woman that has seldom been dealt with in any depth'. Maryemma Graham goes further, considering that the lesbian theme 'muddies the waters' about female bonding.

Maryemma Graham also sees the novel as depicting men as the sole source of female oppression, with which she disagrees. Item 4, however, takes a very different line. Here the writer sees the portrayal of the brutal, abusive stepfather as a tribute to Walker's courage in her refusal to avoid the issue of male brutality. Black men have no excuse for bringing white racist violence into their homes, and internalising white values in their desire to humiliate. The counterpart to this, it is argued, is shown in the improvement in Mr.___ as the economic situation improves, and he is taught by women to respect them. From respect comes love, and the possibility of self-love, a reading deriving from psychotherapy, as the writer acknowledges.

Critics quoted in Item 2 comment that the subject of The Color Purple is the sexual politics of black life, as experienced by ordinary blacks, and that it is a challenge to the black community to fight for the freedom of the entire race. Indeed, Item 4 suggests that white people seem to be 'excommunicated from consciousness'. The coloured metaphors examined in Item 3 also relate to this agenda. The colours chosen by Celie for Shug's room and for the trousers that she makes form a bold denial of the 'humiliating associations' of 'colored'.

Item 4 centres on an interpretation of literary contexts, those of the fairy tale and folk tale, and the morality to be found in black oral culture. The writer sees the happy coincidences at the end of the novel, and what appears to be the excessive reward given to Celie, as belonging to these traditions, rather than as 'a failure of the realist imagination'. The 'authenticity of the folk voice' is also mentioned in Item 2. In Item 4 Walker's work is compared to that of the black women writers Toni Morrison and Maya Angelou, with the writer considering that their treatment of black males is 'less trenchant'. This writer sees quilting not simply as linking episodes and characters, but as showing women sewing in sisterhood, and as bringing peace to Celie. It is suggested that quilting transforms discarded pieces into beauty, as perhaps Celie herself is transformed.

The weight of the interpretations offered in Items 2, 3 and 4 seems to fall on a positive view of Alice Walker as a feminist, or rather womanist writer, more than as a black writer, though of course she is both. Despite some quibbles, the impression formed of this novel is that it is an inspiring work for women, and particularly for black women. Ideas of liberation, forgiveness, and reward occur in readings of the text from a number of angles, so that I am persuaded of the strength of this view of the novel. This is certainly supported by Shug's view of the nature of God in Item 1, especially in contrast to the violence that runs through Item 8.

## Question 3

### Thinking about the question and organising the material

As with Question 2, much of the work for this question can be done on the pre-release material before the examination itself. The question will test Assessment Objective 5ii, so you can identify and mark the various contexts mentioned in the Items given. Once you have done this, you can organise the information into various types of context: historical, cultural, literary, and so on.

The question will give you the second organising principle for your response. In this case, 'sources and values' are referred to, so it may be helpful to separate these as far as you can. You also have to address the issue of which of these 'most influenced' the writer of the extract, so although this question does not ask you to 'compare and contrast', looking at the evidence of all three pieces together may help you to come to a judgement. As with Question 2, there are only half the number of marks awarded on this question compared to question 1, and only 35 minutes allowed for you to write your response. Again, the sample response below shows one way of tackling the question, but there are other, equally valid, ways of responding.

### Sample response

Items 5 and 6 are mostly concerned with contexts around the writer herself, and these help to identify some of the important sources and values of her work. An unusual source mentioned by Walker herself in Item 5 appears to be the characters themselves – she writes about them 'refusing to come out', 'appearing', and interacting with her and her family; this rather muddies the concept of characters as literary constructs. It also leads to a value – she clearly loves the characters, and it is necessary to her that they love her, too. Item 6 gives other personal sources – the sustaining care from her mother, for instance, and her mother's battle with the white landlord. Her mother's labouring beside her father in the fields was clearly formative. Her parents, we are told, talked to their children and encouraged their talents, and her mother's creativity was clearly an important source for Walker: the creativity in planting and quilting can be directly related to the text of The Color Purple. Walker's childhood accident – as a result of which she lost an eye – is also identified as affecting her outlook.

The 'compassion for the earth' of Walker as a black Southern writer, mentioned in Item 6, is reflected in Walker's own words: her characters refuse to speak in the city, but start to appear when they are among the 'sheep, cattle and goats'. A source mentioned in Item 6 is the language context – the language of the characters is related to the natural setting in which they live. Walker mentions the making of her quilt, too, which is both a source and a value of the novel, as the response to Question 2 suggests. The values of the South are also important too, according to Item 6: trust in the community is mentioned, neighbourly kindness, sustaining love, and the importance of giving voice to centuries of bitterness and hate. Although Walker sees The Color Purple as a historical novel, she makes it clear that this is not 'historical' in a male sense: a key source for the story is the remembered narrative about a woman asking the 'Other Woman for a pair of her drawers'.

Item 7 is mostly concerned with historical and literary contexts. One context is both of these: although this is a historical novel, it addresses issues with which Afro-American women's literature has been concerned. These include men's violence against women, sisterhood, women's eroticism and lesbianism, and their economic independence.

One of the most significant contexts seems to be her own work. It is clear that her previous work not only dealt with women, but also offered narratives of rural Southern men and women. As in other novels, she uses the history of a family to explore changes between generations. The image of woman as 'mule' had been used before, in the writings of Zora Neale Hurston. Quilting had been used before, and also 'spirit', as demonstrated in Shug, one of the few examples of female blues singers as heroine in the Afro-American tradition.

The form of the novel provides another literary context. Being written entirely in letters, the novel adopts what has been historically a specifically female genre. The letters are arranged not in the European tradition of the epistolary novel, but in the Afro-American tradition of slave narrative. The ending being set on Independence Day suggests as a source Frederick Douglass, a writer both of slave narrative and a celebrated Fourth of July speech protesting against slavery.

Historically, the beginning of the novel is set not in poverty, but in the land-owning black middle class at the turn of the twentieth century, exemplified by Pa and Mr.___. Women's status is inevitably drawn on, too. Women at this time had few rights, and were generally regarded as inferior to men. They were under the control of men, and blacks were denied equal access to education. This was clearly a source of Walker's writing, but it as clearly gave rise to values — it is black women's liberation from these conditions that lies at the heart of the novel, and forms its most important value.

> These responses to Sample Paper 1 are not intended to be exhaustive, and of course you might well find a number of other equally valid things to say in response to all the questions. They do indicate, however, what the focus of each response should be.

# Sample Paper 2

Time Allowed: 3 hours (including 30 minutes' reading time)

You should spend about $1\frac{1}{4}$ hours on Question 1 and about 35 minutes each on questions 2 and 3.

The Assessment Objectives will be printed on the paper.

### ITEM 1

In this extract from the novel *Sons and Lovers* by D. H. Lawrence, Paul Morel is thinking about ending his relationship with Miriam Leivers. One of his problems is his strong relationship with his mother, who disapproves of Miriam.

He remained staring miserably across at the hills, whose still beauty he begrudged. He wanted to go and cycle with Edgar. Yet he had not the courage to leave Miriam.

'Why are you sad?' she asked humbly.

'I'm not sad; why should I be?' he answered. 'I'm only normal.'

She wondered why he always claimed to be normal when he was disagreeable.

'But what is the matter?' she pleaded, coaxing him soothingly.

'Nothing!'

'Nay!' she murmured.

He picked up a stick and began to stab the earth with it.

'You'd far better not talk,' he said.

'But I wish to know –' she replied.

He laughed resentfully.

'You always do,' he said.

'It's not fair to me,' she murmured.

He thrust, thrust, thrust at the ground with the pointed stick, digging up little clods of earth as if he were in a fever of irritation. She gently and firmly laid her hand on his wrist.

'Don't!' she said, 'Put it away.'

He flung the stick into the currant-bushes, and leaned back. Now he was bottled up.

'What is it?' she pleaded softly.

He lay perfectly still, only his eyes alive, and they full of torment.

'You know,' he said at length, rather wearily – 'you know – we'd better break it off.'

It was what she dreaded. Swiftly everything seemed to darken before her eyes.

'Why?' she murmured. 'What has happened?'

'Nothing has happened. We only realize where we are. It's no good – '

She waited in silence, sadly, patiently. It was no good being impatient with him. At any rate, he would tell her now what ailed him.

'We agreed on friendship.' He went on in a dull, monotonous voice. 'How often *have* we agreed for friendship! And yet – it neither stops there, nor gets anywhere else.'

He was silent again. She brooded. What did he mean? He was so wearying. There was something he would not yield. Yet she must be patient with him.

'I can only give friendship – it's all I'm capable of – it's a flaw in my make-up. The thing overbalances to one side – I hate a toppling balance. Let us have done.'

There was a warmth of fury in his last phrases. He meant she loved him more than he her. Perhaps he could not love her. Perhaps she had not in herself that which he wanted. It was the deepest motive of her soul, this self-mistrust. It was so deep she dared neither realize nor acknowledge it. Perhaps she was deficient. Like an infinitely subtle shame, it kept her always back. If it were so, she would do without him. She would never let herself want him. She would merely see.

'But what has happened?' she said.

'Nothing – it's all myself – it only comes out just now. We're always like this towards Easter-time.'

He grovelled so helplessly, she pitied him. At least she never floundered in such a pitiable way. After all, it was he who was chiefly humiliated.

'What do you want?' she asked.

'Why – I mustn't come often – that's all. Why should I monopolize you when I'm not – You see, I'm deficient in something with regard to you – '

He was telling her he did not love her, and so sought to leave her a chance with another man. How foolish and blind and shamefully clumsy he was! What were other men to her! What were men to her at all! But he, ah! She loved his soul. Was *he* deficient in something? Perhaps he was.

'But I don't understand,' she said huskily. 'Yesterday – '

The night was turning jangled and hateful to him as the twilight faded. And she bowed under her suffering.

'I know,' he cried, 'you never will! You'll never believe that I can't – can't physically, any more than I can fly up like a skylark – '

'What?' she murmured. Now she dreaded.

'Love you.'

He hated her bitterly at that moment because he made her suffer. Love her! She knew he loved her. He really belonged to her. This about not loving her, physically, bodily, was a mere perversity on his part, because he knew she loved him. He was stupid like a child. He belonged to her. His soul wanted her. She guessed somebody had been influencing him. She felt upon him the hardness, the foreignness of another influence.

'What have they been saying at home?' she asked.

'It's not that,' he answered.

And then she knew it was. She despised them for that commonness, his people. They did not know what things were really worth.

He and she talked very little more that night. After all he left her to cycle with Edgar.

He had come back to his mother. Hers was the strongest tie in his life. When he thought round, Miriam shrank away. There was a vague, unreal feel about her. And nobody else mattered. There was one place in the world that stood solid and did not melt into unreality: the place where his mother was. Everybody else could grow shadowy, almost non-existent to him, but she could not. It was as if the pivot and pole of his life, from which he could not escape, was his mother.

And in the same way she waited for him. In him was established her life now. After all, the life beyond offered very little to Mrs Morel. She saw that our chance for *doing* is here, and doing counted with her. Paul was going to prove that she had been right; he was going to make a man whom nothing should shift off his feet; he was going to alter the face of the earth in some way which mattered. Wherever he went she felt her soul went with him. Whatever he did she felt her soul stood by him, ready, as it were, to hand him his tools. She could not bear it when he was with Miriam. William was dead. She would fight to keep Paul.

And he came back to her. And in his soul was a feeling of the satisfaction of self-sacrifice because he was faithful to her. She loved him first; he loved her first. And yet it was not enough. His new young life, so strong and imperious, was urged towards something else. It made him mad with restlessness. She saw this, and wished bitterly that Miriam had been a woman who could take this new life of his, and leave her the roots. He fought against his mother almost as he fought against Miriam.

It was a week before he went again to Willey Farm. Miriam had suffered a great deal, and was afraid to see him again. Was she now to endure the ignominy of his abandoning her? That would only be superficial and temporary. He would come back. She had the keys to his soul. But meanwhile, now he would torture her with his battle against her. She shrank from it.

## ITEM 2

This is an extract from *A Freudian Appreciation*, written by A. B. Kuttner and published in 1916.

We can now return to *Sons and Lovers* with a new understanding. Why has the attitude of the son to his mother here had such a devastating effect upon his whole life? Why could he not overcome this obstacle like other children and ultimately attain some measure of manhood? Why, in short, was the surrender so complete? In Paul's case the abnormal fixation upon the mother is most obviously conditioned by the father, whose unnatural position in the family is responsible for the distortion of the normal attitude of the child towards its parents. The father ideal simply does not exist for Paul; where there should have been an attractive standard of masculinity to imitate, he can only fear and despise. The child's normal dependence upon the mother is perpetuated because there is no counter-influence to detach it from her. But there is another distortion, equally obvious, which fatally influences the natural development. Paul's early fixation upon his mother is met and enhanced by Mrs Morel's abnormally concentrated affection for her son. Her unappeased love, which can no longer go out towards her husband, turns to Paul for consolation; she *makes* him love her too well. Her love becomes a veritable Pandora's box of evil. For Paul is now hemmed in on all sides by too much love and too much hate.

If now we compare Paul's boyhood and adolescence with, let us say, the reader's own, we find that the difference is, to a great extent, one of consciousness and unconsciousness. All those psychic processes which are usually unconscious or at least heavily veiled in the normal psycho-sexual development lie close to consciousness in Paul and break through into his waking thoughts at every favorable opportunity. Everything is raw and exposed in him and remains so, kept quick to the touch by the pressure of an abnormal environment which instead of moulding, misshapes him. The normal hostility towards the father which is conditioned in every boy by a natural jealously of the mother's affection, is nursed in him to a conscious hate through Morel's actual brutality and his mother's undisguised bitterness and contempt. And the normal love for the mother which ordinarily serves as a model for the man's love for other women is in him perverted into abnormal expression almost at his mother's breast, so that he is always conscious of his infatuation with his mother and can never free his love-making from that paralyzing influence. These powerful determinants of the love-life which we acquire from our parents would be too overwhelming in every case were it not for the process of submersion or repression already referred to. This repression usually sets in at an early stage of childhood and acts biologically as a protective mechanism by allowing us to develop a slowly expanding sense of selfhood through which we gradually differentiate ourselves from our parents. In this way the fateful dominance of the parents is broken, though their influence remains in the conscious as a formative and directing impulse.

In Paul this salutary process never takes place because he cannot free himself from the incubus of his parents long enough to come to some sense of himself. He remains enslaved by his parent complex instead of being moulded and guided by it. One turns back to that astonishing scene at Lincoln Cathedral. Here Paul goes to the roots of his mother's hold upon him. For his passionate reproaches hurled at his mother because she has lost her youth, prove that the mother-imago, in all its pristine magic, has never diminished its sway over him; he has never been able to forget or to subordinate that first helpless infatuation. If only she could be young again so that he could remain her child-lover! With that thought and wish so conscious in him nothing else in life can become really desirable, and all initiative is dried up at the source. Paul cannot expand towards the universe in normal activity and form an independent sex interest because for him his mother has become the universe; she stands between him and life and the other woman. There is a kind of bottomless childishness about him; life in a pretty house with his mother – the iteration sounds like a childish prattle. Miriam feels it when she calls him a child of four which she can no longer nurse. Nor can Clara help him by becoming a wanton substitute for his mother. Only the one impossible ideal holds him, and that means the constant turning in upon himself which is death. Paul goes to pieces because he can never make the mature sexual decision away from his mother, he can never accomplish the physical and emotional transfer.

## ITEM 3

This extract is from *The Forked Flame: A Study of D.H. Lawrence* by H. M. Daleski, published in 1965.

If Lawrence's reaction against his mother was the fundamental cause of his hostility towards much of what he characterized as the male principle, Helen Corke, Louie Burrows, and Jessie Chambers were contributory factors in his repudiation of 'idealism' and 'spirituality'. Of these young women Jessie Chambers was the most decisive influence and, as Miriam in *Sons and Lovers*, Lawrence prepared for her both a grave and a monument. But if he dug her grave it does not necessarily follow that he betrayed her. The charge has to be faced, however, for it has been the basis of a considerable body of accusatory criticism.

As was perhaps only to be expected, the cry of betrayal was first uttered by Jessie Chambers herself:

'As the sheets of manuscript came rapidly to me I was bewildered and dismayed at [the] treatment [of Miriam]. I began to perceive that I had set Lawrence a task far beyond his strength. In my confidence I had not doubted that he would work out the problem with integrity. But he burked the real issue. It was his old inability to face his problem squarely. His mother had to be supreme, and for the sake of that supremacy every disloyalty was permissible.'

I quote, too, what I think is a representative example of the way in which her judgement has been followed by critics:

'... as we now know, there is a fundamental falsity in [the history of Paul's relations with the two women, Miriam and Clara]. The moving reminiscences of E.T., Lawrence's real-life Miriam, have now made it clear that not only did he use his novel to give himself imaginatively the sexual gratification he could not find in life, but he refused to face the truth of his difficulty when he insisted on placing the blame for his failure upon the girl rather than the mother, where it belonged.'

In passing, we may remark the egoism of Jessie Chambers' attitude and the unwarranted assumption to which it gives rise – Lawrence was not writing the novel as a task set by her – but I am more concerned with the fallacies inherent in Edward Wagenknecht's argument. In the first place it is not clear on what basis Jessie's word is automatically accepted as better than Lawrence's. Though we can understand her charge of 'disloyalty', the following extract from a letter suggests that Lawrence did not falsify the history of her relations with her:

'I see Frieda has written a defence of me against Miriam – or Jessie, whatever she shall be called. It's all very well for Miss Chambers to be spiritual – perhaps she can bring it off – I can't. She bottled me up till I was going to burst. But as long as the cork sat tight (herself the cork) there was spiritual calm. When the cork was blown out, and Mr Lawrence foamed, Miriam said 'This yeastiness I disown: it was not so in my day.' God bless her, she always looked down on me – spiritually. But it hurt when she sent a letter of mine back: quite an inoffensive letter, I think. And look, she is bitterly ashamed of having had me – as if I had dragged her spiritual plumage in the mud. Call that love! Ah well.'

Moreover, in regard to Jessie's assertion that the Clara episode 'had no foundation in fact',  Harry T. Moore's researches have established – it seems to me conclusively – that the episode was at least in part on an actual experience.  Lawrence's 'imaginative sexual gratification', therefore, was decidedly not imaginary. But that is hardly important. What should be noticed is Wagenknecht's confusion of art and life. If there is a 'fundamental falsity' in the novel, then the critics who take this line should be able to point to the falsity in the text, but this they signally fail to do. There is, no doubt, the unsubstantiated claim that Lawrence places the blame for 'his' failure on Miriam rather than on his mother, but this is simply not true. The extent to which Paul, as a result of his mother's influence, is to blame for the failure of his relationship with Miriam is fully and frankly acknowledged. I have already drawn attention to two passages in which such acknowledgement is made, and they are by no means isolated instances. The plan of the book entails Paul's slowly growing recognition of his own inadequacy and there are numerous references to it, varying from direct commentary: 'He was afraid of her love for him. It was too good for him, and he was inadequate. His own love was at fault, not hers', to explicit admission: "I can only give friendship –" [said Paul], "it's all I'm capable of – it's a flaw in my make-up. The thing overbalances to one side – I hate a toppling balance. Let us have done"' (p.271).

A more recent critic, apparently in reaction against Jessie Chambers and those who follow her, has swung to the other extreme. Mark Spilka finds that 'the chief "split" between Paul and Miriam comes from the abstract nature of their love, and not from the mother's hold upon the young man's soul. And the final responsibility for this split belongs with Miriam'; but this is surely to underestimate the central importance of Mrs Morel and the extent of Paul's own difficulties. The relationship fails because of fatal hindrances on both sides – even if Mark Schorer finds this objectionable:

'The central section of the novel is shot through with alternate statements as to the source of the difficulty: Paul is unable to love Miriam wholly and Miriam can love only his spirit. These contradictions appear sometimes within single paragraphs, and the point of view is never adequately objectified and sustained to tell us which is true.'

The truth which Lawrence presents is, apparently, more inclusive than critics seem willing to admit, and if it is not of the black and white variety that does not mean to say that he is contradicting himself. I hope that in my discussion of Paul's relations with his mother I have sufficiently indicated the nature of the barrier which prevents him from loving Miriam; I shall therefore endeavour to show that, as far as Miriam is concerned, the point of view is not only adequately objectified but that – whatever happened in real life – the way in which she fails Paul is convincingly demonstrated.

Miriam gives Paul, at the crucial stage of his development, much-needed intellectual stimulation – she is 'the threshing-floor on which he [threshes] out all his beliefs' (p. 279) – but what she gives in this way is vitiated by her 'sucking of his soul':

'He felt that she wanted the soul out of his body, and not him. All his strength and energy she drew into herself through some channel which united them. She did not want to meet him, so that there were two of them, man and woman together. She wanted to draw all of him into her. It urged him to an intensity like madness, which fascinated him, as drug-taking might' (p. 239).

The comparison with drug-taking suggest the debilitating nature of the relationship: Paul comes to crave Miriam's stimulation but it is artificially restricted and lacks a healthy physical counterbalance to its dizzy intensity. From the outset sexual conflict is implicit in their relations, and even though Paul is at times satisfied by the pleasure Miriam gives him, there is a clear indication that it is unlikely to prove adequate ultimately:

'Then he began to talk about the design. There was for him the most intense pleasure in talking about his work to Miriam. All his passion, all his wild blood, went into this intercourse with her, when he talked and conceived his work. She brought forth to him his imaginations. She did not understand, any more than a woman understands when she conceives a child in her womb. But this was life for her and for him' (p. 249).

## ITEM 4

This is an extract from the Introduction (written by Gamini Salgado) to the Macmillan Casebook *D. H. Lawrence: Sons and Lovers*, published in 1969.

If the domestic background of the Morels is drawn from life, so to a very great extent is that of the Leivers and Willey Farm. A good deal of criticism has concerned itself with the question of whether Lawrence was 'fair' in his portrayal of the real-life counterparts of Miriam, Mr and Mrs Morel, and the rest. The best and best-known example of this sort of criticism is *D.H. Lawrence: A Personal Record*, by Jessie Chambers, the girl portrayed in the novel as 'Miriam'. (Her book was originally published under the initials 'E.T.', standing for the eponymous heroine of an unpublished novel 'Eunice Temple' by Jessie Chambers.) On all available evidence (which includes not only her own account and letters to Lawrence, but reminiscences by friends and relations), Jessie Chambers was a very remarkable person in her own right. Sharing Lawrence's intelligence and his enormous youthful appetite for literature and ideas, she seems also to have had the capacity to bring out in him that almost subcutaneous sensitivity to experience which is the hallmark of Lawrence's writing. Much of *A Personal Record* is a moving account of the real-life relationship between Lawrence and Miss Chambers, and it ends by showing how, under the dominant influence of his mother, Lawrence distorted the actual relationship between himself and the girl. It is impossible not to respond to the dignity and candour of Jessie Chambers' story or to remain unmoved by the sense of betrayal which vibrates through it. It is quite understandable that the reader's first reaction on reading Jessie Chambers' memoir and the other evidence relating to the triangular relationship between Lawrence, his mother and Jessie should be very similar to Jessie's own. We feel that Lawrence has not really played fair by the girl, that she wasn't really like that at all, that *it* wasn't really like that at all. Indeed, the *Athenaeum* reviewer makes just this point. But it is necessary to try to distinguish between the demands we may fairly make of a novelist as novelist from those we may make of him as an individual. Lawrence's responsibilities to his private relationship are one thing, his responsibilities as a novelist are quite another. To equate the two is to confuse the truth of history with the truth of fiction, to put it slightly differently, the 'truth' that the novelist attempts to portray for us has to be judged in terms of the vividness, internal consistency and inclusiveness of his vision rather than by its accuracy as a chronicle of what in fact happened at a given time and place. There is a perfectly proper sense in which the question of whether the author is 'fair' to his characters may be asked of *Sons and Lovers*, as it may be asked of any novel. But the answer to it involves an account of the characters in their relation to each other and the fictional world they inhabit, and of the author's attitude to them *as it appears in the details of the novel*, not a measuring-off of the fictional characters against their real-life counterparts. The latter may tell us something about the novelist, but nothing of value about the novel. It cannot even tell us *how* the novel fails (where it does), only *why* the novelist fails. 'Never trust the artist, trust the tale.'

From the kind of criticism which sees the novel as illuminating the private life of the author it is a short but important step to that which sees it as illuminating the private life of us all. Almost as soon as *Sons and Lovers* appeared there were critics who saw in it a startling endorsement of Freudian theories about the Oedipus complex. Lawrence had not read Freud when he wrote *Sons and Lovers* (though while he was working on the novel he did hear of Freud's theories from Frieda, who herself came to know of them through meeting a young Austrian disciple of Freud). Of course this does not weaken the case of those who saw a dramatization of Freudian theory in the novel, but rather strengthens it. Practised with a proper regard for the unity and texture of the novel itself, this kind of approach can yield insights that would not otherwise be easily obtained, as Simon Lesser shows. But there seem to be at least two dangers to which this sort of criticism is unusually susceptible. First, it often ignores the palpable surface of the novel, what is really *there*, in its eagerness to get at what is *really* there. It smooths awkward details in its effort to cut the novel into the size and shape that fits the theory. Secondly, it tends to use the theory as a criterion by which to judge the value of the novel (that is, the more the novel endorses the theory, the better it is). Lawrence's own objections to the psycho-analytic approach were rather different, though they have some points of contact with the sort of objections I have listed. The psycho-analysing critics, he felt, falsified the living truths of the novel in the name of the half-truths of intellectual schematizing. Nevertheless *Sons and Lovers* continues to invite this kind of critical approach rather more than most other novels (a recent full-length study by an American critic is called *Oedipus in Nottingham*) and this fact is an interesting and important clue to one of the sources of its power. Even critics who are not wholly committed to a 'psycho-analytic' theory of criticism have been able to make perceptive comments on aspects of *Sons and Lovers* by looking at it in the light of what psycho-analysis has to say about repression and sublimation, about the dark and devious workings of our unconscious desires and how they affect the everyday surface of our lives. It is, however, important to distinguish between the psycho-analytic criticism which honestly tries to relate the 'manifest' content (texture, character, plot) of the novel to its 'latent' meaning, and that which merely reduces the novel to a verbalization of its author's psychological inadequacies. Only the former is the proper concern of literary criticism.

## ITEM 5

This letter written by Lawrence is very close to the plot of *Sons and Lovers*.

*To Rachel Annand Taylor, 3 December 1910*

I have been at home now ten days. My mother is very near the end. Today I have been to Leicester. I did not get home till half past nine. Then I ran upstairs. Oh she was very bad. The pains had been again.

'Oh my dear' I said, 'is it the pains?'

'Not pain now – Oh the weariness' she moaned, so that I could hardly hear her. I wish she could die tonight.

My sister and I do all the nursing. My sister is only 22. I sit upstairs hours and hours till I wonder if ever it were true that I was at London. I seem to have died since, and that is an old life, dreamy.

I will tell you. My mother was a clever, ironical delicately moulded women of good, old burgher decent. She married below her. My father was dark, ruddy, with a fine laugh. He is a coal miner. He was one of the sanguine temperament, warm and hearty, but unstable: he lacked principle, as my mother would have said. He deceived her and lied to her. She despised him – he drank.

Their marriage life has been one carnal, bloody fight. I was born hating my father: as early as ever I can remember, I shivered with horror when he touched me. He was very bad before I was born.

This has been a kind of bond between me and my mother. We have loved each other, almost with a husband and wife love, as well as filial and maternal. We know each other by instinct. She said to my aunt – about me:

'But it has been different with him. He has seemed to be part of me.' – And that is the real case. We have been like one, so sensitive to each other that we never needed words. It has been rather terrible and has made me, in some respects, abnormal.

I think this peculiar fusion of soul (don't think me highfalutin) never comes twice in a lifetime – it doesn't seem natural. When it comes it seems to distribute one's consciousness far abroad from oneself, and one understands! I think no one has got 'Understanding' except through love. Now my mother is nearly dead, and I don't quite know how I am.

I have been to Leicester today, I have met a girl* who has always been warm for me – like a sunny happy day – and I've gone and asked her to marry me: in the train, quite unpremeditated, between Rothley and Quorn – she lives at Quorn. When I think of her I feel happy with a sort of warm radiation – she is big and dark and handsome. There were five other people in the carriage. Then when I think of my mother: – if you've ever put your hand round the bowl of a champagne glass and squeezed it and wondered how near it is to crushing-in and the wine all going through your fingers – that's how my heart feels – like the champagne glass. There is no hostility between the warm happiness and the crush of misery: but one is concentrated in my chest, and one is diffuse – a suffusion, vague.

Muriel [Jessie Chambers] is the girl I have broken with. She loves me to madness, and demands the soul of me. I have been cruel to her, and wronged her, but I did not know.

Nobody can have the soul of me. My mother has had it, and nobody can have it again. Nobody can come into my very self again, and breathe me like an atmosphere. Don't say I am hasty this time – I know. Louie – whom I wish I could marry the day after the funeral – she would never demand to drink me up and have me. She loves me – but it is a fine, warm, healthy, natural love – not like Jane Eyre, who is Muriel, but like – say Rhoda Fleming or a commoner Anna Karenina. She will never plunge her hands through my blood and feel for my soul, and make me set my teeth and shiver and fight away. Ugh – I have done well – and cruelly – tonight.

I look at my father – he is like a cinder. It is very terrible, mis-marriage.

*Louie Burrows, according to Jessie Chambers, one of the models for Clara Dawes.

## ITEM 6

This is an extract from *D. H. Lawrence: A Personal Record* by 'E.T.' (Jessie Chambers), who was the model for Miriam. It was published in 1935.

He asked me if I had written the notes I promised to do, and I told him I had begun to write them before he was ill and just went on. He said he was going to Bournemouth as soon as he was strong enough, and after that he would come and fetch them. That was our first real talk since his mother's funeral. Some of the old magic returned, the sense of inner understanding which was the essence of our friendship....

The writing of the novel (still called 'Paul Morel') now went on apace. Lawrence passed the manuscript on to me as he wrote it, a few sheets at a time; just as he had done with *The White Peacock*, only that this story was written with incomparably greater speed and intensity.

The early pages delighted me. Here was all that spontaneous flow, the seemingly effortless translation of life that filled me with admiration. His descriptions of family life were so vivid, so exact, and so concerned with everyday things we had never even noticed before. There was Mrs Morel ready for ironing, lightly spitting on the iron to test its heat, invested with a reality and significance hitherto unsuspected. It was his power to transmute the common experiences into significance that I always felt to be Lawrence's greatest gift. He did not distinguish between small and great happenings; the common round was full of mystery, awaiting interpretation. Born and bred of working people, he had the rare gift of seeing them from within, and revealing them on their own plane. An incident that particularly pleased me was where Morel was recovering from an accident at the pit, and his friend Jerry came to see him. The conversation of the two men and their tenderness to one another were a revelation to me. I felt that Lawrence was coming into his true kingdom as a creative artist, and an interpreter of the people to whom he belonged.... I began to realise that whatever approach Lawrence made to me inevitably involved him in a sense of disloyalty to his mother. Some bond, some understanding, most likely unformulated and all the stronger for that, seemed to exist between them. It was a bond that definitely excluded me from the only position in which I could be of vital help to him. We are back in the old dilemma, but it was a thousand times more cruel because of the altered circumstances. He seemed to be fixed in the centre of the tension, helpless, waiting for one pull to triumph over the other.

The novel was written in this state of spirit, at a white heat of concentration. The writing of it was fundamentally a terrific fight for a bursting of the tension. The break came in the treatment of Miriam. As the sheets of manuscript came rapidly to me I was bewildered and dismayed at that treatment. I began to perceive that I had set Lawrence a task far beyond his strength. In my confidence I had not doubted that he would work out the problem with integrity. But he burked the real issue. It was his old inability to face his problem squarely. His mother had to be supreme, and for the sake of that supremacy every disloyalty was permissible.

The realisation of this slowly dawned on me as I read the manuscript. He asked for my opinion, but comment seemed futile – not merely futile, but impossible. I could not appeal to Lawrence for justice as between his treatment of Mrs Morel and Miriam. He left off coming to see me and sent the manuscript by post. His avoidance of me was significant. I felt it was useless to attempt to argue the matter out with him. Either he was aware of what he was doing and persisted, or he did not know, and in that case no amount of telling would enlighten him. It was one of the things he had to find out for himself. The baffling truth, of course, lay between the two. He was aware, but he was under the spell of the domination that had ruled his life hitherto, and he refused to know. So instead of a release and a deliverance from bondage, the bondage was glorified and made absolute. His mother conquered indeed, but the vanquished one was her son. In *Sons and Lovers* Lawrence handed his mother the laurels of victory.

## ITEM 7

This extract is from study notes for A Level students.

D.H. Lawrence was born in 1885 in Eastwood – the Bestwood of *Sons and Lovers* – a mining town just outside Nottingham, in the industrial Midlands of England. Like Paul Morel, he was the son of a coal miner, Arthur Lawrence, and a strong-willed, refined, middle-class girl, Lydia Beardsall Lawrence, formerly a schoolteacher, who, like Gertrude Morel, had married 'beneath her.' In fact, the picture of Paul's childhood given in *Sons and Lovers* is as accurate and detailed a picture of Lawrence's own boyhood as any biographer conceivably could draw. Unlike Paul, Lawrence had two older brothers, an older sister and a young sister (Ada, who was to be the family member closest to him after his mother's death), but there the differences end. Like Paul, Lawrence was quiet, 'good,' rather religious as a boy and intensely attached to his mother. Like Walter and Gertrude Morel, Arthur and Lydia Lawrence fought constantly and, to a child, frighteningly. Arthur Lawrence drank, like Walter Morel, and his children hated him, as the Morel children hate their father. Like Paul Morel, Lawrence early began to paint and to exhibit other signs of creativity and extraordinary intelligence. And like Paul, also, 'Bert' Lawrence fell in love with a nearby farm, the Haggs (called Willey Farm in *Sons and Lovers*) and half in love with the girl who lived on it, Jessie Chambers, who became the Miriam in *Sons and Lovers*.

In real life, Lawrence's relationship with Jessie was almost exactly that of Paul and Miriam in *Sons and Lovers*. Indeed, Jessie Chambers herself contributed her own recollections of this early and intense relationship to the manuscript originally called *Paul Morel*, in the form of a number of individual narrations which Lawrence, of course, rewrote and revised, but many of whose central facts and points were certainly incorporated into the book. Like Miriam, Jessie was an intense, 'spiritual' girl who loved the brilliant young writer with an almost religious fervor. Lawrence, for his part, was quite as dependent on Jessie's judgments and on her encouragement as Paul is on Miriam's, and Lydia Lawrence, the writer's mother, felt the same unyielding hostility toward Jessie that Mrs. Morel feels for Miriam. And like Gertrude Morel, Lydia Lawrence finally defeated the girl Jessie in their silent struggle for Lawrence's love. In fact, a day or two after his mother died, Lawrence took Jessie for a walk and told her 'You know, J., I've always loved mother.' 'I know you have,' she replied. 'I don't mean that,' he answered. 'I've loved her – like a lover – that's why I could never love you.'

*Sons and Lovers* was begun shortly after Lydia Lawrence's death in 1910, when Lawrence was staying in Eastwood. His first partial draft of the novel, according to Jessie Chambers, was 'flat and tepid,' with a melodramatic and over-contrived plot. But at Jessie's suggestion he revised his plan of the book, converting it into a more accurate and detailed record of his actual boyhood experiences. In this, as we have already seen, he was substantially aided by Jessie herself, who even supplied narratives of her own for him to work from. Later, when he and Frieda were 'honeymooning' in Germany, Lawrence took up the book once more, and with Frieda providing 'bits' as Jessie once had (especially those dealing with the mother's reaction) plus some helpful letters from Jessie herself, he finally completed this first masterpiece of his.

## Sons and Lovers

Answer **all three** questions.

Read Item 8, printed after the questions.

30 minutes are allocated in the examination to the reading and consideration of this Item.

Question 1 will ask you to compare Item 8 with the passage from *Sons and Lovers* in your pre-release material, Item 1.

1. Compare the ways these two writers deal with love, by examining:

   • the emotions and relationships shown in the extracts

   • the effects of external factors on the couples, including other people and society

   • the effects of viewpoint, and changes in viewpoint

   • authorial voice

   • the effects achieved by the choices of language in each.

   (40 marks)

2. Compare and contrast two of the different interpretations offered in Items 2, 3 and 4. Which did you find most persuasive, and why?

   (20 marks)

3. Using Items 5, 6 and 7, explain what sources and ideas, in your view, most influenced D. H. Lawrence in his writing of *Sons and Lovers*.

   (20 marks)

*This is the unseen extract, printed on the examination paper and not seen before the examination itself.*

## ITEM 8

This is an extract from the novel *Emma* by Jane Austen. Emma has found that her friend Harriet has fallen in love with Mr. Knightley and that she (Emma) might even have encouraged her. She also thinks that Mr. Knightley might return Harriet's affection, and fears it because she has realised that she must marry Mr. Knightley.

Emma could say no more. They seemed to be within half a sentence of Harriet, and her immediate feeling was to avert the subject, if possible. She made her plan; she would speak of something totally different – the children in Brunswick Square; and she only waited for breath to begin, when Mr. Knightley startled her, by saying,

'You will not ask me what is the point of envy. – You are determined, I see, to have no curiosity. – You are wise – but *I* cannot be wise, Emma, I must tell you what you will not ask, though I may wish it unsaid the next moment.'

'Oh! Then, don't speak it, don't speak it,' she eagerly cried. 'Take a little time, consider, do not commit yourself.'

'Thank you,' said he, in an accent of deep mortification, and not another syllable followed.

Emma could not bear to give him pain. He was wishing to confide in her – perhaps to consult her; – cost her what it would, she would listen. She might assist his resolution, or reconcile him to it; she might give just praise to Harriet, or, by representing to him his own independence, relieve him from that state of indecision, which must be more intolerable than any alternative to such a mind as his. – They had reached the house.

'You are going in, I suppose,' said he.

'No' – replied Emma – quite confirmed by the depressed manner in which he still spoke – 'I should like to take another turn. Mr. Perry is not gone.' And, after proceeding a few steps, she added – 'I stopped you ungraciously, just now, Mr. Knightley, and, I am afraid, gave you pain. – But if you have any wish to speak openly to me as a friend, or to ask my opinion of any thing that you may have in contemplation – as a friend, indeed, you may command me. – I will hear whatever you like. I will tell you exactly what I think.'

'As a friend!' – repeated Mr. Knightley. –'Emma, that I fear is a word – No, I have no wish – Stay, yes, why should I hesitate? – I have gone too far already for concealment – Emma, I accept your offer – Extraordinary as it may seem, I accept it, and refer myself to you as a friend. – Tell me, then, have I no chance of ever succeeding?'

He stopped in his earnestness to look the question, and the expression of his eyes overpowered her.

MODULE 6: Exploring Texts

'My dearest Emma,' said he, 'for dearest you will always be, whatever the event of this hour's conversation, my dearest, most beloved Emma – tell me at once. Say "No," if it is to be said.' – She could really say nothing. – 'You are silent,' he cried, with great animation; 'absolutely silent! at present I ask no more.'

Emma was almost ready to sink under the agitation of this moment. The dread of being awakened from the happiest dream, was perhaps the most prominent feeling.

'I cannot make speeches, Emma:' – he soon resumed; and in a tone of such sincere, decided, intelligible tenderness as was tolerably convincing. – 'If I loved you less, I might be able to talk about it more. But you know what I am. – You hear nothing but truth from me. – I have blamed you, and lectured you, and you have borne it as no other woman in England would have borne it. – Bear with the truths I would tell you now, dearest Emma, as well as you have borne with them. The manner, perhaps, may have as little to recommend them. God knows, I have been a very indifferent lover. – But you understand me. – Yes, you see, you understand my feelings – and will return them if you can. At present, I ask only to hear, once to hear your voice.'

While he spoke, Emma's mind was most busy, and, with all the wonderful velocity of thought, had been able – and yet without losing a word – to catch and comprehend the exact truth of the whole; to see that Harriet's hopes had been entirely groundless, a mistake, a delusion, as complete a delusion as any of her own – that Harriet was nothing; that she was everything herself; that what she had been saying relative to Harriet had been all taken as the language of her own feelings; and that her agitation, her doubts, her reluctance, her discouragement, had been all received as discouragement from herself. – And not only was there time for these convictions, with all their glow of attendant happiness; there was time also to rejoice that Harriet's secret had not escaped her, and to resolve that it need not and should not. – It was all the service she could now render her poor friend; for as to any of that heroism of sentiment which might have prompted her to entreat him to transfer his affection from herself to Harriet, as infinitely the most worthy of the two – or even the more simple sublimity of resolving to refuse him at once and for ever, without vouchsafing any motive, because he could not marry them both, Emma had it not. She felt for Harriet, with pain and with contrition; but no flight of generosity run mad, opposing all that could be probable or reasonable, entered her brain. She had led her friend astray and it would be a reproach to her for ever; but her judgment was as strong as her feelings, and as strong as it had ever been before, in reprobating any such alliance for him, as most unequal and degrading. Her way was clear, though not quite smooth. – She spoke then, on being so entreated. – What did she say? – Just what she ought, of course. A lady always does. – She said enough to show there need not be despair – and to invite him to say more himself. He *had* despaired at one period; he had received such an injunction to caution and silence, as for the time crushed every hope; – she had begun by refusing to hear him. – The change had perhaps been somewhat sudden; – her proposal of taking another turn, her renewing the conversation which she had just put an end to, might be a little extraordinary! – She felt its inconsistency; but Mr. Knightley was so obliging as to put up with it, and seek no farther explanation.

Seldom, very seldom, does complete truth belong to any human disclosure; seldom can it happen that something is not a little disguised, or a little mistaken; but where, as in this case, though the conduct is mistaken, the feelings are not, it may not be very material. – Mr. Knightley could not impute to Emma a more relenting heart than she possessed, or a heart more disposed to accept of his.

# Achieving High Marks

In order to achieve high marks, you need to satisfy the descriptors (or Assessment Criteria) for the mark schemes, which are drawn directly from the Assessment Objectives. In this module, the Assessment Objectives are different for each question, so the descriptors for the mark bands are as well.

Here are the descriptors for the top two bands for each question, as they might appear for the two Sample Papers above.

## Question 1

*29–34 marks*

| | |
|---|---|
| AO1 | critical terminology used accurately in detailed commentary |
| AO2ii | detailed critical response to both texts and task |
| AO3 | evaluation of how choices of form/structure/language shape meanings |
| AO3 | evaluation of links between authorial purposes/means |

*35–40 marks*

| | |
|---|---|
| AO1 | accurate use of appropriate critical vocabulary/concepts |
| AO2ii | clear conceptual grasp of issues raised by texts and task |
| AO3 | sophisticated analysis of how choices of form/structure/language shape meanings |
| AO3 | conceptually and analytically links purposes/means |

## Question 2

*14–16 marks*

| | |
|---|---|
| AO4 | clear evidence of critical viewpoint |
| AO4 | clarity of judgement in the understanding of a variety of critical positions |

*17–20 marks*

| | |
|---|---|
| AO4 | positions own judgement in context of other judgements |
| AO4 | synthesises/evaluates a variety of critical positions |

## Question 3

*14–16 marks*

| | |
|---|---|
| AO5ii | detailed exploration of sources/values/ideas |
| AO5ii | detailed exploration of significance of influential sources/values/ideas |

*17–20 marks*

| | |
|---|---|
| AO5ii | analysis of a range of contextual factors influencing Walker/Lawrence |
| AO5ii | analysis of the significance of the various sources/values/ideas influencing Walker/Lawrence |

This is the final module of the course, and this will be your final examination. As you will see through the work you do on these two Sample Papers, it draws together all the skills you have learned during the course. When you approach the examination itself, you need to have this firmly in your mind. Looking at the mark schemes above shows exactly what sort of thinking and writing you need to apply to each question.

The best final preparation for this module is to attempt Sample Papers unaided.

**Assonance**: a rhyme in which the vowels (but not the consonants) are similar, for example *fate* and *save*, which share a long 'a'.

**Ballad**: a poem, often in short stanzas, narrating a story, for example Coleridge's *The Rime of the Ancient Mariner*.

**Comedy of Manners**: a witty comedy satirising the manners and social pretensions of sophisticated society. Examples include Congreve's *Way of the World* and Goldsmith's *She Stoops to Conquer*. See: Restoration Comedy

**Conceit**: a far-fetched comparison in which you are made to admit likeness between two things, whilst always being aware of the oddness of the comparison. An example is George Herbert's poem 'The Pulley'.

**Context**: in AS Literary Study this is the new fifth Assessment Objective. Contexts are the important facts, events or processes that have helped to shape literary works.

**Cordial(l)**: life-giving or restorative; a stimulant to the heart, such as medicine, food or drink.

**Divine right**: the belief that a king's right to rule comes from God.

**Dramatic monologue**: a poem in which a speaker seems to be addressing an imaginary listener.

**Emblem**: a representation or a symbol with a pictorial quality, for example George Herbert's poem 'Easter-wings'.

**Fall of Man**: the Christian doctrine that Adam and Eve fell from grace and so were forced to leave the Garden of Eden.

**Feminist**: a person (usually a woman) who holds beliefs that recognise and advocate the rights of women.

**Generic**: relating to genre.

**Half-rhyme**: in poetry, a rhyme in which the words contain similar sounds but do not rhyme completely. An example, from Wilfred Owen's poem 'Strange Meeting', is the rhyming of *hall* and *Hell*.

**Interlaced**: a medieval principle of construction in which ideas are intricately woven together, as in the poetry of Chaucer.

**Legalism**: a preference for a strict adherence to the law, rather than to the principles of the Bible and Christian virtue. The concept can be seen in Shakespeare's *Measure for Measure*.

**Lyrical**: having the quality of a short, song-like poem expressing the poet's thoughts and feelings.

**Machiavelli**: Niccolò Machiavelli (1469–1527) was an Italian writer and statesman who advocated the use of ruthless means to enable. The adjective Machiavellian is used to describe a person who practises duplicity and scheming in order to win political power.

**Marxism**: the social and political theories of the German philosopher Karl Marx (1818–1883). Marx believed that social change is driven by the conflict between the social classes, in essence between those who have money and power (who own the factories and businesses) and those who have no money or power (who have to work for others). He argued that this conflict was reflected in all aspects of society, even literature.

**Medieval**: relating to the Middle Ages.

**Metaphysical**: 1. literary term invented by the poet John Dryden (1631–1700) to describe a group of seventeenth-century poets, including George Herbert, who were characterised by the use of far-fetched imagery and witty conceits. See: Conceit

**Metaphysical**: 2. in philosophy, relating to theories concerned with the fundamental concepts of thought, such as time, space, immortality, and the soul.

**Milieu**: the particular environment – social, academic, literary etc. – in which a writer lives.

**Morality Play**: a form of medieval verse drama in which the characters are abstractions such as Vice, Faith, and so on; an example is the anonymous *Everyman*.

**Mystery Play**: medieval drama in verse in which biblical stories are retold.

**Narrative poem**: poem in which a story is told.

**Negative capability**: term used by the Romantic poet John Keats (1795–1821) to describe the ability to 'be in uncertainties, mysteries, doubts', in other words to think and experience without the need for proof or reason.

**Psychoanalytic**: relating to the theories of the German psychologist Sigmund Freud (1856–1939). Freud believed that human behaviour is strongly influenced by forces so deeply hidden in the mind that we are not aware of them. These forces, he argued, evolve during an infant's early relationship with its parents.

**Register**: the words and expressions appropriate to specific circumstances, for example in writing about war; a military register can be found in the poetry of Wilfred Owen.

**Restoration Comedy**: a form of comedy that developed in the period after the restoration of the monarchy in 1660. As a reaction against Puritan restraint, Restoration Comedy concerned itself with the witty, the frivolous, and the bawdy, the setting usually being that of fashionable society. The secular concerns of social satire now began to replaced religious themes in drama. See: Comedy of Manners

**Revenge Tragedy**: a dramatic genre which developed in the Elizabethan and Jacobean periods; known also as 'the tragedy of blood', these plays, often bloody and violent, had plots based on the desire for revenge for a real or imagined wrong. Examples include Shakespeare's *Hamlet* and Webster's *The White Devil*.

**Rhetoric**: language designed to persuade or impress.

**Sacramental**: related to a religious ceremony, indicating inner grace or spirituality.

**Satire**: a literary work in which the aim is to amuse, criticise or correct by means of ridicule.

**Sensual**: related to the senses or sensations, usually with a sexual rather than spiritual or intellectual connotation.

**Sensuous**: appealing to the senses, but with no restriction to fleshly or sexual pleasure.

**Shrieve** (or shrive): to hear someone's confession.

**Socialist**: relating to the political and economic theory of socialism, which advocates state ownership and control of the means of producing wealth.

**Specification**: the syllabus for a subject issued by an examination board.

**Stock**: standard or typical (often used of a character in a play).

**Structuralism**: a literary theory that see the meaning of a work as deriving from the subtle interrelationship of its parts, and not from its capacity to reflect 'real life'.

**Suspend disbelief**: to dispense with the need to look at a work of literature realistically; this way, as in the case of *Measure for Measure*, we can accept situations, characterised events which are in themselves unbelievable, but which create the effects intended by the writer.

**Wandering Jew**: a legendary figure who was condemned to wander the world without rest. He gradually acquired great wisdom and encouraged others to avoid sin and turn to God. The story influenced Coleridge's *Rime of the Ancient Mariner*.

**Wit**: intelligence, understanding and ingenuity in dealing with a situation; a characteristic feature of Restoration Comedy.